SMARTER BUSINESS EXITS

Strategies and Toolkits for Corporate Divorce,
Succession Planning and Joint Exits

by
William B. Bierce

Leaders
Press

Leaders Press

Printed in the United States of America

ISBN 978-1-943386-78-9 (print book) | ISBN 978-1-943386-77-2 (e-book)
Library of Congress Catalog No. 2020902440 | First edition: February 2020
Photo credit: Liza Margulies | Cover design: Dalchand Sharma

Selected publications by William B. Bierce:

The Devil's Dictionary of Global Sourcing (2012)

Smarter Business Exits: Strategies and Toolkits for Corporate Divorce, Succession Planning and Joint Exits (Leaders Press 2020), available at https://smarterbusinessexits.com

Business Owner's Strategies for Selling An International Business (e-book 2020), available at https://smarterbusinessexits.com

Multiparty Contractual Networks: New Tool for Global Entrepreneurship and Supply Chains, in Business Law International (Int'l Bar Ass'n, Vol. 20, No. 3, Sept. 2019), available at www.biercekenerson.com/contact

Professional Service Firms: Partner's Guide to Continuity, Succession Planning and Business Divorce (e-book 2020), available at https://smarterbusinessexits.com

Restructuring Strategies for Your Smarter Business Exits (e-book 2020), available at https://smarterbusinessexits.com

Praise

It's a fact that every business owner will exit the business at some point. Preparing beforehand for the inevitable challenges of an exit is not only prudent but also very smart. *Smarter Business Exits* is a book every business owner should read to get a grip on the nuances around various exit scenarios *before* they happen. Bill Bierce, a recognized authority on exit events, walks you through the process of preparing your business for a split, sale, or inheritance and offers the best advice I've seen on the market. Highly recommended!

Tom Fedro |co-founder, Paragon Software Group Corp.; best-selling author of *Next Level Selling*

Beyond commercial success, entrepreneurs, senior executives, investors, consultants, and licensed professionals in privately owned companies will face the challenge of making a clean exit. Don't take that step lightly as being prepared is critical. Bierce takes you through a step-by-step process of "exit excellence" to help you plan to minimize and mitigate any corporate divorce—no matter how complex. Although I'm a seasoned business owner, I have taken Bierce's advice and used his tool kits to prepare my business for exit. I'm supremely grateful for this book and Bierce's guidance.

Tony White | chairman, enChoice

Exit strategies begin with identifying your business model, defining mutual expectations on corporate governance, and ensuring operational excellence for the creation of sustainable value. Once launched, your business needs risk management and resiliency strategies both for obvious threats and unforeseen disruptions. Finally, optimizing value on exit requires careful preparation for liquidity events in a sale, merger, acquisition, or restructuring with new partners. Along the way, other stakeholders could derail your plans. If a business owner like you is not aware of the potential nightmare your exit could become without a solid strategy, you need to read this book and prepare yourself, your business, your team, and your partners for an excellent departure. Don't wait until it's too late.

Ali Razi | founder & CEO, Banc Certified Merchant Services

I had read this book at the right time and could not be better prepared. By identifying classic solutions to foreseeable scenarios, *Smarter Business Exits* helps you plan, adapt, renew, transform, and restructure for exits at different stages of your business's life cycle. It takes you from business prenup to sale, with crucial lessons at different crossroads that might arise from poor business judgments, gaps in leadership or emotional intelligence, personal differences, mismanagement, misconduct, or violation of legal rights. I'm sleeping well at night now, knowing that myself, my business, and my partners are prepared for our eventual liquidity.

Mark Nureddine | CEO, Bull Outdoor Products; best-selling author of *Pocket Mentor*

Are you a business owner with partners? No matter where you are in your business life cycle, *Smarter Business Exits* is a must-read. Whether you and your partners agree or not about how to plan for the sale of the business, in this smart collection, you'll learn all you need to know about getting ready for the eventual divorce. You'll learn how to hire the right advisors, navigate toxic paralysis in co-owner relations, and use governance tools to keep your co-owners fulfilling their promises of service, loyalty, productivity, and commitment. I cannot imagine where my co-owners and I would be today without this book. I highly recommended *Smarter Business Exits*!

Chris Catranis | CEO, Babylon Telecommunications; best-selling author of *Disruptive Leadership*

This is an excellent book for business owners to prepare for that eventual sale. I've been in business for twenty-nine years, and I wish I had read this book earlier! *Smarter Business Exits* made a lot of things come together for me to lay out the steps for my future exit. It hits some great points I'm glad I know now rather than later, such as how to design my business in an exit lifestyle fashion. I highly recommend this book to any business owner! Whether you're just starting in business or a seasoned pro, you can get an excellent general overview of an exit strategy in this read.

Kathy Stack | president/CEO , Grafx Design and Digital

Owning a business comes with specific challenges that any owner will immediately recognize. If you've wondered just how to use to ensure that everyone is on the same page during business exits, then this book is for you. *Smarter Business Exits* is the ABCs of exiting or planning for succession of a business.

Don Zerivitz | president, Pro Clean

Dedication

To Martha and Katharine.

To business owners everywhere, who pursue the journey, pilot the ship, navigate the perils, maintain optimism and support their business, partners and communities.

To investors, who share the journey, encourage entrepreneurship, risk loss and change the world.

To professional advisors, the crew helping to trim and guide the ship.

'Loving each other is not looking at yourselves face to face. It's looking together in the same direction.'
– Antoine de Saint Exupéry, *The Little Prince*

Acknowledgments

In writing a book on strategies for business owners to change some or all ownership of their business, I took inspiration from my clients and fellow professionals. Through the many journeys, we realigned many twisted personal, family and business situations to preserve and transmit optimal value. We planned, negotiated and executed a wide variety of deals with changes in ownership and ownership structures. We resolved some feverish business divorces without destruction. We relaunched businesses with new managers or owners. We acquired closely held businesses and integrated them into larger closely held businesses. Respecting their privacy, I simply acknowledge my fellow travelers here.

In this book, the lessons, classic scenarios and legal and tax frameworks target American businesses. But a much wider world inspired me. Many universal truths of business exit intelligence™ flow from my working with fellow 'business travelers' from many countries including Australia, Brazil, Canada, China, England, France, Germany, India, Ireland, Japan, Romania and Switzerland among others. Indeed, my career path as an international technology and business lawyer would never have ripened (or yielded this book) without the Rotary Foundation's 'Ambassador of Goodwill' scholarship program, which financed my post-graduate studies at a French law school.

A few individuals helped me crystallize my toolkits on a real-time transactional basis and commented on how the book captured insights. Warm thanks to David N. Deutsch on 'prep for sale' and serial entrepreneur André Pagnac for the startup CEO's perspectives from the sojourn from start to joint exit.

Other preliminary reviewers (on three continents) gave freely of their time and insights into key topics and focus on the business owner's path. I thank Bobby Blumenfeld, Rudolf 'Rob' Houck and Leonard Nuara on M&A, Simeon H. Baum and Stephen A. Hochman on mediation, Barbara R.

Hauser on family offices, Paul Tour-Sarkissian on family succession planning within family business planning, Tom Podgurski on insurance, Tim Powell on knowledge management, Mary L. Burton on career coaching for executives, Stéphane Rosenwald on operational excellence, George Guernsey for educational perspectives, and Jeremy Straten on framing a closely held business's launch, startup, business divorce and joint exits into the business legal life cycle. Finally, I want to thank Alinka Rutkowska of Leaders Press for an inspired publication process.

Are you in need of restructuring strategies for your smarter business exit?

RESTRUCTURING STRATEGIES
FOR YOUR
SMARTER BUSINESS
EXITS

WILLIAM B. BIERCE

Go to smarterbusinessexits.com now to grab your free copy of "Restructuring Strategies for Your Smarter Business Exits"!

Table of Contents

Table of Contents

How to Use this Book for Your Smarter Growth, Exit Strategies and Succession Planning

Why read this book? You can avoid many mistakes along the path towards retirement or sale. As a business owner, you undoubtedly want to connect the dots from launch to growth to sale or succession. Here, you can take a self-guided tutorial on smarter business exit strategies (including disputed 'corporate' divorce) without suffering destruction of enterprise value. This book shows what every business owner needs to know, timely positioned at different phases of your business's lifecycle. It gives make-or-break advice on how to plan for succession and/or exit, alone or jointly. It recounts secrets your advisors might not tell you, unless you ask. You can identify solutions to many variations of the exit plan. You might even enjoy case studies and tips to avoid or escape from nightmares.

How to read this book? How can you get the best value from a book on the complex topic of exit strategies for a closely held business, including succession planning?

- *To keep it* simple, each chapter addresses specific issues that might be most meaningful to you in your journey in the business lifecycle.

- *To keep it short* for the broadest audience, the book does not explore the special needs of niche-interest businesses or professional service firms, international businesses, judicial compulsions (such as dissolution and liquidation upon deadlock) or bankruptcy reorganizations. You can access additional information on my websites.

- *To keep it accessible and relevant,* you can skim the detailed table of contents and choose the juiciest relevant chapters that you have time for. (My editor told me so!)

Design and Governance using Business Exit Intelligence. Your journey starts with organizing the business. In Part I (Chapters 1 and 2), you learn about organizational design with the author's framework for *'business exit intelligence'™* and exit-targeted corporate governance. You can make mistakes at startup by working on the wrong exit model or with the wrong people building the wrong business and managing it in the wrong way. So you should look for a smarter exit strategy from the start.

Stakeholder Conflict Resolution. Having navigated startup and created something of value, you now have to protect your business from other shareholders and non-equity stakeholders. In Part II (Chapters 3 and 4), you can anticipate who will give you trouble and consider methods to overcome crises, mitigate disasters and resolve typical disputes, especially on enterprise valuation.

Family Businesses, Startups and other Multi-Owner Businesses. Rather than explore a myriad of business types, you can read here about two of the most numerous business types. In Part III (Chapters 5 and 6), you can focus on a family-owned business or a multi-owner business ranging from a startup to a more mature business.

Toolkits for Smarter Exit Strategies and Succession Planning. Some common denominators arise in every business exit or succession plan. These include legal documentation covering a variety of potential exits scenarios, done at launch or re-launch (with new investors), or mid-stream (such as an agreed or forced individual exit by one shareholder) or upon a joint exit. Throughout your journey, operational excellence is a target for value creation, liquidity and governance, not just an exit tool. For cases where some non-exit restructuring is appropriate, you will learn about alternatives to traditional redemptions, buyouts and joint sales. Part IV (Chapters 7 through 11) covers these common denominators.

Tips. Each chapter includes some tips relating to that chapter.

Self-Assessment Questions. Each chapter invites you to assess your own situation. The answers to self-assessment questions depend on your unique environment, personality, goals, business, legal structures, tax strategies and financial objectives.

Additional Materials for You. For special situations that might apply to your business, you may wish to explore supplemental materials, available at the author's websites, https://corporate-divorce.com and https://smarterbusinessexits.com. Also, please feel free to inquire about additional tools for succession and exits in niche businesses, professional service firms, international businesses, deadlock and restructuring before exits. The sites may also offer information on vendor management of supply chain relationships, supplemental case studies, webinars, consulting and training sessions online.

Introduction

To and Beyond the Next Exit: Business Exit Intelligence™

Greetings to you who work for the success of privately-owned businesses: founders, owners, boards of directors, senior executives, employees, investors, venture capitalists, private equity and lenders. (This book should also help guide professional advisors, friends, family, mentors, mediators, trustees, executors and family offices). Our focus is on family businesses and multi-owner businesses ranging from startups to mid-market companies.

Conflicts among owners and between owners and managers are a fact of life in closely held businesses. Such conflicts threaten deadlock, litigation from disputes on fiduciary duty and wrongful oppression of minority owners, business disruption, loss of value and even liquidation. The book addresses the challenge of how to find graceful and low-risk, low-cost exits with minimal damage to the enterprise, its owners and other stakeholders. This book offers a framework for the efficient management of the business affairs of an industrial or commercial enterprise by smarter exit planning for a change of ownership, control or management. Hopefully, it has educational value for developing a business owner's thinking processes affecting personal, family and business life.

Transformative strategic thinking at all stages can avoid or mitigate internal conflicts and crises. Such thinking has three components:

- '*Business exit intelligence*™ promotes effective relationships among owners and with all stakeholders for a smooth joint exit. Such intelligence addresses all forms of any change of ownership.

- *'Business divorce intelligence'*™ (also known to as *'corporate divorce intelligence'*™) addresses the particular situations of a hostile or disputed exit by a co-owner. Business divorce intelligence can help achieve better financial and emotional results without destruction.

- *'Succession planning intelligence'*™ concerns the process of transition of business management from one CEO to the next. Such transitions may involve a change of ownership, or they could be just another aspect of a family's intergenerational ownership and control of a family business already transitioned to a family holding company or trust. When the founder moves away from day-to-day control, others can learn, adapt, plan and build for the next generation's future.

Let's strategize. Your smarter exit via joint business exit, individual business divorce, succession or other liquidity event must fit within your other enterprise-wide strategies. The success of your enterprise-wide strategies for product development, supply chain and logistics, marketing, technology, finance, human capital and governance are all judged upon an exit or succession event. So all strategies coalesce and culminate as you approach any exit or succession.

Let's design across the full business lifecycle. This book is offered to apply iterative organizational design to avoid or mitigate many stumbling blocks of being an owner of a closely held business. By *designing* your enterprise and your legal relationships to mitigate the disruption of separating from your 'partners,' you can build a collaborative, adaptive, agile and sustainable future. Design is an ongoing process in the business lifecycle, from conception to organization, capitalization, recruitment, funding, product development, alliances, growth and eventual transfer to others in a 'change of control.'

Let's anticipate change. This book aims to help you make wiser decisions and responses on shareholder strategies and structures so you can create and preserve value and your sanity in a business exit or succession. It asks, 'How can you design and manage your business entity to optimize the value to the co-owners and plan for eventual change of management or change of any or all ownership?' By anticipating and planning for potentially 'business exit' and 'business divorce' scenarios, entrepreneurs, investors and managers can adapt to unfolding events. Far-sighted individuals can even look beyond the particular business for their personal "encore," as serial entrepreneurs, private equity investors and interim managers do.

Let's protect adaptively. The shareholder value of your company is vulnerable to many threats. This book takes a holistic view of business exits by identifying many threat vectors that imperil harmony, business continuity and resiliency throughout the business lifecycle. Beyond vulnerabilities and conflicts among owners, threats arise from other stakeholders, digital transformation, online merchants and disruptive online business models. External threats exacerbate intrinsic conflicts among owners. Threats pose the greatest risks just when you want to retire or sell the business. Your ability to defend against threats depends on your prior risk management, mitigation and resiliency planning. The best insurance is to *plan the exits at the start of any business relationship.* Then, with adequate protections, exit events can be managed for enterprise continuity. A well-planned succession or exit can realign and rejuvenate the players.

Let's think like a pro. Many 'lessons learned' for economically efficient business divorce are practiced daily by professional investors. For owners of closely held businesses, this book provides insights into key strategies and practices for corporate renewal, growth, liquidity and sustainability that such professionals deliver every day.

Let's consider key lessons, or 'golden rules,' for longevity, sustainability and thriving success of privately held businesses and their diverse stakeholders. This book seeks to solve fatal problems (and high enterprise mortality) stemming from insufficient planning, execution, monitoring, growth and ownership transition. If every reader were to adopt some of these golden rules, this might improve economic growth, the profitability and sustainability of entrepreneurial private enterprise and reduce business failures.

The first golden rule in design thinking is to plan *now* for a succession, a joint business exit or a 'corporate divorce' without destruction. Failure to plan is just a plan to fail. The last golden rule is to *continue* the planning process. Your company's value depends on ongoing good governance, compliance and risk management ('GCR') to deal with volatility, threats, complexity and ambiguity. Your company faces disruptive digital competitors, risks of safety, security and duties to third parties generally. You might have succeeded over the years at building enterprise value, but you cannot achieve liquidity without 'smarter business exits' from multiple perspectives.

Let's move from volatility to vision. Hopefully, this book will help you replace volatility with vision and value, uncertainty with understanding, complexity with clarity and ambiguity with agility.

You can develop such succession plans, exit strategies and alternatives on your own. Alternatively, you can hire a professional advisor as coach, mentor, corporate advisor, legal counselor, clean-up crew and prep-for-sale consultant or mediator to advise and implement 'business exit intelligence' strategies. Hopefully, this book will help in either case.

Some Terminology

Let's frame our conversation. Can we speak the same language?

For simplicity, '*corporations*' and '*company*' refer to the full range of legal entities for conducting a privately-owned business. Also covered are limited liability companies, partnerships, joint ventures and business trusts. For simplicity (and blurring some distinctions), let's call any owner a '*shareholder*,' any manager or decision-making partner a '*director*' and any legal form of entity as the '*company*' or '*corporation.*'

'*Business exit*' (or '*corporate exit*') refers to any termination of an existing ownership structure for a business. This covers all 'internal' stakeholders: equity owners, employees and investors holding some form of ownership equity rights that have not fully matured or converted to equity ownership. It does not necessarily include a change of CEO or other management.

'*Business divorce*' (or '*corporate divorce*') *is* a subset of business exits. Like the uncoupling of interdependent partners in marital divorce, business divorce can generate emotional and legal conflicts or can be collaborative.. Technically, '*corporate divorce*' refers to ownership changes *in corporations*. '*Business divorce*' covers ownership changes *in any legal business entity*. For simplicity, we use the two terms interchangeably, whether disputed or not.

By contrast, '*commercial divorce*' relates to changes in a business's strategic relationships with its external stakeholders, particularly value chain of customers, suppliers, service providers, licensors and strategic alliance partners. Whether internal or external, your business's stakeholders have invested in relationships, resources and capital investment. All stakeholders nourish a business's continuity and growth, unless there is conflict. Since business divorce can lead to commercial divorce (and vice versa), this book offers parallels for managing termination of commercial contracts in the value chain. The author has extensive experience in design and operation of global value chains and exits in 'commercial divorce.'

'*Succession plan*' refers to the replacement of the top manager ('CEO') as manager. The CEO might be a founder or owner. A succession does not necessarily involve a change of any ownership. Unlike a business divorce, there is no dispute or conflict among owners that precipitates hostilities leading to this owner's exit. But family obligations and emotions can becloud the founder's exit, inciting conflicts both with other owners and with family members.

W.B.B.

PART I

Designing Your organization

1

Organizational Design for the Business Exit Lifecycle

Smarter business exits™ apply organizational design principles for the business and its governance across each phase of the *'business exit lifecycle™.'* In each phase, the owners face particular vulnerabilities that can be mitigated or eliminated by vision. In each phase, the owners build additional enterprise value and face new risks that threaten such value. Smarter organizational design starts with understanding these phases and viewing all stakeholders as sources of both value and vulnerability.

The Phases of the Business Exit Lifecycle

In each phase, business owners face key decisions. By identifying the different phases, you can better navigate through that phase and prepare better for subsequent phases.

Five Phases for Individual Exits ('Business Divorce')

1. Enterprise Startup, Launch and Growth

In this first phase, owners focus on building and growing a viable business. Otherwise, there is no viable exit.

2. Pre-Exit Phase: Acquisition and Restriction of Equity Rights

In this phase, an individual (or entity representing one) acquires equity rights. Unless restricted by contract, such equity rights are freely transferable. Without transfer restrictions and predictable terms of redemption or buyout, any individual exit could quickly become a hostile business divorce involving litigation. Upon becoming a shareholder, each founder or other shareholder needs to appreciate the subtleties of the business divorce process and make or negotiate choices. Sadly, some startup founders neglect such subtleties, jumping in without adequate protection, in an effort to minimize professional fees, focus on developing a minimally viable product ('MVP') and generate cash flow from customers. This phase sets the stage for the exit phases in a business divorce.

3. Exit Trigger Phase: Termination of Non-Equity Rights

In a third phase, a minority owner might have a dispute with the board of directors about such owner's role as employee, consultant or other stakeholder. If not resolved, the dispute can trigger buyout or redemption rights, or, if none, a dispute on alleged misconduct by each party.

4. Exit Phase: Redemption or Buyout of Equity Rights (or Dispute)

This phase of business divorce can be mechanical (following the terms of the shareholders' agreement). Or it can involve a dispute. In any dispute, all owners become distracted from pursuing business opportunities. In the mutual interests of minimizing litigation costs, delays, distractions and lost enterprise value, this dispute phase should be ended quickly to save enterprise value for all. As discussed later, reliance on third-party neutrals can avoid lost value for everyone involved in a disputed business divorce.

5. Post-Exit Phase: Restrictive Covenants

After the actual exit, the former owner may be subject to limited-duration restrictive covenants on competition, solicitation of employees, and disparagement. Disputes may arise over the enforceability of such covenant and on alleged misappropriation of confidential or proprietary information. After the restrictions lapse, the former owner could compete and cherry-pick your employees.

Nine Phases for Joint Exits ('Change of Control')

1. Pre-Exit Phase: Growth and Vulnerability

In this phase, the founders build a viable business capable of being sold to a buyer or transferred to a family member. Here, the company grows, but usually it must make concessions that limit its value on exit or succession. The founders enter into agreements with co-founders, investors, employees and others who may have some rights exercisable upon a future change of control. Such contractual rights may come in the form of 'change of control' clauses that trigger specific rights or prohibit assignability of enterprise assets. The company's licenses from technology suppliers are normally not transferable. The company may have agreed to confidentiality of third-party trade secrets that cannot be disclosed to a possible buyer. The company might be unable to make changes in pricing, terms or supply without the consent of vendors or customers. The company's assets might be commingled with third-party assets under a consignment agreement. 'Transmissibility' thus depends on third party consents.

This phase thus creates the web of value drivers, vulnerabilities and conflicting interests of stakeholders. Such weaknesses often lead to disputes to be resolved in later phases by individual exits, a joint exit or some alternative.

2. Pre-Preliminary Phase: Preparation for Sale

In this phase, beginning at least three years before selling, you scout the market for possible buyers and make your company ready for possible sale or succession. Readiness involves improvements to operations and quality of earnings while identifying potential buyers and cultivating relationships. Here, the owners consider how the sale process might flow: negotiations with just one bidder, simultaneous multi-bidder negotiations or an auction sale. Each process has different impacts on confidentiality and bidder strategies. Readiness requires anticipation of what an optimal buyer will want, identification and remediation of inefficiencies and vulnerabilities, adoption of best practices, and organizational re-design to facilitate a smooth transfer and integration into another enterprise.

Here, the owners look at the company from the buyer's perspective. Buyers want a clear picture of what they get, so this phase invites transparency in the company's profile, its complexities, financial accounts, risk profile, insurance, risk mitigation plan and management processes. The business organization might need to be segmented (mentally) into sellable and non-sellable assets and product lines. The goals are to differentiate low-value and high-value operations and thereby to maximize any key value drivers targeting the optimal buyer's unfilled needs.

Given the years available for this phase, the founders can sequence the pre-sale organizational improvement steps in stages. The first priority should be creating three years of reliable, audited financial statements, to be done early in this phase. All corporate records should be reviewed in due course and updated, perhaps later in this phase.

For compliance with U.S. law on inbound foreign direct investment by foreign acquirers, the owners should identify potential risks of international regulations, such as governmental rejection for national security, antitrust or compliance rules.

3. Preliminary Sale Phase: Introductory Discussions

Here, the owners engage in initial discussions with potential buyers (or a potential successor). Before any discussions, the owners should engage professional advisors to limit the risks of mistakes, like a possible claim of a 'broker' or 'finder.' This phase poses risks since a potential buyer might set a high prospective price and then later seek to reduce it after due diligence discloses negative facts.

4. Letter of Intent Phase: (Mostly) Non-Binding until Final

A letter of intent ('LOI') starts the final sales process. Certain terms are legally binding to ensure exclusivity of negotiations, non-solicitation of employees and confidentiality. Other terms are not binding, particularly the price, deal structure, parties, hold-backs in escrow, post-closing consulting agreement(s), delayed decision-making on future outcomes, financing, contingencies and required approvals. The LOI introduces the due diligence phase.

5. Due Diligence Phase: Vulnerabilities Disclosed to Buyer

The purpose of *'due diligence'* is to build trust with the buyer by showing how well you have built, managed and controlled the business for compliance.

In this phase, the buyer has one goal: to identify reality and force the seller to confront the realities of material risks and previously unknown vulnerabilities of the business. Your company's vulnerabilities can range from possible inefficiencies (lack of synergies) to loss of key employees, misrepresentation by the sellers and illegality of regulated operations.

This phase exposes the sellers to destabilization. Employees might become loyal to the buyer before the deal is signed. Key employees might leave for fear of layoff, reduced compensation, changed roles and new hierarchies, while those who stay might get new opportunities in a bigger organization. You might need to pay retention bonuses. A potential buyer who is a competitor might abuse the process to gain unfair or illegal competitive advantage.

6. Contract Negotiation Phase: Seller on a Tightrope

This phase is the most intense phase in any business exit. The owners will be distracted from 'business as usual,' so that a deal failure will hurt prospects for a backup deal. The sellers walk a tightrope, disclosing only the minimum to avoid a clawback and concealing 'immaterial' flaws that permit a buyer to drive the price down.

7. Post-Contract, Pre-Closing Phase: Vulnerabilities Rumored to the Marketplace

Once the sale or transfer agreement is signed, the sellers must continue 'normal' operations until closing while protecting their interests as sellers. Since the sale contract is technically confidential, rumors might circulate that the company is failing. Employees who know the terms may disclose weaknesses to prospective employers and other marketplace actors. Employees, suppliers, customers and lenders will want assurances. Competitors will solicit customers and employees. Sellers must satisfy pre-closing conditions such as getting consents from third parties or government. A material adverse change in circumstances might kill the deal.

8. Post-Closing Phase: Vulnerabilities Publicized

After closing, the purchase price might become public, eliciting negative reactions by employees, friends or even family. Yet post-closing liabilities may continue for years under representations and warranties, indemnities, personal guarantees, insurance premiums and escrowed funds. All sellers may be jointly liable. Customers might not pay. The former owners could lose status but still might be obligated to provide transitional support services, without employee loyalty. In this phase, you look like you won a windfall but you have to work to keep the benefits of the deal.

9. Post-Post Closing Phase: New Difficulties for Sellers

In a final phase, the sellers have lost all control over the company but may still have duties such as non-competition, non-solicitation and non-disparagement covenants. Meanwhile, family relationships carry burdens, such as resentment by a family member fired by the buyer, family members expecting wealth before the risk of repayment has expired, and feelings of responsibility to different generations of a multi-generational family business. Family co-owners might have other personal jealousies even though they were treated pro rata on the purchase price. This phase can last long beyond the final exit from liability.

Overlay Phases for Succession (Intra-Family Transfer)

Family businesses are illiquid assets that may transition from one generation to the next. The phases for intra-family transfer of *managerial succession* may include intergenerational financial planning and are overlaid on the phases applicable to a joint exit of a multi-owner business. This phase normally begins when the Generation 1 ('G1') founder turns 55 or 60 but can be as late as age seventy or later.

1. Family Intergenerational Planning: Wealth Management and Ownership Transfer

Approaching retirement age or other milestone, the founder engages in family wealth management planning. Such plans typically include an inventory and allocation of the founder's and spouse's assets across generations using strategies for gifting, fiduciaries as owners and family-based governance structures. The family wealth management plan can span multiple generations. Adopting the plan begins with developing – with family input – a list of needs and priorities, such as retirement income, educational expenses for younger generations, liquid assets and wealth management. Here, the founder communicates succession plans to the family and adopts principles that will encourage all stakeholders to support the new family business manager. The founder's company ownership is transferred, whether to a trust, a successor or a combination, whether by gift, sale or a combination. In this phase, the founder and family should resolve family-based conflicts, fair treatment of family members (who might or might not be working in the family business) and intergenerational wealth distribution.

2. Selection and Training of Successor Manager(s)

In a family business succession plan, ownership and control are transferred to the next generation. In a training phase, the founder selects a successor and oversees a program of training and progressive increases in authority ceded to the successor. The founder remains highly visible at the company. Non-employee family members need to be respected and included to avoid resentments.

3. Designation of Successor Manager(s)

In this phase, a new CEO is appointed and assumes day-to-day control. The founder might remain on the Board to provide strategy and consulting, with only an occasional visible presence at the company. If well planned, this phase will add value and enable further intergenerational wealth transmission.

4. Post-Succession Phase

This phase marks the 'complete' retirement of the founder. After the transition of control and ownership, the exiting generation will need to manage the financial plan and retain family cohesion.

Organizational Design for Resolution of Stakeholder Conflicts

Throughout these business exit lifecycles, owners need to focus on organizational design to limit or manage stakeholder conflicts. Otherwise, the closely held business lacks any planning for survival when stakeholders behave selfishly in potentially destructive ways. Adaptive organizational design for conflict resolution becomes all the more critical as digital transformation, the gig economy and virtual businesses disrupt 'traditional' companies and challenge cohesion among a more diverse suite of stakeholders. Adaptive organizational design is a continuous process of listening to stakeholders and the marketplace using *'emotional intelligence,'* *'business intelligence,'* *stakeholder interest analysis* and 'elastic thinking.'[1] Armed with such thinking, we can design your closely held business with strategies and agreed tools for efficient and fair 'business divorce,' joint exit or succession. Such designs can reduce the waste and hostility of conflicts. I call this *'business exit intelligence.'*

Organizational Design Intelligence

'Organizational design intelligence' refers to the culture of continuously redesigning the organization for collaboration, mutual success, innovation and trust among all stakeholders.[2] When considering business divorce, exit or succession structures, your closely held business comprises interdependent components:

- people (serving the governance model for decisions and the talent model for implementation);
- process (the operational model producing the customer experience, including rules on transparency, repeatability and auditability);
- technologies that enable operations; and
- internal controls, serving both compliance with *internal* governance for the owners' benefit and *external* regulatory mandates.

Given these interdependencies, your ownership structure, incentive compensation and exit tools should be recalibrated to reflect any loss of components or synergies when there is a change in ownership or allocation of such components by competing businesses. By changing one component, you can adjust for disruption in other components.

---

[1]   Leonard Mlodinow, ELASTIC (Pantheon Books 2018).
[2]   See generally, Robert Porter Lynch, BUSINESS ALLIANCES: THE HIDDEN COMPETITIVE WEAPON: HOW TO PLAN, NEGOTIATE AND MANAGE STRATEGIC PARTNERSHIPS FOR INCREASED CORPORATE PROFITS (John Wiley & Sons, Inc. 1993); Larraine Segil, INTELLIGENT BUSINESS ALLIANCES: HOW TO PROFIT USING TODAY'S MOST IMPORTANT STRATEGIC TOOL (Century Business 1996); Stephen M. Dent, PARTNERING INTELLIGENCE: CREATING VALUE FOR YOUR BUSINESS BY BUILDING STRONG ALLIANCES (Davies Black Publishing 1999); Naomi Stanford, GUIDE TO ORGANIZATIONAL DESIGN: CREATING HIGH PERFORMANCE AND ADAPTIVE ENTERPRISES (The Economist 2nd ed. 2015).

Business Intelligence

Business operations can be improved using data-driven *'business intelligence'* ('BI'). BI refers to the use of data, analytics and technologies for decision support. Using BI, a technical analyst can benchmark operations, gain insights from marketplace metrics and internal data and adapt the enterprise for growth and competitiveness by pointing to new opportunities. Combining external marketplace data and internal operations data, BI can thus create an 'intelligence' to point an enterprise in new directions and improve the auditable quality of business processes. Thus, BI institutionalizes a firm by converting a business owner's instinctive process assessments into 'business process management' and 'continuous process improvement.' Business owners can use the 'preparation for sale' period to explore whether any business operations need to be beefed up, dropped, restructured or accelerated for faster 'time-to-value.'

Emotional Intelligence

'Emotional intelligence' (or 'emotional quotient') intersects the range of human emotions and personal awareness. When we are aware of our emotions, we can put them into perspective, not allow them to dominate, and use our time to evaluate the technical aspects of our challenges, such as how to structure and implement a non-hostile business exit. The use of emotional intelligence to manage our own emotions and those of others generally requires three skills: '(1) emotional awareness; (2) the ability to harness emotions and apply them to tasks like thinking and problem solving; and (3) the ability to manage emotions, which includes regulating your own emotions and cheering up or calming down other people.'[3] Inspired by your own awareness, you can choose your best 'heroic self.'[4]

Happy people look positively on life's daily opportunities and challenges. Happiness starts with contributing to the happiness and connectedness of others. In addition to daily mindfulness of how one feels and interacts, happy people select, identify with and contribute daily to a positive

---

[3] *'What is Emotional Intelligence?,'* Psychology Today, https://www.psychologytoday.com/basics/emotional-intelligence, accessed Jan. 31, 2018.

[4] Todd Herman, THE ALTER EGO EFFECT: THE POWER OF SECRET IDENTITIES TO POWER YOUR LIFE (Harper Collins 2019).

community (which could start with a positive marriage). With personal goals that give meaning to living and an acceptance of weaknesses in one's self and others, happy people take initiatives, experiment and learn new things for personal growth, satisfaction and achievement. With an emotionally balanced perspective, happy people bounce back from disappointments with resilience, putting past failures behind them and adapting their goals, direction and emotions to renewal. With a resilient attitude, happy people can transcend mistakes in personal and professional relationships and rebuild anew without losing sight of their direction and achieving emotional meaning to life.[5]

In any business, amicable resolution (by negotiation or mediation) can not only limit dispute resolution costs, but it also preserves commercial relationships. This explains the popularity and wisdom of mediation, arbitration and negotiation for emotionally intelligent exits.

Business Succession Intelligence

In stable private companies, destabilization can result from a founder's failures. The founder might have a 'control' mindset with refusal to share operational knowledge and to support progression towards the next generation of leadership. The founder might engage in early self-dealing that later investors might overlook until the IPO is withdrawn and the founder is forced out of management.

The harmful consequences of dependency on a founder (or other key manager) can be mitigated by effective succession planning. Such planning is necessary to respond to the threat of loss of an organization's key leadership, whether at the executive level or on the shop floor. The succession planner starts by identifying the essential attributes, skills and knowledge base of the key incumbent employees. Then the parties need to understand the timing of a possible transition, retirement or exit. Finally, the implicit knowledge of the key employee needs to be made explicit and transferred to the organization. This latter step is a matter of employment law, where the bargain involves an exchange of incentive compensation for the individual's transfer of such knowledge in an orderly exit.

---

[5] For a framework on the pursuit of happiness, see Vanessa King, 10 KEYS TO HAPPIER LIVING: A PRACTICAL GUIDEBOOK FOR HAPPINESS (Headline Publishing Group 2016).

Training programs for succession can focus on knowledge management and transition. As the organization evolves towards succession, lower-level employees can be moved up by cross-training and upskilling. The entire process may inspire greater loyalty among employees, customers and clients that results in continuous improvement in the customer experience.

Succession planning should address the risk that the company might not be in a good financial condition when the founder leaves the position of control. Business succession intelligence thus invites financial decisions whether to distribute 'wealth' early or defer 'gains' until a joint exit, and how to protect against foreseeable risks. The answer requires some balancing of present versus future liquidity for the founder and other stakeholders. Given the normal imbalance, succession planning is critical for all.

Conversely, effective succession planning can strengthen the organization and increase entity viability and value for all. For startups, restricted stock purchase agreements and stock option awards are thus structured to reward collaboration (including grooming and training of successors) before and after an individual exits. Assignments of intellectual property rights are imposed as a condition of employment, so the organization retains the benefits of the knowledge worker's specialized knowledge. But in larger organizations, the succession plan requires board oversight and management.

'Business succession intelligence' thus requires analysis of talents and future needs for talent, criteria and selection of a successor and managed transition. Done well, succession planning can preserve and add value to any organization. Done poorly, succession planning can wipe out the enterprise.

Business Exit Intelligence

'Business exit intelligence' reflects the product and interplay of emotional intelligence, business intelligence and business design intelligence, applied to the existing legal structure of the enterprise. Ideally, since inception, the legal structure defines rights and duties in various scenarios (such as shareholder disputes, retirement, incapacity, death, family divorce, withdrawals, or lack of full participation, or exit planning for one, a few or all owners).

As explored below, smarter business exits occur when you satisfy three key components of '*business exit intelligence*':

- giving an emotional backstop to your co-owners to enlist reciprocity for a smarter exit design, including an acknowledgment of interdependencies and various legitimate interests;

- looking outside your own limitations (cognitive biases) to find smarter possibilities; and

- reinforcing smarter decision-making by emotional intelligence about your self-esteem attributable to your personal identity and your evolving business 'community' or 'tribe.'

'*Business exit intelligence*' explores possibilities for reasonable exits by individual owners or by all owners who must choose a best joint exit. Like a Monte Carlo simulation of value-weighted, multi-level probabilities, the best solutions come from opening the mind to multiple alternative scenarios, to escape the bias of our own individual perspectives and spontaneous foregone conclusions. You can uncover your winning strategy, learn to put everything at risk but adopt a risk-balanced plan for pursuing new goals for yourself and your business.[6] For good timing, you should evaluate business exit, business divorce, exit and succession scenarios at all key junctures in the business lifecycle and the exit lifecycle. You can overcome your procrastination by taking small steps towards small goals that lead to a smarter business exit. Become an informed opportunist.[7]

Business Divorce Intelligence ('Corporate Divorce' Intelligence)

Realistically, your existing legal structures might not anticipate the particular scenario that you encounter. Such gaps expose the parties to dispute resolution mechanisms such as litigation, negotiation, mediation, arbitration, and liquidation.

'*Business divorce intelligence*' (alternatively, '*corporate divorce intelligence*') is based on the negotiation principle of creating alternative outcomes that

---

[6] See Tracy Goss, THE LAST WORD ON POWER: EXECUTIVE RE-INVENTION FOR LEADERS WHO MUST MAKE THE IMPOSSIBLE HAPPEN, pp. 24-25 (Doubleday 1996) and Jeff Keller, ATTITUDE IS EVERYTHING: CHANGE YOUR ATTITUDE... AND YOU CHANGE YOUR LIFE (INTI PUBLISHING & RESOURCE BOOKS 1999).

[7] See Robert H. Waterman, Jr., THE RENEWAL FACTOR: HOW THE BEST GET AND KEEP THE COMPETITIVE EDGE (Bantam Books 1987), at pp. 6–7.

permit all parties to win something. Game theory teaches that adversaries achieve better outcomes by developing trust and working collaboratively than if they remain hostile and distrustful. You should listen to the other side's stated and implicit needs and design a win-win solution. By opening the door to innovative and responsive possibilities, you can achieve your own goals, particularly the goal of escaping a grinding dispute. Your approach should be supportive, rather than purely defensive. You should continue to ask questions to understand and then identify and explore collaborative solutions. By showing spontaneity, empathy and respect, you can experiment, innovate and find a creative solution.[8]

If you are still blocked from finding a solution, consider reciprocity strategies, or at least empathy and mindfulness of your larger impact. You can then ask yourself how you would act if you were in your co-owner's shoes. Would a coin-toss work? Why not?

Organizational Design for Synergy, Risk Management and Resiliency

A smart exit depends on a smart start, both as to the right design and the right people. At inception, you can lay the groundwork for exit (and manage the risk of a hostile business divorce) by adopting a business model and teaming with the people who fit well into the model and your own temperament. Corporate governance rules can mitigate conflicts, but weeding out the wrong partner early in the game will have a greater impact on your successful exit.

Business Model Risk: Choosing the Right Balance between Piggybacking and Ownership

Your business model should identify all essential assets and business functions that you do not need to own and find ways to minimize capital expenditures. Your innovation will be wasted if you invest too early in long-term assets such as real estate, equipment and other 'wasting' assets. Otherwise, your assets become silent, illiquid partners. Use your capital for your Minimally Viable Product, not for the tools to make it. Your model

---

[8] Gerard I. Nierenberg, FUNDAMENTALS OF NEGOTIATING (Hawthorn Books, Inc. 1973), at pp. 182–195.

must identify opportunities for renting, leasing and outsourcing as well as purchasing from future cash flow as you scale up.

'People Risk': Choosing the Right Personalities for Team Synergies and Corporate Culture

An ugly business divorce usually starts with a mistake in selecting your co-owners or in some failure to manage personal relationships. If you are to exit happily, identify people who meet the criteria for a happy business marriage: industriousness, commitment, flexibility in seeing multiple sides to a problem or opportunity, loyalty, courage, listening skills, respectfulness, humility, low-friction and emotional stability. Ask yourself how each founder fits into the business model. In my view, the most important personality attributes are a combination of analytical acuity and adventurous sharing in both fun and problem-solving. Open, mindful personalities lead to flexibility, collaboration, synergies and mutual respect for mutual rewards.

Look for the high-risk personality traits of a flexible mindset. Do you have any hoarders, screamers, divas, dreamers, parasites, back-stabbers or domineering controllers? Does one leader undermine another by stealing credit for accomplishments or demeaning name-calling? Is this what you want? Can you insure against the risks?

Having chosen the right personalities, you need to train, retain and encourage them for a time when you will no longer be giving the orders. By promoting culture of self-actualization, you will make your business more valuable by internal teamwork and low employee turnover.

Choosing the right personalities applies to choosing investors. All investors impose some rules to protect their investment. But what happens when the company runs out of cash? Will the investor continue to contribute new funds in time? What are the terms for a new contribution? Will one investor dominate a suite of other investors who are tied together under pre-existing relationships? Many startups have gone bankrupt when a single influential investor became hostile to the founders and decided to pull out rather than put more cash at risk.

Supply Chain and Service Provider Risks

Your business depends on third parties providing goods, logistics, services, licensed technology and intellectual property. Any failure by your suppliers can threaten your business. You should manage your outsourcers with appropriate master agreements with audit rights and contingency provisions. You can hire vendor management consultants to audit your vendors' performance and intervene to obtain price reductions and apply penalties for non-performance. Vendor management becomes a necessity where transition to a new supplier would be impracticable. Any change in vendor could fail due to industry concentration, ingrained personnel habits, new training, portability of data or systems and other transition costs.

Ownership Dispute Risk Management

Organizational design to limit risks of disputes among owners starts at the level of defining the scope of business. With a broad scope, all opportunities belong to the company. With a narrow scope, the risk of conflicts of interest can be sharply reduced. A narrow definition allows all owners the flexibility to pursue non-competing ventures and perhaps even act as a captive supplier of commodity goods or services, so long as all owners consent.

Risk Management and Resiliency Plan

The viability of a business organization can be measured by how its design and operations limit risks of toxic threats and facilitate 'disaster recovery.' Begin with compliance with the minimum requirements for existence as a particular type of legal entity. Protect the assets, supply chain and brand name that have been won at the 'sunk cost' to the founders and prior managers. Retain essential knowledge by manuals, records and intellectual property rights. Plan for change in your markets and your personnel. Anticipate crises.

Every organization depends on teamwork. Top management defines the business vision and mission and designs and oversees the business model, strategies, tactics and tools. The 'front office' team faces the customer with sales and marketing. The 'back office' administers human resources, finance, accounting, information technology, legal and compliance. Without individuals in each key role, the organizational design will fail.

Sustainability and growth depend on a complete team and separation of functions (operations, accounting and audit).[9]

Risk management includes taking actions on known risks that you do not expect to occur. It's like skiing into an avalanche. You choose to ignore the risks. Succession failure and corporate stakeholder risks can be your avalanche. Risk management focuses on value at risk, targeting first the biggest risks and the biggest probabilities.

In today's risk-averse B2B environment, enterprise customers require their providers (like your company) to provide business continuity plans, disaster recovery plans and, now, 'risk management and resiliency plans.' Such plans include detailed procedures for business impact analysis of changes in the business environment or in internal procedures. Indeed, reflecting increasing interdependence and operational integration, enterprise customers are requesting suppliers to divulge sensitive proprietary operational information. Such confidential information should be protected in the procedures for requests for proposals ('RFPs'): codes of conduct, business impact analysis, security measures, monitoring, auditing, business continuity planning, crisis management planning, risk management, corporate governance, anti-fraud measures, software escrows for contingent use, step-in rights, customer protection, compliance with new regulations identified by the enterprise customer under the master services agreement, records information governance, physical security, remediation plans, information relating to any company employee or prospective employee, and reports with respect to such supplier processes.

Without risk management and resiliency plans, your business will have difficulty in becoming a trusted service provider to enterprise customers. With such plans, you will not only gain in marketing and sales. You will also optimize enterprise value upon a corporate divorce, change of control or succession. Such plans require your constant vigilance and updating.

---

[9] See Thomas S. Coleman, A PRACTICAL GUIDE TO RISK MANAGEMENT (The Research Foundation of the CFA Institute 2011).

Organizational Processes for Knowledge Management

Business Process Design and Management

Smarter organizational design and exit planning require persistent transition planning for succession or change of control. Without a well-defined, well-managed business, there is nothing to transmit in a sale or succession plan. You have no going concern if your operational processes are not repeatable and auditable under a capability maturity model.[10] Hence, quality assurance should be designed into your operations, including quality checks by internal inspection.

To ensure viability after a change of control, business processes need to be defined and managed. Business process management ('BPM') tools have evolved from simple flowcharts and logic statements to artificial intelligence (AI) tools such as voice-directed robotic process automation. For large, complex organizations, AI-driven chatbots, data collection tools and data analytics can supplant human interaction with customers. Even for startups, data-driven software-defined processes are essential to survival. Even family-owned businesses depend on pre-defined and managed business processes.

For corporate survival, all essential processes need to be anchored in technologies, written procedures and trained personnel. Ironically, process failures arise most often from human failures.

Thus, smaller companies need to institutionalize the operational knowledge of the founders, owners and partners. At the start, a small business's brand value might reside in the founder's personality, skills and availability. If the founder is to create a salable business, the founder must convert the founder's implicit knowledge and experience into repeatable managed business processes that others can apply. This conversion process faces numerous obstacles, such as a controlling founder or CEO or other information hoarder.

---

[10]   See Capability Maturity Model Institute's offerings for process and controls, available at https://cmmiinstitute.com/, accessed June 23, 2019.

Smaller companies can fail because they cannot attract or retain large enterprise clients. BPM helps overcome this weakness. Global enterprises have their own regulatory mandates that will flow down to their supply chains. Whether you provide services online ('SaaS'), on site or remotely, if your company performs outsourced services that affect the financial statements of another company, you may be required to document and be audited for process compliance. Thus, in any services industry, adoption of international standards and annual self-audits has become a tool not only for risk mitigation but also for branding, qualification for RFPs, talent recruitment and individual performance measurement.

BPM requires continuous vigilance and possibly investment for continuous process improvement. Enterprises must continuously analyze, redesign, and improve their end-to-end core business processes.

A BPM approach delivers several benefits throughout your entire business lifecycle:[11]

- Sequencing of operations for efficiency and responsiveness (if repetitive) by improved access to automation via robotic process automation ('RPA'), machine-learning and artificial intelligence;
- Training of knowledge workers for effective service to clients as well as helping your organization conduct post-mortems for post-transactional self-improvement queries and adjustments to the underlying business algorithm;
- A framework for your business continuity plan and risk resiliency program, both of which augment enterprise value as a going concern;
- Improved awareness and compliance with legal mandates, especially privacy, data protection and cyber-security;
- Auditability of business processes for self-certification (under an ISO standard) or third-party certification, which in turn enhances your reputation for compliance, predictability of performance and quality; and
- Credibility as a trustworthy 'enterprise-level' supplier or service provider to global companies.

---

[11] For an analogous life cycle approach aligned with building a business that will sell well in a strategic exit, see Jeremy Straten, THE BUSINESS LEGAL LIFECYCLE: HOW TO SUCCESSFULLY NAVIGATE YOUR WAY FROM STARTUP TO SUCCESS (Michael Hanrahan Publishing 2019).

Intellectual Property Management

Business value depends upon patents, copyrights, trademarks, trade secrets and know-how. Such intellectual property rights ('IPR') has no value unless it is validly acquired and constantly updated, used for competitive value and, for trade secrets, maintained confidential. Your business also receives IPR from licensors and service providers. Sustainability of your business thus depends on having a good program for collecting, evaluating, protecting and deploying IPR.

Knowledge Management

Knowledge management ('KM') addresses the problem of creation, retention, exploitation, adaptation and renewal of business processes. At inception, as a team, the founders of a startup possess all enterprise knowledge (other than 'commodity' services that are outsourced such as accounting, tax preparation and HR administration). As the founders begin to build a team, they hire and delegate discretionary tasks to knowledge workers to execute the business mission, vision and resulting procedures. An organization that fails to capture the explicit rules and implicit cultural intelligence of its knowledge workers exposes its owners to collapse upon the departure of a key knowledge worker.

How can a company retain its cohesion upon the loss of key knowledge workers who retire or leave? If the company does not have a clone, it must fill the gap quickly. A KM consultant can help by interacting with the key knowledge workers. At some point, this interaction results in 'knowledge capture' might have become sufficient for a 'lift and shift' outsourcing of certain high-volume, relatively low value tasks to external service providers, locally or offshore for wage arbitrage. Today, learning organizations are designed for continuous process improvement by teams of knowledge workers who support, challenge and interplay with each other for enterprise agility, using rapid-development thinking like 'lean' and 'Kanban' methodologies to create, test, revise and perfect operational procedures.[12] Further, online software tools ('software as a service') enable

---

[12] For knowledge as an enterprise function, an economic resource, a value chain and a core business strategy, see Timothy W. Powell, THE VALUE OF KNOWLEDGE: THE ECONOMICS OF KNOWLEDGE AND INFORMATION (Walter de Gruyter GmbH 2020).

virtual organizations, so knowledge workers are dispersed, leading to a need for on-site team-building and 'community' activities.

Tips: Designing for Your Smarter Exit

Ignore Succession Planning at Your Peril: Succession planning supports enterprise resiliency and long-term viability. A founder's or board's failure of succession planning invites loss and potential personal liability for imprudence in management.

Share your Business Exit Intelligence: When associating with a business partner, use your business exit intelligence. Identify, share and get agreement on shared exit goals, even if exit is decades away.

Design for Focused Narrow Scope: This will help you dedicate resources only to shared goals. This will avoid distractions and minimize disputes over conflicts of interest.

Design to use Technologies (or Intellectual Property: Without trademarks, copyrights, patents and trade secrets, your enterprise might have negligible value.

Design for Recurring Cash Flow – Digital Transformation and Annuity Revenue Streams: Your enterprise value will be greatest if you can demonstrate stable, recession-resistant cash flow that could be leveraged (with debt) for the buyer to comfortably pay a higher price. You should transform your business model into one that delivers necessary business services with a visible, recurring customer base centered on non-discretionary spending.

Design for Knowledge Management and Process Control. Identify repetitive processes, such as customer intake and onboarding, and automate them by simplifying to the bone! Transform your business model to 'Software as a Service' (or some 'Business Process as a Service'). This requires a minimum investment in technologies such as chatbots, databases, customer relationship management software, and digital media marketing that targets your ideal customer (and their influencers).

Design for the Buyer's Sweet Spot (Joint Exit): For a joint exit, design your company to fill a gap in your target buyer's portfolio. To orchestrate demand by competing buyers for a prized business for sale, the sellers must generate reliable revenue streams with a solid core business that can grow further a new owner's care. As discussed in later chapters, exit planning thus involves short-term strategies to boost revenues and reduce costs. Invest in buy-sell insurance.

Design for Possible Leveraged Buyout (Individual or Joint Exit): For an individual's exit, design your company to have adequate funding, or ability to be leveraged, for the leveraged buyout of an individual co-owner. Avoid chronic undercapitalization. If you are planning to borrow to pay off a departing co-founder, you need to design your organization to meet the lender's sweet spot.

- Understand loan covenants relating to financial ratios and sources and uses of funds and uses of borrowed funds.
- If you cannot justify a high valuation for your borrowing on a value basis, then consider a rationale for a revolving credit to support your growing current cash flow and growing related current liabilities.

Your Professional Advisors

At launch, you can get valuable assistance from business attorneys, accountants, marketing consultants, industrial psychologists, commercial and personal bankers, insurance broker, personal wealth advisers, information technology consultants, information service providers, vendor management consultants and human resource consultants.

Your Self-Assessment

- In your business's organizational design, what value do you get from interactions with your co-owners? Does this create synergies and value? How can this be optimized?
- Consider whether you want to be a 'serial monogamous entrepreneur' (with multiple exits from different high-growth companies) or just a one-company entrepreneur.
- What are the emotional needs of current and prospective new co-owners? How will this interplay with your needs and those of existing co-owners?
- How mature and institutionalized are your business processes that add the most value? Is the business run by 'the seat of the pants' with important operational 'implicit knowledge' being controlled

by one or two individuals? What investment would be required to improve and institutionalize those processes?

- Have you adopted policies and procedures for business process management?
- How could you outsource certain operations to minimize capital investment while retaining core competencies and competitive advantage in-house? Do your suppliers or service providers compete with you?
- What targets do you want your business to achieve in the next two years? Five years?
- What would your 'retirement' look like?

PART II

Governance, Conflicts and Dispute Resolution

2

Corporate Governance for Owners

Governance is the process for managing an organization based on authorized decisions, policies and actions at all levels for operational survival and sustaining shareholder value. Good governance builds value. Poor governance magnifies poor decisions, generates conflicts and can shut doors on opportunities.

In any company, conflict prevention and resolution depend on governance, not simply on culture or strategy. Corporate governance defines written principles and rules for interactions. By contrast, corporate culture flows from unwritten rules and environmental context.

'Corporate culture eats strategy for lunch,' as Peter Drucker would say. 'Renewing' companies 'treat information as their main strategic advantage, and flexibility as their main strategic weapon.'[13] A corporate culture that does not embrace the promise of continuous business growth and transformation will die like Darwin's endangered and extinct species. Thus, company founders do best by embracing a culture that adapts to changes in markets. The business must grow and thrive through share values that translate to shared direction. Adaptability is reflected in the agreements for

---

[13] Waterman, *supra,* at p. 6 ('informed opportunism').

shareholders, employees and the 'value chain' (suppliers, lenders, licensors and customers). Every agreement needs to support termination and renaissance. Hopefully, good relationship management and an adaptable corporate culture can avoid termination.

Basic 'Corporate Governance' for All Owners

Governance is a tool for verifying continued trustworthiness and alignment to the collaboration. Governance processes take the temperature periodically for the corporate vision, mission, goals, strategies, tactics, roles and responsibilities, performance evaluation, accounting and audit. Governance mechanisms therefore are used to decide upon and enforce the trappings of culture, with periodic reviews for adaptation and possible transformation.

Organizational Design: Elements of Corporate Governance

Design for effective corporate governance starts with principles for segregating (or including) the role of business owner from the role of employee manager. Corporate governance describes the methods and procedures required or permitted to duly authorize an action in the corporate name.

Building Trust

How should you define the rules for corporate governance in your company? You cannot just rely on a culture of collaboration and trust each other and work hard for effective collaboration. That's what married people do, until they lose full trust or get regulated (in community property jurisdictions). Trust has many sources and can grow (or fail) over time. Trust can be promoted by a fair 'pre-nuptial' or other agreement that defines the terms of exit.

Before jumping into a 'governance' relationship, consider how to identify key elements that create, build and sustain trust. Trusting relationships generally embody availability, mutuality of interest, competency (though not necessarily in identical roles or functions) and qualities of character such as integrity, persistence and communication. At peak levels, trust also includes personal and social respect and enjoyment, friendship, and treatment as valued family members. The loss of trust in a business relationship thus has all the harm and hurt of a personal divorce. For this reason, by creating duties and rights despite a possible total loss of trust, corporate governance serves as a protection for all stakeholders in case of a loss of trust.

The Formalities

For meetings of the shareholders or the Board, corporate governance requires attention to the drab questions of quorum, majority voting, number of days of advance notice for action by the decision-making body and whether a vote is required at all. In short, the owners must take care to define roles and responsibilities carefully in advance. Without such care, the 'default' rules of the governing laws will apply.

The documentation depends on the form of entity. In corporations, corporate governance derives from the terms of the certificate of incorporation, by-laws and internal operating procedures adopted by the Board of Directors. In LLCs, the certificate of organization and operating agreement define who governs, often with no participation by the members. In limited partnerships, the general partner decides, and any action by a limited partner to govern would normally make that partner personally liable to third parties for any infringement of third-party rights by the partnership.

In a private company, the founding owners define the mission, vision and spirit of closely held enterprises. Since ownership and management are legally separate under corporate law (and can be separated under LLC law), the company's formation and operation reflect governance rules, policies and procedures established by law and internal action. In turn, governance is impossible without the exercise of control by the owners, whether by just appointing corporate directors or LLC managers, or by appointing themselves to such roles. In business exit, disentanglement requires some combination of change of ownership (and resulting control of governance), governance (management). Business exit may also include recapitalization, a new mission or vision, new business models, new strategies, and some new human resources. Sometimes, the company founders have the insight to design a smooth transition for their personal disentanglement. In other cases, a company founder may be expelled by others, or all founders may be expelled by a sale or bankruptcy. Thus, strategic planning for any business needs a plan for such contingencies.

Under corporate law, the board of directors (or other manager under the applicable entity form) has two duties: to adopt and govern according to a long-term strategy (adapting to short-term exigencies) and to appoint and supervise the CEO.

'Braided' Governance for Owners with Non-Owner Roles

Like a braided rope, a 'braided' governance structure enjoys the strengths of multiple strands. Each strand may be strong on its own, but the introduction of multiple governance structures can mitigate the separations (and risks of non-collaboration) among different enterprise teams, leaders and other stakeholders. Thus, a modular, or 'braided,' governance structure will have different teams, or leaders, with overlapping authority to review operations and decisions from different unique perspectives. The strands could be vertical or horizontal. While the board of directors has overall responsibility, it depends on advice from all participants. The board can establish multiple committees of the board, as well as multiple committees of key employees, to keep separate functions and allocate tasks, each with a defined role and perspective. Typical committees include audit, nominating, compensation and special committees for particular issues. Thus, employment issues can be overseen for employment law compliance, finance, legal compliance, marketing, sales, R&D and other perspectives.

In a co-ownership context, preferred shareholders may have special rights in governance, such as veto rights, exclusive decision-making rights for a particular scenario, or other decision-making authority. Such preferences can result in exclusion and expulsion of common stockholders in an extreme scenario.

Protecting Minority Owners

Corporate Law: Duties of Majority and Managers to the Minority

Several state and federal statutes as well as common law doctrines underpin the obligations of shareholders (or 'members' for LLCs), investors, company founders and promoters, directors and officers of corporations, managers of LLCs and general partners in partnerships.

Corporate laws define management duties. Shareholders act as founders or investors in reliance on such duties and can force a business divorce when such duties are breached. So, a brief discussion will help frame the nature of business divorce from the standpoint of a management's breach of such duties. And since the holders of a majority of voting rights can choose or fire the management, any breach of duties by managers that 'oppresses' the holders of a minority of voting rights could instigate business divorce, or litigation to make the minority 'whole' after dilution of 'shareholder value' from 'mismanagement.'

Management by Board of Directors: Fiduciary Duties

Under corporate law, the business and affairs of every Delaware corporation are managed by or under the direction of the corporation's board of directors.[14] In discharging their duty to manage or oversee the management of the corporation, directors owe fiduciary duties of loyalty and care to the corporation and its stockholders.

Management for Shareholder Benefit

Traditional corporate law mandates that the board of directors and officers of a corporation must focus on optimizing 'shareholder value.' Shareholder value generally means profits payable to shareholders in the form of dividends, plus long-term capital gains from holding shares while the corporation operates. This focus on shareholder value defines the obligations of management under duties of loyalty (or 'fiduciary duty,' to put the shareholder interests first ahead of those of management) and due care (prudent business judgment). Let's consider these rules under Delaware law, which is the de facto 'corporate law' in the United States for many reasons despite some drawbacks.

Normal Discretion by the Board: Business Judgment Rule

Under judicial interpretations of state corporation in Delaware, New York and elsewhere, the 'business judgment rule' insulates directors from being second-guessed by a court where a majority of the board has no conflict of interest (see 'duty of loyalty' below) and exercises its discretion to adopt long-term business plans, hire and fire senior officers and generally

---

[14]   See, e.g., Del. Gen. Corp. Law, § 141(a).

'manage' business operations, even where the decision later proves unwise, if not disastrous. Delaware courts apply various flavors.

First, in making a business decision, the directors of a corporation may be presumed to have acted on an informed basis, in good faith and in the honest belief that the action taken was in the best interests of the company. Absent a conflict of interest, in exercising business judgment, boards generally 'are fully protected in relying in good faith upon the records of the corporation and upon such information, opinions, reports or statements presented to the corporation by any of the corporation's officers or employees, ..., or by any other person as to matters the member reasonably believes are within such other person's professional or expert competence and who has been selected with reasonable care by or on behalf of the corporation.'[15] However, when the neutrality and competency of the advisors may be disputed, the board cannot rely on the 'business judgment' rule.

Second, the complaining shareholder must allege breach of fiduciary duty and some conflict of interest. Then the directors must prove 'entire fairness,'[16] such as in a fairness opinion by an independent investment bank.

This common law rule raises problems in business divorce. In closely held corporations, a director may also be a shareholder. By definition, this creates a conflict of interest between roles as shareholder and as director. What if the entire board is composed of shareholders with conflicting personal interests? In such cases, the impacted minority might validly claim a conflict of interest at the board level that violates the director's or officer's duty of loyalty, if the controlling stockholder adopted an interested transaction to protect the director's personal interests and was not reasonably or necessarily related to the best interests of the corporation. In an incipient business divorce, such breach of fiduciary duty might be achieved by having a shareholders' resolution to avoid such conflicts, assuming substantial benefit to the corporation and thus all shareholders generally.

---

[15]   Del. Gen. Corp. Law, § 141(e).

[16]   See Lyman P.Q. Johnson, *Unsettledness in Delaware Corporate Law: Business Judgment Rule, Corporate Purpose*, 38 Del. J. Corp. L. 405, 411–413 (2013), available at https://scholarlycommons.law.wlu.edu/cgi/viewcontent. cgi?article=1346&context=wlufac

Each state's law may apply different requirements before insulating directors from a shareholder's claim of mismanagement. New York's corporation law expressly allows a corporate director to consider a wide variety of factors in deciding on a potential or actual offer for a 'change of control' (for example, sale or merger). Such factors include not only the best interests of the corporation and its shareholders, but also those of current and retired (pensioned) employees, customers, creditors and the prospects for future growth, development, productivity and sustainability for providing goods, services, employment opportunities and employment benefits and other contributions to their communities.[17]

Duty of loyalty

Broadly stated, the duty of loyalty requires directors to act in good faith to advance the best interests of the corporation and, similarly, to refrain from conduct that injures the corporation's interests, as set forth in the certificate of incorporation and any shareholders' agreement. The duty of loyalty prevents a director or officer from putting personal interests ahead of the corporation's, such as in self-dealing, unreasonably preventing shareholder action to replace the director, or profiting from the corporation's confidential information. Likewise, the directors must exercise good-faith efforts to implement corporate policies to comply with the laws relating to its operations and to monitor internal compliance, at least by senior management. This duty of loyalty likewise requires a duty to balance all considerations to produce the best solution for the stockholders.

Sometimes a majority of the board has conflicting personal interests in a proposed corporation. In that case, the 'business judgment rule' cannot apply. The directors will then have the burden of proof to show the self-dealing transaction is entirely fair to the corporation. This burden of proof might be satisfied if the board relies on impartial and independent decision-makers for professional advice and even a 'fairness opinion.' But even then, minority shareholders may succeed in showing unfairness.

---

[17] N.Y. Bus. Corp. Law, § 717(b). It defines 'control' as 'the possession, directly or indirectly, of the power to direct or cause the direction of the management and policies of the corporation, whether through the ownership of voting stock, by contract, or otherwise.'

Misappropriation of Corporate Opportunity

The corporate opportunity doctrine is a subset of fiduciary duty. A 'corporate opportunity' is a business opportunity that belongs to the business entity and meets three criteria. First, the opportunity fits within the company's line of business, broadly interpreted. Second, the company has a legitimate interest or expectancy in the opportunity (determined by reviewing the corporate governance documents). Third, the company is financially able to pursue the opportunity without further funding. For usurping a corporate opportunity, the breaching party (whether co-owner, director, officer, manager or employee) must disgorge all profits and equity from the usurpation or secret advantage.[18] To counteract a party's inequitable conduct, a court may also impose a constructive trust on the property, interests and profits so acquired.

You can avoid such a disaster by playing fair. First, at inception, you can narrowly define the company's goals and thus its opportunities. Maybe you should carve out and reserve specific opportunities that the governance documents bar the company from pursuing. Second, if there is any doubt, you can offer the opportunity to the board of directors and hope they decline to pursue it, either for lack of fit with the company's line of business or lack of finances.

Duty of reasonable care

Managing a company requires creativity and risk-taking. How much risk-taking can a director take without being legally liable for gross negligence or 'wasting' the company's assets? Under the duty of care, the directors must make prudent business decisions by being careful. The duty of care requires directors to make informed business decisions but recognizes that directors must make decisions constantly and cannot spend forever on each one. Thus, directors are not required to review all information in making their decisions — only the information that is material to the decision

---

[18]   *In re: Mobilactive Media*, LLC, (Consol. C.A. No. 5725-VCP) (Del. Ch. Jan. 25, 2013), slip op. (Parsons, Vice Chancellor), at pp. 56-61 (a 50--50 owner of joint venture was liable for usurpation; court denied dissolution due to deadlock as inequitable due to consequences of usurpation). See also Delaware's Uniform Fraudulent Transfer Act, 6 Del. Code § 1304 *et seq.* (transfer of a company's assets includes corporate opportunities and must be supported by reasonably equivalent value, or it is fraudulent).

before them. Nevertheless, in evaluating information provided to them by management, directors are expected to review the information critically and not accept it blindly.

In each disputed case, courts will generally consider the level of effort and quality of analysis. How much time did the directors have to review information on a proposed action? What information did they review? Did they ask critical questions about that information? Did they obtain expert financial or legal advice? Were they informed and did they consider all reasonable risks?

Directors without a 'conflict of interest' are not liable for reasonable decisions, but if they fail to analyze the proposed actions without regard to identifying and analyzing potential risks, they may be held liable under Delaware's 'gross negligence' standard. Further, Delaware law allows corporations to immunize, by a charter provision, directors from personal monetary liability for violating their duty of care.[19] This does not shield directors from liability for violating their duty of loyalty. In a business divorce, the minority will thus gain more traction claiming a breach of duty of loyalty (such as self-dealing) than for a breach of the duty of care (such as taking a risk in good faith without conflict of interest).

Selecting Special Corporation Laws: Modification of Normal Duties

Until recently, most state laws followed the traditional duties of loyalty and duty of care for all managers, with a duty to work for the best interests of the owners. Recently, two twists apply: exoneration (and permitted self-dealing) and a duty to work for social welfare beyond the interests of shareholders.

Where to Create your Legal Entity

Why incorporate in Delaware?

In the United States, business entities are creatures of the individual states and territories (and the District of Columbia). Certain state legislatures (such as Delaware, Nevada and Wyoming) have developed local laws in a

---

[19] Del. Gen. Corp. Law, § 102(b)(7).

manner to attract non-residents to choose such local laws as the framework for a new business entity.

The 'advantages' of Delaware as a situs for entity formation may include choices to enable LLCs to exclude fiduciary duties by LLC managers or to avoid some other corporate law (such as New York's) that holds the ten largest shareholders personally liable for employment payments.[20] The advantages may also arise in business exit scenarios discussed later.

Effective August 1, 2013, the Delaware General Assembly amended its LLC Act to allow the members to choose whether or not to waive any fiduciary duties of care and loyalty to the LLC and its members.[21] Before this amendment, while LLC operating agreements might have previously expressly permitted managers (or managing members) to enter into commercial transactions with the LLC, the operating agreements could not clearly waive fiduciary duties of care and loyalty. After this amendment, LLC operating agreements can exclude any duty of fiduciary duty and loyalty. This change promotes harmony by eliminating the possibility of a challenge by minority members about 'self-dealing' or about 'theft of corporate opportunity' by the managers.

This distinction may promote business divorce, or at least result in oppression of minority owners. With an understanding this technical difference, founders and investors in LLCs need to decide whether the risks of such misconduct are outweighed by the benefits of encouraging the managers to provide goods, services, finance or other benefits to the LLC as if they were not managers.

Social Benefit Corporations ('B Corp' or 'B LLC'))

A business manager's normal duty of loyalty and due care is owed only to business owners. Exceptionally, to promote social benefits using private enterprise, states have adopted special corporation laws to enable a corporation to consider and allocate resources to promoting some defined scope of social benefits, in addition to shareholder welfare. The 'B Corp' structure requires that the shareholders approve a provision in the corporate charter to define the targeted social benefits. The 'B Corp' corporation laws (and corresponding 'B LLC' laws) generally require that a member of the

---

20   N.Y. Bus. Corp. Law, §630.
21   Del. LLC Act, §18-1104.

board of directors be appointed to give an annual report to shareholders on the relative success of such targets.

B Corporations thus become more complex to manage. By allowing management to pursue vague social welfare goals, the shareholders accept profit dilution with society. This profit dilution is accepted as part of becoming a shareholder. However, if the majority owners wish to convert to a B Corp, any minority shareholder disagreeing with that conversion would need to act to redeem or sell the shares and exit the ownership role.

Triple Play: Shareholders, Community and Ecological Sustainability

Imagine a B Corp that is managed not only for shareholders and a defined 'community' of target beneficiaries of corporate operations. Imagine a B Corp that also pursues sustainable ecological protection, such as organic farming, electric automobiles, solar panels for reduced dependency on the electrical grid, and so on This is your new 'Triple Play' next generation company.

Designing and managing a business that supports shareholders, community and the ecosystem is easy to imagine. But owners must understand the dilution of profits that will flow from investments in social and ecological externalities. Compared to a traditional corporation, in such a B Corp, dividends might be smaller, but moral sensitivity might be greater. 'Triple play' companies may be easy to invest in. But, with triple dilution, they can be difficult or impossible to exit, restructure, sell or regrow upon a business divorce.

Shareholder Rights and Remedies

Shareholders can challenge the validity of board decisions under corporate law. And they can also assert rights as creditors, employees, whistleblowers, civil rights victims and harassment victims.

In a shareholder derivative suit, a shareholder may sue the board of directors for actions by the board that breached the integrity of the corporation during the shareholder's ownership of any shares.[22] Claims are treated as

---

[22] Del. Gen. Corp. Law, § 327.

'derivative' when they 'naturally assert that the corporation's funds have been wrongfully depleted, which, though harming the corporation directly, harms the stockholders only derivatively so far as their stock loses value.'[23]

In effect, the Board's failure to act justifies the shareholder's suit. In common law jurisdictions, the court might also grant 'equitable relief' separate from 'legal remedies' for contract breach. Equitable remedies target the non-compliant individual (or entity) to compel performance or pay *quantum meruit* ('what it was worth') where there was no adequate consideration for a contract but where such payment would be necessary to avoid unfairness and unjust enrichment. And, under the principle of 'unjust enrichment,' compensation is owed where it would be inequitable to allow the person performing the services to get less than fair value and to entitle the recipient of those services to be 'unjustly enriched.'

Oppressed minority shareholders may have a claim against the majority, or the directors and officers appointed by the majority, to return any misappropriated assets that have been converted to personal use to the corporate entity. 'Restitution' is a judicial remedy to force disgorgement of property obtained through misrepresentation or other misconduct.

In equity, a court might order an injunction. It might compel specific performance of a task previously agreed by the defendant. It might compel an accounting for profits (to be allocated by prior agreement or by the court). To prevent unfairness, the court might order rescission of the bargain and mutual restitution of prior transfers. The remedy might be as simple as ordering the rectification of a record or declaring 'equitable estoppel' to prevent someone from claiming a right that was already waived or abandoned. Where the assets are unique, the court could impose an equitable lien to prevent the sale of a unique asset without the court's further permission, or, after such a sale of the unique asset, impose a constructive trust on the proceeds of joint operations. Where a party has indemnified the damaged victim, the court could enforce a common law right of subrogation, allowing the indemnitor to enforce the rights of the victim against the wrongdoer.

---

23 *El Paso Pipeline GP Co., L.L.C. v. Brinckerhoff*, 152 A.3d 1248, 1261 (Del. 2016).

Claims by Minority Owners under Corporate Law

Resolution of shareholder disputes triggers the interplay of competing public policies. Laws governing corporate and commercial entities protect shareholders, directors and officers. But other laws set up a cascade of potential conflicts of law. Hence, resolving shareholder disputes and planning any succession of management or control entails a balancing of public policies and rights.

There are multiple legal theories of an owner's misconduct. In litigation against an oppressive majority owner or director or officer, the aggrieved minority may claim personal damages for injury to the value of the minority owner's shares arising from misconduct. Typically, such misconduct might allegedly include usurpation of corporate opportunity, looting (shifting assets from one company to another), self-dealing, securities fraud, breach of fiduciary duty or common law fraud. Other claims may include defamation or tortious interference with existing business relationship or prospective business relationship. In a hostile corporate divorce, the claims might also include actual and constructive fraudulent conveyance and transfer, insider preferences, illegal dividends, breach of contract, intentional interference with contractual relations, aiding and abetting breach of fiduciary duty and unjust enrichment.

Standards for Judicial Validation of Actions by Directors or Controlling Owners. Court decisions highlight the procedural steps needed to seek an 'equitable' remedy (not just for damages). This enables courts to impose a 'constructive trust' and seize a director's or controlling owner's personal assets purchased improperly with corporate monies.

- *Stringent 'Entire Fairness' Test (if Conflict of Interest).* Directors owe the shareholders a fiduciary duty to act in the best interests of the entire company and all shareholders. Controlling shareholders (measured by voting rights or other form of control) owe a similar fiduciary duty. Where there is a potential conflict of interests between personal and fiduciary roles, the courts will review the 'entire fairness' of the challenged transactions. For this, fairness opinions by third parties can be persuasive evidence.

- *Deferential 'Business Judgment' Test (if no Conflict of Interest).* Normally, courts do not intervene where the board of directors or controlling owner have no personal interest in a transaction and exercise some valid 'business judgment.' Thus, a controlling owner is not held to the stringent 'entire fairness' standard where the benefits of the challenged transactions are distributed to all shareholders pro rata and the controlling owner does not also receive a 'unique benefit.' No unique benefit arises merely because the transactions provide an ancillary benefit to the controlling shareholder such as providing urgently needed personal liquidity.[24] But the controlling owner may be held to the 'entire fairness' standard if he or she has a financial interest in a corporate transaction, exercises a position of control over the board to force it to provide him or her with a unique benefit, and taints the transactional negotiations so as to prejudice the minority stockholders.[25]

- *'Step-Transaction' Test (Collapsing Multiple Transactions as One).* Sometimes controlling owners adopt a series of steps that, if done as a single step, would clearly breach fiduciary duty. Courts interpreting corporate laws have adopted a 'step-transaction doctrine' to collapse and judge component transactions as a single event. Delaware courts apply this doctrine in any one of three scenarios.

  o Under the *'end result test,'* the doctrine will be invoked 'if it appears that a series of separate transactions were prearranged parts of what was a single transaction, cast from the outset to achieve the ultimate result.'

  o Under the *'interdependence test,'* transactions will be treated as one if 'the steps are so interdependent that the legal relations created by one transaction would have been fruitless without a completion of the series.'

  o Under the *'binding-commitment test,'* a series of transactions will be combined if, at the time the first step is entered into, there was a binding commitment to undertake the later steps.[26]

---

[24] *Gamco Asset Mgt. Inc. v. iHeartMedia Inc.* C.A. No. 12312-VCS (Del. Ch. Nov. 29, 2016).

[25] *New Jersey Carpenters Pension Fund v. Infogroup, Inc.,* C.A. No. 5334-VCN (Del. Ch. Oct. 6, 2011).

[26] *Liberty Mutual Corp. v. The Bank of New York Trust Company, N.A.,* C.A. No. 5702-VCL (Del. Ch. Apr. 29, 2011), slip op., at p. 19, available at https://courts.delaware.gov/opinions/download.aspx?ID=154060.

Damages get more complex when an owner also owed duties under a contract, such as a manager's duties under a shareholders' agreement or LLC operating agreement. In that case, in addition to corporate governance principles, the other owners could obtain damages under a contract theory, claiming a breach of the implied covenant of good faith and fair dealing in the performance of such contracts.

Where multiple owners controlling a majority act in concert to defeat the rights of the minority, the minority could seek damages for the fact that they aided and abetted each other in the underlying breach of rights. This is an after-thought, to use a phrase from criminal law in civil cases. In civil cases, the tort of 'aiding and abetting' does not constitute the underlying claim or a basis for supplemental damages. Such a claim might justify punitive damages in an egregious case, so a minority owner can be expected to point out how the majority interacted to defeat the minority's rights.

Who Can Claim What under 'Derivative' and 'Direct' Claims? When making claims, minority owners must distinguish between direct claims targeting them personally and derivative claims targeting all minority owners. The courts look at 'whose ox was gored' and 'who is entitled to damages': '(1) who suffered the alleged harm (the company or the suing stockholder, individually); and (2) who would receive the benefit of any recovery or other remedy (the company or the stockholder, individually).'[27] For claims that are derivative (for the benefit of the entire company), the board has inherent power to rectify its own neglect of its duties. So courts require any complaining owner to first demonstrate that the board has been notified of its objectionable conduct and requested to rectify it, or that any complaint to the board would be fruitless. Otherwise, the court will dismiss a derivative claim.

For 'direct' claims, the minority must show how the minority was targeted individually.

Some claims can be both 'derivative' and 'direct.' 'Dual claims' occur when the dispute involves a controlling stockholder and transactions 'that resulted in an improper transfer of both economic value and voting power from the minority stockholders to the controlling stockholder.'[28] Thus, direct claims cannot be asserted by a minority without a claim that the

---

[27] *Tooley v. Donaldson, Lufkin & Jenrette, Inc.,* 845 A.2d 1031, 1033 (Del. 2004).
[28] *El Paso Pipeline GP Co., L.L.C. v. Brinckerhoff,* 152 A.3d 1248 (Del. 2016).

controlling stockholder also diluted voting rights. And claims of breach of fiduciary duty and corporate waste (decisions that waste company assets) are not 'dual claims.'[29]

Claim by Minority for Asset-Stripping by Majority. Majority owners have a fiduciary duty to include all shareholders in the cash received from the sale of all (or substantially all) company assets. The logic is simple. Such a sale will kill the joint business, so it should be treated as a sale of the business, with payments to the equity owners for their proportionate shares. Otherwise, the majority might find some artifice to strip the company assets and pay the proceeds to themselves as a bonus or other special compensation.

Suppose the majority had lent money to the company and used the proceeds of an asset-stripping sale to repay loans made by the majority in good faith. In this scenario, the controlling owner receives repayment of a prior loan before sharing with the minority only the net after such loan payoff. Not so fast, the minority will say. Under the 'thin capitalization" test for piercing the corporate veil (and holding directors and controlling owners liable for company obligations), loans are normally not considered loans where the borrower has no capacity to repay. The minority would claim that, if the company was unable to operate without the loan, and the loan could not be repaid under ordinary business conditions, the loan was disguised equity and the loan should be treated as equity for purposes of distributing assets on a sale of substantially all assets.

---

[29] *Dietrichson v. Knott*, C.A. 11965-VCMR (Del. Ch. Apr. 19, 2017), slip op., at pp. 12-13.

From the case files

What difference does it make if you sell substantially all assets instead of selling substantially all shares (or merging to eliminate all shares)?

A tech startup had a mission to facilitate online charitable donations. It developed an online donation platform and licensed it to clients. But the company never reached the point of sustainable positive cash flow. After developing the software platform, the founder adopted an exit plan. He fired those employees who had not already left, sold substantially all assets (the platform, copyrights, trademarks and all client contracts) to a customer (a non-profit corporation), and resigns as director, President, Secretary and employee shortly after the sale. Without these assets, the company had no operations and no ability to stay in business. From the proceeds of the asset sale, the founder repaid to himself the loans he had made to the company and any excess proceeds of sale.

As director, the founder never informed the handful of other owners of the sale. The other owners consisted solely of former employees with vested shares from the stock option plan. In effect, he had stripped assets without accounting for self-dealing. The repayment of a loan might have been legal, but only if the company had a viable future after the sale. The former employees filed claims for breach of fiduciary duty, self dealing and collusion with the buyer (who was named under a conspiracy theory).

How ironic! Some of the employee-owners had sacrificed market-level wages to 'do good' by quitting a better-paying job to support the company's charitable mission. By structuring the exit as an asset sale, the founder deprived them of the value of their work, their personal sacrifice and their self-respect. This tragedy could have been avoided by proper corporate governance. The majority owner should have called a shareholder meeting for disclosure, discussion and a vote to consent, with a plan to use the sale proceeds to pay equity to the minority shareholders as if in a liquidation. Or the founder might have bought out the few owners before the asset sale.

How entangling! If you are the asset buyer and the deal would cover substantially all assets of another company, beware! Here, by his self-dealing and fraud on the selling company's shareholders, the seller's founder also exposed the buyer (a regulated non-profit company) to litigation for aiding and abetting and reputational injury. As a non-profit corporation, the buyer also became vulnerable to disciplinary action by the state Attorney General.

Claims against Minority Shareholders under Corporate Law

Similarly, if a minority owner 'exercises control over the business and affairs of the corporation,' the minority owner may be held liable for self-dealing or abuse of control that gives it special benefits at the expense of other shareholders.[30]

Tools for Good Governance to Manage Predictable Conflicts

Like governmental constitutions, corporate governance that concentrates all decision authority in one person invites corruption. A one-person board of directors for a startup might suffice for a while. Adding others to the board, inviting professional advisors to 'board' meetings or having other checks and balances can help avoid the corrupting influence of absolute power.

In corporations, the duty of loyalty may be infringed when a director has a conflict of interest. To minimize such conflicts by executives who are directors, board committees are normally established with independent directors to whom certain limited functions are delegated by the corporate by-laws. Such powers may be very broad, such as audit or approval of a management buyout proposal. The existence and charter of board committees thus insulates all board members from shareholder claims of self-dealing (or collusion that allows some others to engage in self-dealing.

Interplay of Operations and Governance

Operational excellence addresses business opportunities through new or disruptive business models, digital transformation, cost-cutting, outsourcing, extension of lines of business or territories, vertical integration, and so on. Operational excellence refers to the efficiency and efficacy (like a drug to cure a medical condition) of the enterprise at all levels and operations. Each department or function can be measured against key performance indicators, such as cost per unit purchased, speed of processing and speed delivery to client. But operational excellence also depends on taking the appropriate actions steps under the particular conditions and goals for continuous process improvement.

Failing operations might not necessarily mean that corporate governance was a failure. Operational decline points to mismanagement and thus a 'governance' failure by the owners to supervise and replace deficient managers. Replacement of the manager might suffice. But if the manager

---

[30] *In re Primedia Inc. Derivative Litig.,* 910 A.2d 248, 257 (Del. Ch. 2006).

is also an equity holder, then the resolution will involve employment, management and shareholder rights. In short, failing operations do not automatically result in failed corporate governance.

Conversely, a failure in corporate governance will undoubtedly harm operational excellence. Conflicts among owners distract them from running the business.

So enterprise survival depends on resolving governance disputes. In some cases, business divorce hurts the smaller company (or prevents it from achieving its full potential). In other cases, business divorce creates new opportunities for refurbishing a failed operation through new leadership, new capital, new business channels and new customers. So business divorce and innovation (and further innovation) play a symbiotic role in the global economy.

Interplay of Compliance and Governance

Compliance with laws, regulations, contracts and company policies is part of the duty of the board of directors under the heading of acting prudently and staying informed so their decisions are protected by the business judgment rule. Shareholders are therefore entitled to expect the board to protect enterprise value from losses due to non-compliance, breach of contracts and miscellaneous third-party litigations. Business owners who are directors or officers can be held accountable in a dispute involving ownership, owner expulsion, owner resignation or owner employment. Without a compliance program that is vigilantly policed, such owners are vulnerable in a disputed business divorce.

Compliance programs might be designed for protecting the company and others dealing with the company, as well as for a clean joint exit by sale to a buyer. However, compliance programs are essential to your self-protection from unnecessary or unjustified hostilities among shareholders. In short, adopt and manage your compliance programs as if your happiness and wealth (and potential personal liability) depended on it.

Protecting Holders of Rights Convertible to Equity

Traditional corporate finance tools include payments convertible to equity. Such payments can be characterized as debt, warrants or equity with an indefinite conversion ratio. The original character of such payments may determine the method for a business exit.

Handshake Deals between 'Co-Owners': No Rights

There is no business exit without a business to split up. If there is only an 'agreement to agree,' no valid or enforceable contract exists. Neither party owes the other anything. Each can walk away. An invalid 'agreement to agree' occurs when it omits 'a material term that is left for future negotiations'[31] or is so vague, indefinite and uncertain that the full intention of the parties cannot be 'ascertained to a reasonable degree of certainty.'[32] In such conditions, no amount of explanations can overcome the fundamental unenforceability.

But the lack of any agreement to be in business together does not prevent a party acting in good faith, and in reliance upon an express yet vague inducement by the other party, from demanding compensation for the loss incurred in relying on that inducement. Hence, clear contracts, with defined deliverables and deadlines, can help avoid confusion and disputes with owners and other stakeholders.

Delayed 'Co-Ownership': Rights Convertible to Equity in the Future

Some investments are structured as something other than vested ownership. For holders of equity-flavored rights, a business exit might occur before the conversion to a debt obligation or contract rights to full equity. The mechanism depends on the legal structure.

Convertible Notes (Debt)

Lenders take priority over shareholders if the company goes bankrupt. A 'convertible note' is a debt obligation of the borrower to pay a fixed sum according to a fixed payment schedule, with interest.

The timing and rate of conversion to equity must be negotiated. The lender has the right to convert the principal and maybe also the unpaid

---

[31] *Joseph Martin, Jr., Delicatessen v Schumacher*, 52 N.Y.2d 105, 110 (1981).
[32] *Varney v. Ditmars*, 217 N.Y. 223, 111 N.E. 822 (1916).

interest into equity at a ratio determined in the note. Typically, this ratio is determined by reference to some agreed form of valuation. Such valuations can come in the form of a new capital contribution by a new investor, thus creating an artificial market. Or the valuation can be based on some expert's appraisal, which can be expensive, time-consuming and subject to dispute.

Convertible debt is problematic. First, the conversion ratio is guesswork because actual valuation is pure guesswork. Second, the lender has no voting rights or shareholder rights (especially for alleged breach of fiduciary duty) until conversion. Third, for the company, convertible debt has the downside of requiring payments of interest (or even principal) when there might be no cash flow. Finally, because conversion is a choice for the lender, a distressed company and its lender/investor might dance around the outcomes of a conversion or non-conversion during a downward spiral.

'Simple Agreements for Future Equity' ('SAFEs')

Sometimes contractual rights give the right to convert a payment to future equity at a ratio to be determined by reference to a future equity contribution by a third party. In a Simple Agreement for Future Equity (SAFE), the business contractually promises to issue some form of securities to an investor who receives the SAFE. The SAFE approach was conceived by a startup incubator to respond to two problems. First, a convertible note requires payment of interest, but any outflow by a startup company starved for liquidity can set back its growth. Second, a preferred stock issuance to an early investor is complex and would likely be undone by a later-round venture capital investor seeking rights superior to all founders, investors and holders of equity rights. Unlike shares, however, the SAFE does not entitle the holder to vote. Nor is there a maturity for payments. SAFEs contain a preference in liquidation, to repay all assets of the company to the SAFE investors before any distribution to shareholders. So the SAFE investors are protected ahead of common stockholders in liquidation.

Warrants

Like a purchase option, a warrant is the contractual right to be issued shares (or other equity). In a business exit, the value of the warrant is nil until such issuance. Typically, warrants are issued for services to startups (such providing a finder's services to introduce investors). Customarily, a change of control of the startup does not trigger any right for the warrant holder to demand issuance of the shares. Thus, except when the warrant becomes exercisable, warrant holders are effectively disenfranchised in any matters involving a business exit.

Preferred Shareholders

Under the certificate of incorporation, a preferred shareholder may convert preferred shares to common shares at will. The conversion ratio will be pegged to a fixed ratio, but a more favorable ratio may apply to protect the investor against declining valuations. In a 'down' round where new investors pay less than the existing preferred shareholder paid, the preferred shareholder can be protected from value dilution by receiving additional shares as if all its shares had been purchased at the new lower purchase price.

Professional investors generally insist on purchasing preferred shares in startups. On the upside, such investors might get two payouts on a joint exit. First, they can get a minimum multiple return on investment before any payout to common stockholders. Second, after this preferred return, they might get a negotiated share of the remaining purchase price on a pro rata basis as if the preferred shares had been converted to common stock. Thus, if agreed, the preferred stockholder can also participate *pari passu* on equal footing with the common stockholders in the next slice of the proceeds of sale of shares to the strategic buyer, thus double-dipping. On the downside, the investor may be paid 100 percent of its investment in liquidation or dissolution.

Compared to common stock, preferred stock has preferential rights. Preferential rights for preferred stockholders depend on the negotiated terms. Preferences vary. For dividends, preference can be given for timing and priority of payments of dividends. For change of control (or loss of control), preferences can be given for priority in the distribution of net assets upon liquidation (or 'deemed' liquidation by change of control). A preferred shareholder might have a right of first refusal to subscribe to additional capital upon admission of a new shareholder (thus preserving parity and avoiding dilution).

Stock Options and Other Rights Convertible to Equity

Equity interests in a business are frequently used as incentive compensation for service providers. In light of the risk of forfeiture, what is the framework for the rights and responsibilities of key employees when a business exit is imminent?

Deferred Vesting of Equity Compensation

A corporation or LLC may agree to issue equity ownership to employees or independent contractors as incentive compensation. Such options or grants may be immediately taxable in full, unless vesting is subject to substantial risk of forfeiture.[33]

Conditions of Vesting

Usually, for employees and independent contractors providing services partially in consideration of the issuance of some equity ownership interest in the business, the absolute ownership may be delayed, so their rights are not 'vested' until after performance of services over a period of years. Vesting can be gradual, based on a percentage each month, quarter or year or upon achievement of particular pre-defined performance milestones. Vesting can be based on one event, such as a future change of control (sale or merger). Deferred vesting of equity as compensation for services is key to an intelligent design for business exit. Deferral can help ensure that the entity receives the intended benefits over a reasonable time frame.

For startups and emerging growth companies, delayed vesting of equity compensation is a critical factor in attracting and retaining capable and motivated talent. For startups, the typical requirement for vesting is based on time spent.

For senior executives in a mature public company, equity incentive compensation (as well as bonuses) can depend on achievement of one or more key performance metrics (for instance, KPIs) linked to multiple measures of company financial performance of the company or a subdivision (for example, revenue, net revenue, return on investment, return on equity, and so on), elimination of particular hazards to company viability, or fulfillment of some transition plan decreed by the board of directors.

---

[33] See Internal Revenue Code ('Code'), 26 U.S.C. §§ 83(b), 421-424 and 409A.

In exceptional cases, a founder might be rewarded with benefits *after* death. In March 2018, Blackstone CEO Stephen Schwartzman designed a compensation package that includes a car and driver for life (not just while employed at the world's largest private equity firm by assets). If and when he retires, he will be reimbursed for all business-related travel and legal fees for matters relating to the firm. For a decade after his death, his estate will be entitled to invest in, or alongside, Blackstone's funds without paying participation or management fees. Such exceptional terms could only be available to a founder who created a vast successful company and whose post-retirement role contemplates some ongoing role as a public face of the company. The private equity firm will enjoy the benefits of this founder's deep institutional knowledge and reputation as an industry leader with political connections.[34]

For family-owned businesses, employee might not be fully vested at any time, but only get the right to collect on the appreciation in value of the company's shares. Such arrangements could be structured as phantom shares (which generally are taxable as ordinary income) or an Employee Stock Option Plan.

For private equity, the investment manager's 'carried interest' aligns the interests of the investors and the managers. However, to prevent the managers from getting a free ride on a normal appreciation in the market (for example, from inflation or other events external to portfolio management), fund managers' rights to the carried interest may be subject to achievement of a minimum 'hurdle rate' of return. At the fund level, this hurdle rate can encourage the fund managers to beat the benchmarks of stock and bond indices for comparable types of risk investments. At the individual fund manager level, the partnership or LLC operating agreement keeps loyalty by justifying distributions of the individual's percentage share of the entity that is the fund manager, but only upon achievement of persistent performance over the life of the particular fund entity. Investors in VC and PE funds should understand the contingencies embedded in the reward system before investing.

Terminability of Employment or other Services 'At Will'

---

[34] Dawn Lim, '*Blackstone CEO Schwartzman Gets New Rewards,*' Wall St. J. (Mar. 19, 2018), p. B2, cols. 1–2.

Business owners may provide incentive compensation with equity interests under 'deferred vesting.' But problems will arise if the individual's relationship as employee or other service provider cannot be terminated 'at will' by the controlling individuals.

For employees, termination of employment normally terminates the stock options. Where the employee has legal grounds to dispute the validity of the involuntary termination of employment, the settlement agreement might include vesting of some or all of the unvested equity in addition to some cash as wages, bonuses and commissions. In a settlement, the employer may gain substantial value by allowing some vesting of stock options, since any action by the former employee or former service provider to disparage the reputation, to compete or to solicit employees, suppliers or customers to abandon relations with the company could be used to invalidate the extended grant of vesting. In short, contingent vesting puts the departed employee or service provider at risk of loss and continues the alignment of interests after termination of services.

The symbiotic relationship between an employer and its employees (who may include owners) flows from pre-mercantile common law of master and servant. The servant owes a duty of loyalty to avoid conflicts of interest with master's business, such as competition or misappropriation of business opportunity. Added to these fiduciary duties are any contractual commitments that could expand or add to these generic duties. Where there are multiple owners, documentation of such contractual duties is essential to an intelligent design for corporate governance and possible business exit.

Most well-governed startups define the conditions under which co-founders, as employees, might enjoy equity compensation or other incentive compensation. Such compensation might include commissions or bonuses for achieving defined targets. Where such documentation is sloppy or lacking, the company might be justified in denying such incentives (or recovering incentives already paid) because the employee, though achieving the targets, engaged in competitive conduct that harmed the employer. Under this 'faithless servant' doctrine, the employer can thus recover some damages.

Forfeiture of Unvested Equity Rights

Your company's incentive compensation plans and awards should give the board of directors the discretion to cause the forfeiture of incentive compensation including equity rights in case an employee engages in misconduct prejudicial to the company, including competition while employed, or that would constitute a reason to terminate employment 'for cause.'

Clawback of Vested Options and Equity Rights

A company executive receiving stock options or restricted shares as incentive compensation may lose vested rights under limited defined circumstances. The employer might 'clawback' the equity-based compensation if the executive engaged in specific types of misconduct, such as proven sexual harassment, misconduct that requires the company later to restate its financial condition, failure to participate as a witness in civil proceedings against the company, breach of fiduciary duty, or other act that might be 'good cause' for termination of employment. The clawback can be made retroactive since the employer was not aware of the misconduct when it happened.

Protecting other Stakeholders: 'Change of Control' or Succession

A 'change of control' or 'change in control' can trigger contractual rights in favor of other owners or non-owner stakeholders. Generally, 'control' means the ability to control the election and replace the board of directors or equivalent supervisory individuals. As a matter of corporate governance and relationship governance, you should understand and be aware of the impact that a change in control might have on ownership, governance and stakeholder rights. Pay attention to the 'termination' and 'assignment' clauses in your contracts.

Tips: How to Avoid Disputes on Fiduciary Duty and Corporate Governance

You can avoid unhappy partners by taking several key steps at the beginning of your new venture with others.

- Stay focused. Limit the scope of your business expressly in corporate governance documents. This will serve as a clear guide for future conduct to avoid allegations that you (or others) usurped the company's business opportunities.

- Get authorization. Get all owners and managers to approve sensitive transactions where your integrity might be challenged. If you ask your board or managers for their decision, they will have a duty to exercise business judgment and be fair. If you don't ask, any owner or manager can claim you abused your fiduciary duty by not presenting the transaction to the owners or managers.

- Argue to the other owners and board. Lobby and persuade so they see your point of view. Do this before the decisions are made.

- Anticipate disputes in governance and avoid dissolution by stalemate. In your corporate governance documents, select and agree on how irreconcilable disputes will be resolved.

- If you are caught in a breach of fiduciary duty, allow for an exit plan that includes sale of the company or sale (or redemption or purchase) of your shares. Consider how you wish to have shares valued based on actual scenarios of good or bad conduct by you or your fellow shareholders.

- Use reciprocity as a guiding principle for fairness in governance.

- Build share repurchase rights into all stock options and shareholder agreements in case of a shareholder's death, disability or death. You might also consider additional repurchase rights of vested shares on termination of a shareholder's employment, subject to a defined method for fair valuation and payment.

- Hold board meetings quarterly (or more frequently) to cover standing agendas for:
    o review and approve prior meeting minutes
    o a report by the president and management team on steps taken to implement the Board-approved strategic plan for the year
    o highlight of the company's progress on each functional area
    o a report on financial results and the likelihood of realizing the current goals under the current financial plan
    o issues requiring board approval, modification of a plan, resource allocation and decisions on executive-level personnel

- o risk analysis (regulatory, litigation, competition, resources, personnel, technology and other operations)
- o possible establishment of *ad hoc* committees of the Board to address specific issues
- o 'Executive Session' discussions without the President or managers
- o review of management's documentation to the Board on the client roster with revenue and a pipeline report with target revenues and probabilities.

Your Professional Advisors

During growth when you are acquiring new employees, new partners and new investors, you can get valuable assistance from business attorneys, intellectual property attorneys, accountants, industrial psychologists and personal wealth advisers.

Your Self-Assessment

- Do you know what your financial investors want for a desired exit plan ('liquidity event')? What roles do your investors and employees play in deciding on governance issues? What preferred rights do they have, or do they want, in governance, dilution of ownership and joint sale?

- Which individual(s) have authority to make decisions binding on your business entity? How are they designated and identified internally and externally?

- How are decisions taken if the 'normal' decision-maker(s) cannot address an urgent matter in a reasonable time?

- Do you follow any regular schedule for formal decision-making in matters of corporate governance, shareholder decisions, and operational management?

- If so, what is the schedule, and how does the outcome become validated by all necessary corporate authorization? What procedures are followed to ensure prompt implementation of 'corporate' decisions?

PART II

Dispute Resolution

3

Stakeholder Ecosystem, Conflicts and Crises

In this chapter, we identify stakeholders in your company, your vulnerabilities and consider how to anticipate, resolve and escape from crises caused by intrinsic conflicts among them. Here are some suggestions on how to avoid becoming a story of a failed business divorce.

Smarter Operations and Smarter Business Exits to Survive a High Mortality Rate

Privately owned businesses are the engine for economic growth and employment, but they suffer from a high rate of mortality. Based on U.S. Department of Labor statistics, small businesses employ about 47.5 percent of the private workforce, but twenty percent of newly formed businesses disappear within the first year, only 31 percent survive ten years and just 24 percent survive twenty years. A 76 percent mortality rate during a twenty-year generation shows the long-term unsustainability of small businesses.[35]

---

[35] U.S. Bureau of Labor Statistics, Business Employment Dynamics, *Establishment Age and Survival Data,* Total Private, Tables 5, 6 and 7, available at https://www.bls.gov/bdm/bdmage.htm#TOTAL and links, accessed Nov. 27, 2019.

The owners of those businesses who cannot sell advantageously will thus suffer personally from organizational unsustainability.

The primary causes of such mortality are lack of demand, insufficient capital, the wrong team, competition and poor pricing.[36] For any type of business, *internal conflicts* and *lack of succession planning* account for many business failures.

For *'tech startups,'* persistent cash shortages are a chronic vulnerability. This leads to potential internal conflicts with different levels of investors. Startup founders must define their business strategies both narrowly and with a high level of projected growth ('scalability'). With their business plan in hand, the founders must solicit investments from 'friends and family' and venture capitalists. With investments realized, they must then rapidly develop the product into a beta form (showing 'proof of concept'), entice buyers (whether B2B, B2C or B2G) despite some long sales cycles, and rapidly scale to large size sales for early exit by sale to a strategic acquirer, merger into another enterprise or initial public offering. Each new level of funding creates conflicts over pre-money valuation, dilution, voting and governance. Startups can die due to lack of continued funding of deficit operations, changes ('pivots') in business model that destroy the investment value of an abandoned business model, and competition by larger or more agile tech companies.

Family businesses are especially risky. They depend on the limited skills, funding and time of founders. For their success, family-owned businesses need to identify and hire talent for special skills, or outsource and supervise independent suppliers of such skills. 'About one in five firms (19.3 percent) are family-owned. Of these family-owned firms, about half are 'equally-owned,' that is, fifty percent owned by one or more men, and fifty percent owned by one or more women. Hence, about one in ten firms is both family-owned and equally-owned.'[37] Without a succession plan to identify

---

[36]   Chad Omar, *'What Percentage Of Small Businesses Fail — And How Can You Avoid Being One Of Them?,'* Forbes Finance Council (Oct. 25, 2018), available at https://www.forbes.com/sites/forbesfinancecouncil/2018/10/25/what-percentage-of-small-businesses-fail-and-how-can-you-avoid-being-one-of-them/#5cffd1ee43b5, accessed November 15, 2019.

[37]   SBA, 'Frequently Asked Questions about Small Business,' Aug. 2018, available at https://www.sba.gov/sites/default/files/advocacy/Frequently-Asked-Questions-Small-Business-2018.pdf.

and train a successor leader, a family business can die when the primary owner retires, dies or becomes incapacitated, without a successor for leadership.

Professional service firms die from a combination of poor business model, poor governance, sudden declines in revenues and departures of professionals taking clients to new firms.

As a common denominator, owners of any type of closely held business can ensure enterprise longevity by acting early and often to protect enterprise value from a *hostile* business divorce. A *'smarter business exit'*™ allows one or more owners to terminate ownership without causing material damage to the enterprise, its reputation or future prospects. A business exit that enables the business to survive will provide substantive benefits to direct and indirect stakeholders one's community and economy.

The next section examines how business owners and their advisors can structure a split to minimize adverse impacts on third party stakeholders as well as the owners. Stakeholder conflicts exist in any privately-owned business, regardless of the stage of formation, growth, maturity or exit. This section explores intrinsic conflicts from a legal perspective.

Equity and Quasi-Equity

Equity means the ownership of your company's shares, whether unconditionally owned ('vested') or subject to a substantial risk of future forfeiture. Quasi-equity consists of the future right to shares or the proceeds of sale of the company. Some quasi-equity has, or will have, voting rights, while other quasi-equity has no voting rights but represents a claim to be paid on a change of control. This is a matter of capital structure, which includes:

- vested owners with full voting rights, such as founders, initial investors ('friends and family'), incubators that take shares in return for training, marketing, networking and co-working services) and other service providers who get some payment in shares;

- vested owners without voting rights (non-voting shares);

- invested owners whose ownership can be terminated as a result of future termination of employment (typically, employees with stock options);

- unvested owners who have only a contractual right to become vested owners, and meanwhile have no voting rights and no status as shareholders, such as:
    o holders of debt convertible to shares, or
    o holders of a contract ('Simple Agreement for Future Equity' or 'Simple Agreement for Future Tokens' of bitcoin) to convert to shares upon some future event such as a Series A round investment by a financial investor; and
- unvested contingent owners (your family) under the law governing families and wealth transfers, as community property spouses, heirs, legatees, trust beneficiaries and their personal representatives).

For your strategies for exit or succession, you are vulnerable to your fellow co-owners and quasi-owners. Your best exit strategy or succession thus depends on your ability to own or collaborate with owners of 'control' of the business. While 'control' generally means a majority of ownership and voting rights, majority rule does not apply under contracts for governance or commercial transactions that have their own rules, such as veto rights, super-majority voting requirements and rights that spring up only on some event such as a contract default.

Claimants

Being in business exposes the company to claims by third parties. Like debts, such claims must be paid first (or accounted for by reducing the net sales price of the company) before owners can take or sell the assets. Your strategic exit depends on the amounts and conditions of repayment of debts to a variety of creditors:

- employees (for wages, wage taxes, health insurance, pensions, expense reimbursements and so on);
- suppliers of goods, services, real estate and technologies (such as vendors, outsourcing service providers, independent contractors, landlords, licensors and SaaS service providers);
- lenders;
- customers;
- anyone who is a potential victim of wrongdoings by your company, such as:

o victim of misappropriation or abuse of intellectual property rights or one's personal identity;

o victim of civil rights discrimination;

o whistleblowers (who can obtain financial rewards if your company is a supplier to the federal government or if you cheat on your income taxes);

o victims of sexual harassment in the workplace, supply chain or value chain;

o individuals whose personal information your company receives, controls, uses or transmits);

o victims of fraud, misrepresentation, intentional or negligent infliction of emotional distress;

o victims of actions that otherwise violate the law (such as debtors who are harassed by your collection agents);

o others potential orphans before or after a change of control, such as Kickstarter contributors and others who expected some benefit from contributing value to your business.

Influencers

Your company's value on sale or succession can be affected by influencers who can help or harm your company's good reputation. Influencers include:
- any current or former claimant.

- competitors;
- the press, social media, hostile and favorable self-publishers of commentary; and
- professional observers, advisors and investment analysts in your industry.

Regulators

Finally, your business depends on obtaining and retaining valid regulatory approvals by governmental and industry regulators. These include regulations on finance, marketing, sales, medicine, education, insurance, transportation, e-commerce and commerce, professional services, ethics, land use, real estate rentals and many more aspects of doing business. Regulators may affect the value of your company by imposing penalties, fines, adverse publicity and thereby inviting civil actions by individuals and classes of alleged victims. Your exit strategies should therefore keep compliance and good housekeeping in mind.

Red Flags Leading to Crisis among Owners

Common Triggers of Crises

Every business divorce arises from governance disputes, sloppiness or mistakes that trigger conflict and crisis. By identifying and dealing such mistakes early, you can perhaps redirect the operations towards a successful and happy exit. By ignoring the red flags, you will be sucked into toxic conflict with losses of value and your personal sanity. Before recommending solutions, it's useful to identify those red flags and anticipate a potential crisis.

- Governance design failures
    - o Poor governance design or implementation, or both
    - o Confused or flimsy governance structures
        - Missing legal formalities and/or adequate operating capital
        - Missing systems, methods and tools for coordination (and collaboration)
        - Missing contingency planning and risk management
        - Missing audit (and accountability)
    - o Misguided reward systems
    - o Confused roles and responsibilities among co-owners
- Governance failures in practice
    - o Breach of express or implied verbal 'agreement' about ownership or governance
    - o Breach of organizational or governance documents
    - o Neglectful leadership style by majority owner(s)
    - o Abuse of 'control'

- o Hoarding of knowledge, intellectual property, trade secrets, relationships and other attributes of control
- o Hoarding, delay or failure to share a corporate opportunity with the board, and other hoarding activity.
- o Hoarding of control by controlling owner's failure to delegate authority or define sharing and institutionalization of organizational culture and operations
- o Nepotism
- o Financial abuses, including use of corporate funds for personal purpose ('cash cow' accounting methods and disguised dividends), accounting errors, 'cooking the books' or maintaining multiple accounting books
- o Self-dealing, fraud and other abuses of power
- o Selfish intent: oppression and abuse, with disproportionate allocation of burdens, risks and rewards
- Governance disputes
  - o Unresolved disputes over succession planning or exit planning (timing and control disputes; restarting after a failed sale, inadequate prep for sale or unrealistic expectations on pricing or terms), control of the future business direction (disputes on policy and change management) or any personal demands.
  - o Deadlock under broad veto rights
  - o Deadlock under 50–50 ownership
- Operational vulnerabilities or distress
  - o Financial distress; persistent need for new infusions of capital
  - o Failed integration of an acquisition
  - o Unfair competition in commerce
- Marketplace conditions
  - o Failure to predict or adapt to disruptions caused by the marketplace or government
- Psychological conditions
  - o Personality disorders of 'sinners' from Dante's 'Inferno,' mainly (1) 'incontinence' (lust, gluttony, greed, wrath, heresy), (2) violence, and (3) fraud (simple fraud by

willful misrepresentation to deprive another), or complex
fraud against someone in a special relationship of trust
(betrayers of kin, country, guests, benefactors and god)

o   Emotional disconnectedness for a needed transition

o   Personality conflicts

o   Psychological deficits: the childhood friend and con artist
as your partner

o   Mental illness

o   Unsportsmanlike conduct: favoritism, self-interest, bias,
deception

- Family problems

o   Personal divorce

o   Family cash flow shortfall.

Delays in Starting the Resolution Process

In any business divorce, time is money. Continuing unresolved conflicts
accentuate emotional distress. Once a serious reason for separation of
owners has arisen, or a serious reason for terminating a strategic alliance
with another business has occurred, time is of the essence. The parties
should not delay the resolution process. Too much delay could enable a
faithless 'partner' to continue existing misconduct. Delays can entrench the
parties in a positional dispute about individual wants, not mutual needs.
Excessive delay might even constitute a deemed waiver (or 'laches') by the
other 'partners' who are aware but take no remedial action.

Crisis Management of Stakeholder Conflicts

Once a decision has been made to split, consider that a decision to expel
a partner could backfire. Proceed only after investigation and planning. If
two or more founders 'gang up' against a third, are their actions personal (as
shareholders) or corporate (as directors)? If they are acting as shareholders,
they will have to pay the buyout costs and legal fees. If they act as directors,
it's the company that pays. But the third owner may complain they acted
personally, and thus acted in bad faith as directors to expel him or her
as director and owner. So, when making the decision to split, the two in
the 'cabal' need to carefully identify their roles and their compliance with
their fiduciary duties, not just to act selfishly. This issue can become a

counterclaim by the expelled owner-manager. Hence, expelling a partner requires some planning and justification.

In general, some level of internal investigation of wrongdoing (or incompetence or incapacity) should be conducted before hostile actions are taken. In a company with several policy statements for employee governance, a suspected breach of such policies can unmask willful or negligent mismanagement, fraud, embezzlement, bribery and other justifications for termination for cause. Sometimes one founder will conduct a personal audit and identify and document such misconduct, for eventual confrontation and demand for appropriate resolution. In other cases, the authority, specialized investigation skills and speed of an external forensic investigator may be necessary.

Some company owners might panic upon discovering surprising misconduct by others. Panic-driven decisions frequently result in mistakes. The worst mistake is the failure to adopt a recovery plan after creating a dispute. Even embezzlers might agree to an amicable plan for resolution, since that would resolve the misconduct, perhaps avoid prison and maximizing enterprise value for a shared exit.

Once it appears necessary to take action, planning becomes the most important and valuable use of limited time to limit the continued distrust and 'bleeding.' If a generalized 'business continuity plan' has been in place for a long time, then the transition will be smoother. Recovery requires interim steps along with more permanent remedies. Founders should consult legal and tax advisors and other professionals that deal in finance, insurance, company sales and redesign of the enterprise.

First Aid: Minimizing Harms; Recovering Quickly

In medical parlance, the first responder to a crisis must first stop the bleeding. Similarly, corporate crisis managers focus on avoiding the enterprise's quick death. 'Stopping the bleeding' means curing (or starting to cure) the underlying failings, bringing in additional support, demonstrating managerial skills and intervention and proactive public relations. Interim managers can be hired to fill a gap left upon death, disability or departure of a co-founder or other key owner, or a series of departures of C-Level executives.

Crisis response is not succession planning. While perhaps effective to sustain the enterprise in the short term, emergency intervention has high costs, is highly distracting and usually leaves more casualties than implementation of an existing, albeit stale, succession plan. Scared employees might begin to look for employment elsewhere. Scared clients might seek an alternative provider. Scared lenders might call in their loans, or refuse additional credit desperately needed for operations during the crisis.

Interim Executives

A crisis response may involve hiring interim specialists to capture implicit knowledge of departing executives and coach the remaining team in collaboration skills. For instance, senior managers might be required to stabilize the company during infighting between owners and owner-managers. Interim CEOs, CFOs and CIOs abound. They can step in and perform day-to-day operations while the business divorce is being structured and implemented. For example, if a co-owner 'borrowed' corporate funds without authorization for personal uses, an interim CFO could be appointed to handle all finances and report transparently to all owners while a joint exit might be negotiated.

While perhaps not fatal, the costs of interim managers can be very high. Where the company's founders or senior managers have been expelled, a 'turnaround' manager might be needed not only for interim operations but to provide new structure, new culture and new professionalism. Turnaround managers may reasonably expect equity compensation, and the negotiation of their employment or consulting agreements can be complex and exacerbate the owners' declining powers to govern.

Interim Knowledge Managers / Business Process Manager

An alternative is using a 'knowledge management' ('KM') consultant. Through structured conversations with key persons (especially any departing employees), the KM supports a business's intellectual property rights by capturing hidden trade secrets and other know-how that might become patentable processes. In the context of business divorce, the KM promotes institutional resiliency by improving business continuity, transparency, resource allocation, project management and disaster recovery management. In the crisis of a departing key employee, the KM consultant mitigates risks of transition to a successor employee.

Tips as to Stakeholder Conflicts

Identify Stakeholder Conflicts before they Erupt

Conflicts arise in two ways: a conflict of roles and governance accountability, or a conflict of personality. You must identify where a personality can fit a role, with a focus on where the intrinsic conflict will lead. Consider how much value will be at risk of a bad choice.

Identify, evaluate and make decisions based on acceptable levels of conflicts with potential stakeholders. If your investor wants an early exit, your startup might not have staying power. If your family member wants too much control up front, wants 'equality' and lacks humility, look for a non-family member as a potential successor.

Identify the Crisis as it Unfolds

When do you know you have an inescapable stakeholder conflict? You will know you must consider a business divorce in any one of several scenarios.

1. *Willful Misconduct.* A senior stakeholder abuses your dependency on him or her at a critical moment in an important project. It starts with express non-compliance with a request to share power. It continues with non-cooperation and disparaging gossip about anyone who holds that senior stakeholder to be accountable, or to share power. It's the bully who started the fight and then blames the victim for aggression in a defensive move. The bully acts like an opera diva, who cannot be upstaged. Aside from going on strike, willful misconduct includes self-dealing, embezzlement, harassing, disparaging, backstabbing and other behaviors learned in childhood.

2. *Incompetence.* A co-founder demonstrates an inability repeatedly to perform any task of value to the company. You made a bad choice.

3. *Divergence.* You have built your business on certain key goals, missions, strategies, tactics and tools. A key stakeholder raises a policy-based objection to any of these foundations. You have listened openly, but you cannot agree. Your interests diverge. The rest will be a power struggle.

By failing to declare an easily identifiable crisis, you encourage the bad behavior and will pay more to resolve the problem. It's time to rouse the governance body and take action.

Take Action to Anticipate and Avoid Crisis

Most crises are predictable. You can anticipate that a certain key employee or co-founder might precipitate a crisis to obtain unfair advantage. With selfish intent, the individual might refuse to perform a direct order or a task that fits into his or her job description. The individual could demand some benefit immediately as a condition of further performance.

Avoiding a disaster in a crisis can be as simple as three action steps:

1. *Constantly Seek to Limit your Vulnerabilities.* Avoid being in a compromising weak position. Good management is the first lesson in crisis avoidance. You should manage your relationships so that you are not vulnerable to an extortionate demand. Maintain your control by fulfilling your promises.

2. *Communicate; Defuse.* Effective interactive communication is the second lesson in crisis avoidance. 'Manage' by walking around and taking people's temperatures. Don't let someone's frustrations fester to boiling point. Talk them down from the ledge. Give the challenger an opportunity to back down and cooperate for the immediate moment.

3. *Resolve for the moment, not for eternity.* In a crisis, you do not have time to negotiate resolution of all grievances. So do not try to resolve all disputes. Just get through the current dispute. Schedule a plan for resolution of the long-term dispute together.

Risk Management

Identify tools for risk management of potential stakeholder conflicts. Communicate and encourage the stakeholders to participate in planning to use such tools. For each prospective and existing stakeholder relationship, stay aware of how you would try to resolve the potential crisis without destroying the enterprise. Prepare contingency plans, with reminders to update the plans as relationships change.

Crisis Mitigation

You have a richer scope of choices for crisis mitigation if you identify risks and plan well. Even without a plan, *ad hoc* problem-solving can avoid aggravation of the mess.

1. *Internal Investigation and Strategic Alternatives.* Working with your trusted advisors, you can identify why the conflict arose, possible short-term and long-term solutions. By considering alternative outcomes for both the company and the 'hostile' stakeholder, you can save face, save time, money and avoid distraction. This efficiency is valuable to all parties.

2. *Select a Respectable Alternative for Both Sides.* In business divorce, expulsion of a non-conforming 'hostile' stakeholder should show respect for the value brought to date. You might offer to provide a future benefit or personal recognition to the departing person who must be relocated to another environment. Such human value recycling can be agreed subject to certain conditions. You might offer some opportunities to the departing person for recover of past earned-value, rehabilitation and recycling into a new role elsewhere.

3. *Negotiation with the 'Hostile' Stakeholder.* Most crises in trust among owners can be resolved effectively by mutual agreement, even where someone has been guilty of self-dealing, fraud, embezzlement or other serious breach of trust. Effective resolution may depend on negotiating reasonable exit plans that range from removal of one individual (by redemption or expulsion) to spin-off to sale of the enterprise. We explore these possibilities in later chapters.

4. *Crisis Management Planning.* If you fail to plan, you may be planning to fail. To avoid a succession crisis, all owners and directors should plan for a succession crisis. The team should include all disciplines that would be affected by such a crisis. A crisis management plan could define roles and responsibilities and rules and tools for coordination for a coordinated response. A particular spokesman might be appointed in advance, subject to consultations with particular owners, managers and other stakeholders. The crisis scenarios should anticipate the possible simultaneous loss of access to one or more key individuals. The 'solutions' might be interim or permanent, such as the contingent appointment of a successor or a decision-making team pending appointment of a successor to each key individual.

Your Professional Advisors

For crisis management and dispute resolution involving individual shareholders or separate stakeholders, you can get valuable assistance from attorneys in business, employment, compliance and dispute-resolution; mediators and/or arbitrators, appraisers, accountants, crisis public-relations advisers, insurance brokers and personal wealth advisers. To keep your suppliers and service providers aligned with your business needs, you can hire a vendor contract management team to deliver strategy, program and plan design, implementation, and long-term maintenance.

Your Self-Assessment

- In your business, what conflicts do you face that could have the highest potential damage to your investment and opportunities for your entity?

- What events or threats are most likely to trigger a crisis in your business?

- How will digital transformation benefit or harm your business operations, clientele and value?

- Have you already experienced any pre-crisis warnings from any strategic relationships? Describe what happened, how you handled the situation and whether the risk has been eliminated?

- What is your plan to eliminate, mitigate or insure against such risks?

- By when do you anticipate completion of your plan?

- If a crisis in strategic relationships arose tomorrow, what actions would you take to overcome the crisis?

- What metrics would you use to determine that you have resolved the crisis in strategic relationships? Would you say your crisis resolution tools are weak or robust?

- After resolving the anticipated crisis, what measures would you put into place to ensure the future good reputation, viability and continuity of your business?

4

Crisis Resolution via Alternative Dispute Resolution

This chapter considers a variety of tools to stay out of court. Every tool has its slants and benefits. Since disputed business divorce can be contentious, the more you know about tools for resolution, the more you can appreciate the various choices. Each solution has elements of a game of chance and possible choices to make (or avoid) maneuvers for gamesmanship. Your professional advisor can help you assess any bias implicit in an alternative dispute resolution ('ADR') method. You can skim this chapter to get an overview, or you can dig in and develop a spreadsheet of the attributes and scenarios available for your use of ADR in resolving a dispute in business divorce.

This chapter highlights ADR for disputes on valuation in a disputed expulsion, redemption or buyout. ADR can be useful to resolve many other conflicts and bundle them into a settlement, such as a post-sale dispute over a buyer's alleged breach of the sale contract. ADR can avoid not only the lawyers' costs, time spent on the dispute and the emotional focus on winning, freeing the parties from emotional distress.

'Corporate Divorce' Litigation

Litigation consists of the submission of dispute to a court of competent jurisdiction that has both personal jurisdiction over the parties and subject matter jurisdiction over the nature of the claims.

Some litigations can be complex and expensive. Such is the case for disputes over breach of fiduciary duty and abuse of 'business judgment.' Other litigations can be simple, as in deciding the value of a corporation's shares under an appraisal proceeding after a 'cash-out' (or 'squeeze-out') merger.

Once litigation is commenced, the parties can still engage in settlement negotiations and mediation. Indeed, many courts (like many family courts) require that the parties at least attend a mediation before continuing business divorce litigation.

Choice of Jurisdiction for Organizing Your Business

By choosing the jurisdiction for organizing your business, you also choose the laws governing the internal functioning and relationships among owners and managers. This decision is critical to confidence and collaboration of founders, investors, creditors and other stakeholders.

For international businesses, you may choose to establish a global holding company in a jurisdiction that satisfies multiple frameworks: corporate laws, judicial supervision, local taxation applicable to your type of business, international tax treaty networks, residence of the founders, substantial economic relationships, location of primary operations and political risk factors. For our purposes, the key factor is corporate law.

State Court Litigation: Governance by Owners and Squeeze-Outs

Courts decide governance issues under local corporate and LLC laws. In a squeeze-out merger, the court will decide whether the merger was validly administered and whether the valuation was fair.

The quality of judicial review of business divorce has been a prime selling point in the choice of Delaware as a jurisdiction for corporations and

LLCs. 'As a court of equity, the Court of Chancery has jurisdiction to hear and determine cases involving equitable rights (such as trusts and fiduciary duties) and equitable remedies (such as injunctions and specific performance).'[38] This court adjudicates claims of abuses in corporate governance, shareholder relations and other internal affairs, enforcing the rights, remedies and protections of owners of shares and equity equivalents, directors and officers. For example, where a Delaware corporation elects to be owned by fewer than thirty shareholders and makes no public offering of shares, the Court of Chancery may enjoin or set aside any transfer or threatened transfer of stock of a close corporation which is contrary to the terms of its certificate of incorporation or of any transfer restriction permitted by local law.[39]

Bankruptcy Court Litigation: Restructuring of Ownership

Bankruptcy courts can reallocate ownership of insolvent companies and assets under judicial supervision. Under a plan of reorganization in bankruptcy, the owners can lose most or all of their equity and creditors (or new investors) can become the new owners. The management might remain in place (as a 'debtor in possession') or a new manager (the 'trustee in bankruptcy') may be appointed by the court.

Bankruptcy offers 'vulture investors' an opportunity to purchase assets at a 'fire sale' price. After bankruptcy, the new owners are protected from claims of the former creditors, who are barred from any claims if they fail to submit their claims to judicial administration by a court-ordered deadline.

Alliances of Owners: Common Interest Agreements among Owners

Alliances in litigation can be important to cost-effective and strategic value for litigants who share a common interest against a particular adversary. By sharing costs and/or information under a 'common interest agreement,'

---

[38] State of Delaware, *Litigation in the Delaware Court of Chancery and the Delaware Supreme Court,* available at https://corplaw.delaware.gov/delaware-court-chancery-supreme-court/ (accessed Sept. 21, 2019).
[39] Del. Gen. Corp. Law, § 348(b).

you can preserve the confidentiality of attorney-client communications and joint strategies.

Factions among Owners: Claims against Directors

If you are a board member, you can get sued by your fellow shareholders for breach of fiduciary duty, even where there is no claim of self-dealing. One or more other shareholders could threaten such litigation as leverage in negotiations with you in your personal capacity as a shareholder.

While the board of directors has discretion to make business judgments, this discretion is not absolute. Where the board has neglected its duties, and a shareholder has made a demand that the board resolve the breach of duty, the shareholder could sue the board on behalf of all shareholders for damage to the company. This is like a class action lawsuit because the plaintiff seeks recovery to benefit all members of the class of owners. It is different from a class action because the claim is for injury to the entity. Shareholder derivative claims thus cover claims that the managers (board of directors, LLC managers or general partners) diminished the value or assets of the entity (such as for sale of assets at an artificially low price).

The requirement of making a demand upon the managers before suing them under a derivative action is excused in certain cases. The complaining owner must allege particular facts that either (i) rebut the threshold presumption of the [manager's] disinterestedness or independence, or (ii) create reasonable doubt that the challenged transaction was the product of a valid exercise of business judgment.[40] Or the complaining owner must claim that making a demand would be futile, such as where there were two general partners and one had a conflict of interest that prevented both from acting together to remediate the alleged breach of fiduciary duty[41] or where the general partner had already refused to provide access to the partnership's books and records.[42]

---

[40] *Katell v. Morgan Stanley Group, Inc.*, 1993 Del. Ch. LEXIS 5 (Jan. 14, 1993) [partnership].

[41] Id.

[42] *Curley v. Brignoli, Curley & Roberts Assocs.*, 746 F. Sup. 1208 (S.D.N.Y. 1989), *aff'd* 915 F.2d 81 (2d Cir. 1990), *cert. denied*, 499 U.S. 955 (applying Delaware law to a partnership).

Possible Conflicts of Interest by Law Firms and Professional Advisors

When hiring a law firm (or other professional advisor) in a business divorce, both the party and the proposed law firm should be careful to avoid conflicts of interest. Such conflicts can result in disqualification and resignation of the law firm if it advises multiple parties who later decide, quite predictably, to act adversely among each other.

For example, in litigation, the parties might request a stay of proceedings to allow for a negotiated or mediated settlement. Later, during negotiations or mediation, the parties discover adverse positions that render it impossible for the same law firm to represent them all. The law firm withdraws, one party demands copies of all the files, the law firm delivers only part of the files and claims privilege as to the undelivered files. This process requires judicial recourse[43] and explains why each stakeholder needs separate legal representation.

Complaints to Governmental Administration

Employees and others are protected from unlawful discrimination based on protected classes, such as age, sex, race, religion, national origin, veteran status and sexual orientation. In a business divorce involving employment status or civil rights, the settlement should include a release of such claims.

Choosing Smarter Tools for Resolution of Disputes

In his Devil's Dictionary,[44] nineteenth century journalist Ambrose Bierce defined 'litigation' as a machine that one enters as a pig and exits as a sausage. A 'litigant' is one who willingly gives up his shirt in the hope of saving his skin.

---

[43] See *TCV IV., L.P. v. Tradingscreen Inc.*, C.A. No. 10169-VCL (Apr. 23, 2018), involving arbitration, court litigation and negotiation in the saga of the *Buhannic* corporate divorce, available at
https://courts.delaware.gov/Opinions/Download.aspx?id=271790.
[44] Ambrose Bierce, THE DEVIL'S DICTIONARY (Dover Publications, Inc. 1958).

Distressed business owners can choose from a panoply of alternative methods for resolving disputes with their co-owners. These alternative dispute resolution methods have gained in popularity as the costs, burdens, uncertainties and delays of litigation have grown. Litigation procedures include electronic discovery, giving access to virtually every electronic record of a long-term relationship of all the parties, and requiring high costs of evaluation for possible exclusion under some theory of legal privilege. Indeed, mediators and arbitrators sometimes rightfully joke that the term 'ADR' has a hidden meaning, namely, for a disputant's litigator, ADR represents an 'alarming drop in revenues' because ADR can quickly stop a litigated business divorce.

Shareholders have a choice of dispute resolution about the inevitable question of a buyout or redemption to force or permit one or more owners to exit. Such disputes can be narrowed by adopting a valuation methodology or dispute methodology in the shareholders' agreement. Or you can negotiate *ad hoc*. Your selection will affect not just the value so 'decided.' It will affect your speed to resolution, costs, certainty of outcome, fairness, predictability, levels of distraction and impact on all stakeholders. You may choose depending on levels of control by one side, unequal bargaining power and other factors. By choosing the right tool, you can either tailor or hammer toward a resolution of a shareholder divorce.

Negotiation within a 'Zone of Reason'

Negotiations occur because of mutual uncertainty. Each party risks some loss. Facing such uncertainty, both parties might find it reasonable to make some concessions just to avoid or settle litigation. So you will always have a 'zone of reason' for negotiated dispute resolution, unless a party is irrational. The simplest zone is one that looks at a probability of losing and the amount of the loss, balanced against similar metrics for winning, in a Monte Carlo 'multiple probability simulation.' Such simulations require scenario analysis and some simple algebra.

Negotiation offer several benefits. The process retains each party's autonomy. Negotiations allow each party to make proposals and, if rejected, make different proposal to get closer to settlement. The outcomes are limited by each party's creativity to spot viable alternatives and each party's responsiveness to such alternatives. As in any negotiation, any owner can use threats of litigation to demand accommodations. To cover all issues, all parties should understand the problems and the other side's point of view.[45]

Negotiations, with or without a mediator or facilitator, can help the parties *create new opportunities* from current circumstances. To achieve any new opportunity, you must let go of certain emotions – revenge, hurt, fear, anger – and open up to new possibilities in a problem-solving approach, based on each party's interests.

Urgency and openness to negotiate in good faith are the keys to a possible negotiated settlement. The broad outline can be presented, and each issue can be whittled away until a 'balanced' composite agreement is reached. Without such urgency and openness, your choice might be full-bore litigation.

Confidentiality is a further requirement. Happily, judicial rules on evidence generally protect the actual negotiations from being subject to pre-trial discovery.[46]

Preparation for Negotiations

Innovation in relationships comes by everyone's agreement to temporarily let go of their immobilizing instincts to defend one's unquestioned tribal roots — beliefs, rituals, allegiances, values and emotionally meaningful experiences. By untethering from the tribal lures, the parties can engage in a three-step process.

1. First, by brainstorming, you can identify possible new scenarios.

2. Second, with an open mind about emotional issues, you can change yourself from within, to assimilate to an 'order' that permits

---

[45] For negotiations generally, see Roger Fisher & William Ury & Bruce Patton, GETTING TO YES: NEGOTIATING AGREEMENT WITHOUT GIVING IN (Penguin Books 1981, 1991) (2nd ed.); Roger Fisher & Daniel Shapiro, BEYOND REASON: USING EMOTIONS AS YOU NEGOTIATE, (Viking Press, the Penguin Group) (2005); Daniel Shapiro, NEGOTIATING THE NON-NEGOTIABLE: HOW TO RESOLVE YOUR MOST EMOTIONALLY CHARGED CONFLICTS (Viking, an imprint of Penguin Random House LLC) (2016) ('Shapiro, Non-Negotiable'); Harvard Bus. Review, HBR's 10 MUST READS ON NEGOTIATION, Harvard Bus. Review Press (2019).
[46] See Fed. R. Evid. 408, Fed. R. Civ. Proc. 26 and relevant state statutes, such as NY Civil Prac. L. & Rules, 3101-3140.

harmonious co-existence with mutual benefits. As with sovereign nations yielding some elements of sovereignty and autonomy for harmonious co-existence by treaty to avoid war, protect security and promote mutually beneficial commerce, remember the necessity of sacrifice of some degree of your own autonomy.

3. Finally, after mutual assimilation of each other's concerns, under a larger framework that accommodates the basic needs of all, you can both synthesize a resolution that respects the basic needs of each side.

Negotiating the Non-Negotiable

Negotiating the 'non-negotiable' requires identifying the other side's key tribal roots, building cross-cutting relationships that reflect empathy, attachment, care and kinship, and finding a way to allow both parties to embrace a resolution without destroying or dominating. 'Don't battle over the relationship; jointly build it.'[47] In short, an innovative solution can be framed through imagination that benefits all concerned.

The Elephant in the Closet: Business Valuation Disputes

This chapter highlights some of the technical problems in finding a fair market value so that the parties can agree on a fair exit in a redemption or buyout of a minority owner. Each shareholder has different views of what the business is worth to an unrelated buyer. Each shareholder might want to include some special premium or discount that relates to the 'unique' circumstances of their mutual relationship, the contributions and efforts by each, and the value created or lost by each.

There is no shortage of valuation principles. Smarter exits depend on a basic understanding of the issues in selecting and applying different valuation principles. Finding agreement on a valuation can be difficult, even assuming such an understanding and that all shareholders are acting in good faith.

---

[47] Shapiro, *Non-Negotiable*, p. 199.

Fair Market Value

The fair market value of an asset is generally defined as the price at which a willing buyer and a willing seller would agree to enter into a purchase and sale transaction, where each has equal access to reasonable knowledge of all relevant information about the asset and the markets and neither is under any compulsion to enter into the deal.[48] This definition poses intrinsic conflicts. A seller's willingness to sell may be 'accelerated' by his or her eagerness to escape from oppression, which is not a factor that an arm's length seller would consider. Similarly, the oppressed minority might have unequal access to the company's financial information and business prospects, since the majority might not be voluntarily disclosing such information. Indeed, such non-disclosure frequently accompanies oppressive actions by a majority seeking to squeeze out a minority.

Valuation is admittedly a speculative art form for businesses with little or no income and little history. As a result, early-stage company values can vary widely. In this context, fair market value depends on some form of negotiation, whether as to overall value, methodology for valuation or what constitutes a 'comparable' transaction.

Timing

Timing can have a huge impact on valuation. Before any 'final' valuation can be agreed, the co-owners must agree (or, in litigation, the court decides) on the date of the valuation for the business divorce. As with family divorce, the date can be delayed or accelerated by one of the parties. As with any market for securities or commodities, the value of a closely held business will change when sales are good, new products are discovered, developed and put into production, new sales channels are secured, governmental permits are granted, financing is obtained to help hire new team members or to finance sales to customers on open account. Or the price can decline when one 'partner' chooses to walk away from the common pursuit and uses his or her time for personal ventures.

As a result, the valuation date normally is delayed until the final terms are agreed. However, special circumstances frequently exist to justify a fixed date that is not simultaneous with the actual exit. Such circumstances could involve the health of one party, the time to negotiate a deal and get

---

[48] 26 C.F.R. § 20.2031-1(b).

all necessary approvals both internally and externally, or the timing of one shareholder's additional capital contribution that is not matched by the other.

Discounts for Tax-Driven Valuations

For tax reasons, owners may seek their own independent valuations. For such owners, valuation may be subject to possible discounts for a minority owner's lack of control and, in privately owned companies, lack of marketability for sale to the public. But tax authorities may ignore such valuations when the actual exit transaction occurs shortly after the valuation, under the argument that the transaction reflects fair market value. To avoid such tax risks, valuations should be completed several months before any exit transaction is negotiated.

Factors for Valuation of Your Company for Financial Accounting

Appraisers use basic three principles for valuation to determine a company's fair market value:

1. *Market Value:* Comparable transactions by similar companies;

2. *Income (Cash Flow):* A multiple of cash flow (earnings before interest, taxes, depreciation and amortization, *or 'EBITDA');* and

3. *Net Asset Value (or Net Liquidation Value):* Replacement value to purchase the assets (which is basically a liquidation value), net of liabilities.[49]

In the opinion of the valuation expert, the final indication of value may be a result of one, or a combination, of these approaches. Each approach has its weaknesses, inviting adjustments.

- Comparable transactions are never identical. The appraiser must make adjustments for differences in size, industry, maturity, geography and other variables.

---

[49] See generally, Financial Accounting Standard Board ('FASB') ASC 820 (2011), available at https://asc.fasb.org/imageRoot/81/118196181.pdf.

- EBITDA multiples may vary by industry and defining a particular industry may be difficult where there are multiple lines of business or multiple countries of operation.

- The replacement value of assets gives no value to the benefit of synergies and costs of having assembled the company and its assets, personnel and operations. So asset values might be useful only for startups or companies that have not assembled a management team, developed a minimally viable product ('MVP'), obtained regulatory approvals, established strategic partnerships for a new value chain or acquired key customers.

Such difficulties might make it more appropriate for 'drive-by' valuation by founders when splitting up just to finalize the deal. But each party should identify and address the many factors and assumptions that could materially change the valuation.

For high-growth private companies, a blend of valuation methodologies might be appropriate under guidelines for venture capital and private equity firms.[50]

Development Stage	Valuation Approach
Early stage: no cash flow; no comparable market transactions; no minimally viable product	*Asset approach* (using the asset accumulation method): Negotiated investment transactions involving friends, family and/or angel investors. Further analysis would be appropriate for subsequent investments to review the assumptions of the participants as to valuation.

---

[50] FASB, FINANCIAL SERVICES—INVESTMENT COMPANIES (TOPIC 946): AMENDMENTS TO THE SCOPE, MEASUREMENT AND DISCLOSURE REQUIREMENTS ('FASB 946') (Pub. No. 2013-08, June 2013); American Institute of Certified Public Accountants, VALUATION OF PORTFOLIO COMPANY INVESTMENTS OF VENTURE CAPITAL AND PRIVATE EQUITY FUNDS AND OTHER INVESTMENT COMPANIES - ACCOUNTING AND VALUATION GUIDE (Aug. 19, 2019).

Development Stage	Valuation Approach
Middle stage: momentum in development of significant intangibles and internal goodwill	*Income approach:* While an income approach may be justified, it may require a high discount rate due to unreliability of forecasted income in an early stage
Mature stage	*Market approach:* The company's maturity enables analysis of demonstrated trends in income and comparability to other enterprises whose values have been determined by change of control in the marketplace.

Factors for Valuation of Your Company for Tax Accounting

Tax valuations may differ from accounting valuations in principle, under different rules. However, accounting valuations may be sufficient for tax valuation. IRS Revenue Ruling 59–60 provides the basis for all business appraisals. It specifies that the appraiser must address eight factors:

- Nature and history of the business
- Economic outlook: book value and financial condition
- Earning capacity
- Dividend paying capacity
- Goodwill and other intangible assets
- Prior sales
- Market 'comparables.'

In addition, the IRS has given unofficial 'job aids, articles and white papers' as informal guidance (not reliable as official policy)[51] on applying these eight factors to special situations, such as:

- Discount for lack of marketability[52]

---

[51] IRS, Valuation of Assets, available at https://www.irs.gov/businesses/valuation-of-assets.
[52] IRS, Discount for Lack of Marketability, Job Aid for IRS Valuation Professionals (2009), available at https://www.irs.gov/pub/irs-utl/dlom.pdf.

- Determination of 'reasonable compensation' for services[53]

- S Corporation valuation for valuation of a non-controlling interest in an S Corp.[54]

Getting to Yes: Techniques for Agreeing on an Exit Deal

Resolution of a dispute on valuation or terms of an individual exit can be achieved by direct negotiations, facilitated negotiations (early neutral evaluation or mediation) or adjudicated resolution (arbitration or court). Mediation and arbitration can flip between formats if the parties agree to move from one method to the other.

In a business divorce, each party should consult a valuation advisor, with or without a detailed valuation. If the parties cannot negotiate the valuation, they could decide to appoint a valuation expert and share the cost. Since valuations can take substantial time, delays might result in changes in valuation due to tectonic decisions or actions by mutually hostile owners. The certainty of a professional valuation might be less valuable than the certainty of a deal for business divorce. If there are no hostile antics expected, a third-party valuation can give all owners confidence in the negotiated terms.

Direct Negotiations by the Parties

The 'simplest' method for valuing the enterprise is an internal negotiation. This approach adopts the real 'buy-sell' scenario that valuation experts, acting on the sidelines, consider as the hypothetical scenario of 'willing

---

[53] IRS, Reasonable Compensation, Job Aid for IRS Valuation Professionals (2014), https://www.irs.gov/pub/irs-utl/Reasonable%20Compensation%20 Job%20Aid%20for%20IRS%20Valuation%20Professionals.pdf and an appendix to this job aid, available at https://www.irs.gov/pub/irs-utl/S%20Corporation%20 Valuation%20Job%20Aid%20for%20IRS%20Valuation%20Professionals.pdf
[54] IRS, Valuation of Non-Controlling Interests in Business Entities Electing To Be Treated as S Corporations for Federal Tax Purposes, Valuation Aid for Industry Analysts, https://www.irs.gov/pub/irs-utl/S% percent20Corporation% percent20Valuation% percent20Job% percent20Aid% percent20for% percent20IRS% percent20Valuation% percent20Professionals.pdf (2014).

buyer, willing seller, each having equal knowledge and neither being under any compulsion.'

Prior Agreement

Ideally, an existing shareholders' agreement signed at startup will specify the method for valuation, how the valuation process will work and terms of payment of the buyout price. To ensure fairness, the shareholders might agree principles, such as elimination of any discounts for illiquidity and minority interest. Then the shareholders can defer to the expertise of an appraiser, who makes judgments based on circumstances such as development stage, current and recent financial condition, changes in management, competition, evolving regulatory frameworks and political risks.

Ad Hoc (No Prior Agreement)

The parties might decide to negotiate *ad hoc*, particularly where there is no shareholders' agreement defining valuation method or payment terms.

A directly negotiated valuation can resolve a business divorce. If two co-owners of a business each has equal access to confidential technological, financial, sales and human resource information, each owner can be, or quickly become, a valuation expert for that business at that moment. This intimate business knowledge can accelerate and facilitate negotiated resolution. By a 'quick' resolution through rough-estimate valuation, each co-owner can escape the heavy opportunity cost (and consequential damages, in litigation parlance) of delay. The departing owner can use the time saved to pursue new ventures, where opportunities might be short-lived and must be seized or abandoned. Likewise, the remaining co-owners can focus on pursuing the company's vision without costly litigation, formal appraisals and distractions.

Ironically, valuation uncertainty can promote such resolution of a business divorce! But the conditions must be ripe. Each owner must have adequate confidential information about the business to have a 'ballpark' estimate of its value. Such rough-estimate 'analysis' should consider estimated values both at the moment of business divorce and in the near future as the business faces known challenges (inadequate funding, slow sales cycle, unshakeable fixed and variable costs, insufficient management talent, poor prospects, and so on).

In making the business decision to use the informal, 'rough-estimate' valuation method, each owner must identify how much uncertainty is acceptable. This 'uncertainty margin of error' thus enables the owner to balance the high value of immediate certainty and immediate resolution against the low value of maybe a five percent or ten percent valuation error that could have been avoided by more formal appraisal. Even a higher 'uncertainty margin of error' could be useful in special situations, such as where the emotional satisfaction of quick dispute resolution would be high (due to emotional, physical and/or financial fatigue, outright hostilities, or imminent family rupture, for instance). Such special situations could justify an owner's accepting an 'uncertainty margin of error' that might be twenty percent or even thirty percent.

From the Case Files

Two 50–50 owners had no agreement on buyout, valuation or terms. One owner, an investor, had no capacity to run the business alone, while the manager-owner did. The investor offered a low price, thinking that he would keep some profit by getting a new manager and showing a high value. In fact, the investor made a mistake because the manager then offered to pay the low price to buy out the investor. The manager bluffed when he said he had a replacement investor. As a result, the investor agreed to pay a higher price to buy out the manager.

For startups in the business divorce process, each founder usually has access to all essential data, knows the strengths and weaknesses of the team, the funding, the product and also understands the risks of competition from new entrants, known and unknown. This knowledge of the company and its role in a rapidly changing industry can help prioritize 'value' along financial, technological and emotional sensitivities.

For family-owned businesses, each owner has grown up with the business. Each can balance the value of family harmony as well as traditional valuation principles when considering an acceptable level of 'uncertainty margin of error.' Since family-owned businesses usually have no immediate rapid growth opportunities, and the departure of a family-business owner for another job or investment can be planned without hurry, 'drive-by' valuations are not very helpful in most family businesses.

Facilitated Negotiations by Early Neutral Evaluation / Expert Determination

At any time, disputing owners can request the expert services of a neutral party to evaluate the merits of their position and determine relevant 'facts.' Such an approach is a mini-step towards dispute resolution, but can be useful to narrow the scope of the dispute for eventual submission to court, arbitration or mediation.

Facilitated Negotiations by Mediation

In a mediation, the parties consent to hire a neutral mediator to help them find a mutually agreeable resolution. The mediator and parties agree to maintain the confidentiality of the information disclosed in the mediation process, so that personal feelings as well as legal positions and risk analysis can be discussed frankly. A mediator is most effective when, in mirroring the intent of the disputing parties, he finds a way to lead them along the path for finding an equilibrium, bringing the peacefulness and balance of mirrored reflections, as in the balance of an object and its reflection in still water. The mediator confronts each party with analysis, possible choices and justifications for possible resolutions.

As a neutral, the mediator focuses on the interests of each party. By inviting discussion on interest-driven intentions, the mediator helps the parties identify objectively their opportunities, balance the risks and find mutually acceptable solutions. In this role, the mediator facilitates resolution. At the same time, the mediator is a cheerleader for dispute resolution, encouraging as to resolution, showing good cheer, responsive listening and tenacity to bridge gaps,

Mediations are conducted under a multilateral agreement among the parties and the mediator defining the goals and roles of the parties as well as compensation of the mediator. Normally, the dispute is not considered settled without a written settlement agreement.[55]

Each party brings its authorized decision-makers and attorneys to the mediation. Unlike a court hearing, the attorney's role is to argue and propose alternative resolutions, as well as evaluate and counsel the party on strategy and terms. A savvy attorney will use the mediation to collect information and inspire fear and concessions by the other side. If the mediation resolves quickly, the attorney loses possible future fees. For this reason, some lawyers argue that the mere agreement to mediate should be avoided since it is considered a sign of weakness. But the attorney's interests cannot take priority over the client's. Indeed, in many courts, mediation is a mandatory first step before judicial intervention for resolution.

The mediator's role begins with fact-finding, where each party can express his or her legal and business claims in a joint caucus with all parties present. The joint caucus phase is essential to enabling each party to sense the ability to present the issues clearly and assert rights and claim obligations by the other owners.

After a joint caucus, the mediator's role shifts to asking questions in private with each party, being a good listener. Based on responses to the mediator's questions, the mediator's role then shifts to probing each party not only for possible resolution but also for the emotional attachments that prevent a business owner from 'getting to yes.' This process involves 'shuttle diplomacy' made famous by Henry Kissinger, President Nixon's Secretary of State, in negotiating with Egypt and Israel for a cease-fire and the recognition of Israel as a country.

To succeed, the parties need to select a mediator who will continue to push each side for a resolution, even after the failure of the typical one-day 'all-

---

[55] In some rare cases, courts have enforced mediation agreements without a written settlement agreement, for example, where mediation was annexed to a court proceeding, where the court found that the parties had verbally agreed to a settlement, the parties and counsel had agreed, the settlement amount was reasonable in relation to the possible range of recovery, the objecting party failed to object for seven weeks after a court clerk's notice of settlement, and where the mediation agreement lacked any reservation of right not to be bound without a written settlement. *Rivera v. The Crabby Shack LLC*, Slip Op., Magis. J. Steven Gold, Docket 17-CV-4738, __ N.Y.S.3d __, NYLJ (May 7, 2019, p.21) (E.D.N.Y. May 6, 2019).

day' mediation session. The mediator should also be a skilled negotiator, understanding the give-and-take of quid pro quo, reiterating constantly the benefits of achieving mutual resolution and the risks and costs that each party incurs by pursuing hostilities in court or by failure to resolve pre-litigation disputes. The mediator might inquire about possible agreement that includes a remedy that could not otherwise be obtained by a court or arbitrator, such as an apology, a post-exit limited business relationship or some benefit for a relative. A mediator can also help identify feints and threats, or unreasonable demands, that might stymie a separately negotiated solution.

This role highlights one reason why mediation should be sought early in the dispute resolution process. Early mediation occurs at a time of maximum fear, uncertainty and doubt affecting each party as it contemplates a judicial or arbitral solution imposed on it. Early mediation offers a greater window of opportunity for resolution, and thus a larger zone of reasonable outcomes.

However, mediation offers no guarantee. A party might participate grudgingly, or as tool for 'free' exchange of confidential 'discovery' information, or in bad faith with intent to litigate for retribution or punishment, not merely to obtain a fair outcome.

For business divorce, the parties should be careful to investigate and select experienced or certified mediators who, as professional advisors, are experienced both in structuring of a variety of equity transactions and in negotiating the details, such as valuation, shareholder rights and corporate governance. And they should look for good, empathetic listeners who respect and nurture each party as a worthy person and who invite conscious and commercially reasonable resolutions.

More generally, mediators can play different roles that can be seen as a continuum, not wholly exclusive styles.[56]

- *Facilitative Mediation.* As a non-judgmental facilitator, the mediator solicits the parties to express their positions, understand the relative strengths and weaknesses of each side and ask questions

56   See Zena Zumeta, *Styles of Mediation: Facilitative, Evaluative and Transformative,* available at www.mediate.com/articles/zumeta.cfm, accessed Dec. 6, 2019.

to elicit ultimate goals within a field of reasonableness. The mediator controls the process, the parties control the decisions. The mediator may caucus separately with the parties or their attorneys to brainstorm for possible solutions to discuss with the other party.

- *Evaluative Mediation.* The mediator may 'evaluate' the positions of the parties, only testing the waters to ensure both parties would be receptive, propose a mediator's proposal for settlement.

- *Transformative Mediation.* The mediator may encourage the parties to take control of the settlement process and to 'recognize' the other parties' needs, interests and points of view. The mediator does not meet with the parties or their attorneys separately.

When choosing a mediator, you should ask about the use of different styles of mediation, the mediator's rationale for using such style and related assumptions about the relative usefulness of that style.

Settlement agreements facilitated by mediation are enforceable internationally under the Singapore Convention on Mediation.[57] Intended to cover only 'commercial' disputes between businesses, it excludes disputes between merchants and consumers, employees and employers and between family members. The 'mediator' must certify the settlement, and the parties must have full autonomy to decide, since the 'mediator' must lack the authority to impose a solution upon the parties to the dispute.

Mediated Auction Process between the Parties

In economic theory, an auction achieves the fair market value because it matches a willing buyer and a willing seller, each being under no compulsion, and each having equal access to information. To be fair, the auction process must bring together a sufficient number of potential buyers to enable the seller to feel the process has been fair. Auctions occur in commodities and stock market, where the publicity and disclosures are available through publicly available databases and securities disclosures filed with bodies like the Securities and Exchange Commission.

---

[57] United Nations Convention on International Settlement Agreements Resulting from Mediation, signed July 25, 2019, by 46 states. For text, see https://uncitral.un.org/sites/uncitral.un.org/files/singapore_convention_eng.pdf. Or https://www.uncitral.org/pdf/english/commissionsessions/51st-session/Annex_I.pdf.

But how can one achieve such fairness in mediation? The 'auction' could be achieved in several ways. In each case, sufficient publicity and the presence of at least two sophisticated buyers are key. Thus, in a 'private auction' between the parties, a mediator in a business divorce can use the auction process

In one scenario, the mediator could focus on a sale to a third party. The mediator would invite the parties to agree on a method of co-sale to a third party. One party could be responsible for finding a buyer (such as by a business broker or investment banker) or for holding an auction. The co-sale could involve drag-along and tag-along provisions. If one owner has lent money or assets to the company, then the parties would normally agree that such party would get priority payment as creditor, as if in liquidation.

In a second scenario, the mediator could invite the parties to agree that one would buy and the other would sell. In this case, each is a sophisticated buyer after having been a corporate insider for a reasonably long time. So the 'auction' would be limited to the parties.

In this scenario, the mediator could ask each to submit a sealed bid, under agreed terms and conditions of purchase and sale. As noted elsewhere under 'baseball arbitration,' this only works if there is equal bargaining power and capacity to buy and benefit from controlling the business after the purchase.

Or the mediator could suggest a 'rotating buyer' approach. To be effective, the conditions necessary for this approach include adequate capital to purchase, fungibility of the assets so that the rotating buyer feels that he or she has purchased (or received in gift or liquidation) the item having the highest value to that buyer.

As a variation on the 'rotating buyer' approach, a piecemeal auction might apply by inviting unrelated bidders to bid on one or more of the assets and give to one co-owner (who is the rotating 'insider' buyer) a right of first refusal by matching the third party's bid. (This 'stalking horse' approach is harsh on the third party who puts in effort at analyzing and bidding. As a result, there should be some benefit to the third-party bidder for allowing any such preferential approach. This approach is common in rebidding an existing long-term supply or services contract in outsourcing, and stalking horse bidders are wary.)

Mediation can be highly effective in a multi-party dispute, where several different parties have adverse interests but share a common desire to resolve a dispute that has little benefit for them if it continues. Mediators can use techniques to identify high and low estimates of liability (in the case of sharing obligations to third parties) or of rights to recover claims (in the case of aggrieved parties). By identifying such ranges of highs and lows, the mediator can then invite each party into a zone of compromise. While this process could take several rounds of one-on-one discussions and shuttle diplomacy, the tables of values would be shown to all parties, who could thus see trends and opportunities for consensus.

Mediator's Proposal; Mediator's Valuation

Where the mediator discovers that the parties are willing to compromise within some high-low parameters, the mediator might offer a 'mediator's proposal' as the mediator's act under narrow time constraints. Before making a proposal, the mediator should arrange for prompt responses by the parties.[58] In a valuation dispute, a mediation could turn into an arbitration under the 'final offer arbitration' approach described below, if the parties ask the mediator to become an arbitrator and to choose one of the two proffered final numbers.

Arbitration

In arbitration, an arbitrator (or arbitrators) appointed at the request of the parties acts as a judge and renders a verdict in the form of an 'arbitral award.' Most arbitrations are administered by an institutional arbitral authority, such as the American Arbitration Association or JAMS chosen by the parties. The arbitrator is chosen for expertise in the law of the particular subject matter of the dispute, as well as for neutrality and fairness. An arbitrator gains a reputation and thus repeat referrals by attorney litigators who want their clients' disputes resolved by arbitration.

Arbitration depends on the mutual agreement of the disputing parties. In contracts, the arbitration clause can be as short as one sentence or as

---

[58] See Stephen A. Hochman, *'A Mediator's Proposal – Whether, When and How it Should Be Used,'* in Molly Klapper, DEFINITIVE CREATIVE IMPASSE-BREAKING TECHNIQUES IN MEDIATION (NY State Bar Ass'n. (2011), at pp. 225-236. See text below for discussion of mediator's role.

long as two pages. For example, to simplify any future dispute resolutions, parties to a contract may:

- adopt pre-arbitration 'confidential escalation' processes for negotiation between the parties;

- prescribe the arbitrators' required experience, skills and language competencies;

- decide whether to allow the arbitrator(s) to grant interim equitable relief such as injunctions pending final adjudication;

- define what constitutes 'irreparable harm' (such as cessation of contract performance) that justifies an injunction;

- prohibit the arbitrators from granting certain kinds of damages, such as punitive damages or other non-compensatory damages);

- allocate the arbitration costs to the loser, thereby encouraging settlement;

- allocate enforcement costs to the loser to accelerate compliance with the arbitral award.

Such choices can be incorporated into a shareholders' agreement or commercial services agreement before any dispute arises. Or the choice can be made *ad hoc*, after the dispute arises. It is easier to get consensus on adopting arbitration as the ADR method before a dispute arises. So all parties should be aware of this possible choice and consult with their attorneys in drafting an appropriate method for dispute resolution.

Stung by shareholder derivative litigation, boards of directors (and their professional advisors) invented a solution to limit mandatory arbitration of shareholder's claims against managers and controlling shareholders with a waiver of the right to assert any class action against management or the controlling shareholders. By requiring such disputes to be arbitrated, controlling shareholders may achieve several goals.

Arbitration has many benefits.

- *Confidentiality with 'Adjudication.'* Like mediation, arbitration is not normally public, so adverse publicity may be avoided. While the confidentiality of negotiations and mediation can be protected procedurally, the confidentiality of the arbitral proceedings is intrinsic to this form of dispute resolution. As a result, only the arbitral award would be made public, since, for enforcement, a court would have to see, publish and ratify it. What distinguishes arbitration from negotiation and mediation is the added benefit that it is an adjudication by a third party. As such, it is not subject to the staged arguments, bluffing, minimally credible claims, and other psychological gamesmanship that can be played in negotiations and mediation.

- *Cost Management.* Arbitration procedures can limit costs by restricting the amount of pre-hearing discovery and disclosure of information leading to possible evidence. However, arbitration can be more expensive than mediation because the parties must pay arbitrator's fees, the administrator's fees and legal fees. But the parties save by avoiding delays, inconvenience, travel time and travel costs.

- *Arbitrator's Competency.* Like mediators, arbitrators can be chosen based on choice or criteria, such as particular professional credentials, practical experience in the subject matter of business divorce, bilingual skills and/or locale.

- *Enforceability.* Like mediation settlements, arbitral awards (decisions) are enforceable under the U.S. Federal Arbitration Act so long as the agreement to arbitrate was valid and the arbitrator acted fairly. Fairness is determined by impartiality, lack of corruption or fraud, procedural fairness and acting within the scope of authority.[59] Thus, an arbitral award can have the same effect as a court judgment, but only if it is ratified by a court of competent jurisdiction.

- *Case Management by Arbitrator.* Like mediation, the arbitrator can serve as case manager to limit the scope and intrusiveness of classic judicial 'discovery' procedures. Depending on the rules of the organization administering the arbitration, the arbitrator can suspend proceedings to allow negotiation or mediation for a while. The arbitrator might also have authority to decide several disputes among different parties, all in one proceeding. For private companies, the parties can even define the case-management terms (such as number of depositions and interrogatories) in a detailed arbitration clause.

- *Case Management by an Administrator.* Dispute resolution requires some minimal level of administration at various key

---

[59] Federal Arbitration Act, 9 U.S.C. §§ 2 *et seq.*, available at https://www.law.cornell.edu/uscode/text/9/2.

stages. In mediation, the mediator usually is the administrator. For arbitration, an administrator may be required to compel a recalcitrant party to participate in the process, which includes the selection and appointment of an arbitrator (or arbitrators). An arbitration can take place in one country yet be governed by the arbitral procedures of an administrator located in another country. This gives parties a choice as to procedures while retaining the venue requirements for the UN Convention on the Recognition and Enforcement of Foreign Arbitral Awards.

- *Suspension for Negotiations or Mediation.* The rules of the administrator (or the arbitrator's decision *ad hoc*) may allow the parties to suspend the arbitration so they can pursue negotiations, with or without mediation.

- *Allocation of Winner's Legal Fees and Costs to the Losing Party.* Depending on the wording of the arbitral clause in a contract, the parties can dissuade each other from abusive recourse to arbitration, and can encourage settlement, by agreeing in advance that the arbitrator shall have the power to require the losing party to pay the winning party's legal fees and/or costs. Such allocations can be powerful incentives to negotiate a settlement before the arbitral award is issued. Indeed, such clauses can even instigate a mediation during the course of an arbitration, which might then be submitted to the arbitrator by stipulation, so that the arbitrator renders the award that contains the negotiated settlement. (This gets a little tricky since the arbitrator's authority derives from the existence of a dispute, and a complete settlement thereby deprives the arbitrator of any basis for 'arbitrating' a 'dispute.)

- *International Enforceability.* When confirmed by a court for compliance with the Federal Arbitration Act or other arbitration statute, the arbitral award is normally enforceable under an international convention.[60] Such flexibility can be a great advantage in shareholder disputes and commercial contract disputes involving residents or entities in different countries.

---

[60] United Nations (or 'New York') Convention for the Recognition and Enforcement of Foreign Arbitral Awards, 1958 (hereinafter the 'New York Convention'). For signatories, see https://treaties.un.org/Pages/showDetails. aspx?objid=080000028002a36b.

However, like any other form of dispute 'adjudication,' arbitration is not perfect.

- *Limited Recourse where Arbitrator Not Correct.* Where the arbitrator's award (decision) is not clear, or not 'reasoned' (with references to law or precedents), it might still be valid. The law permits attacks on clearly biased or unjustified decisions, but the arbitrator's decision is generally cannot be overturned in court. Parties have limited opportunities to invalidate the award.

- *Fees of Arbitrators and Administrative Agency.* Judicial dispute resolution might be cheaper than arbitration in some cases due to administration costs for arbitrator fees and administrative fees. Such costs can be reduced by tailoring the dispute resolution process creatively. In disputes over a relatively large value, most arbitral administrators (or arbitration clauses) require three arbitrators. To reduce arbitrator costs, the parties could appoint three arbitrators but use only one (selected by the two nominees of the disputing parties) to act as single arbitrator. (The AAA has such a procedure for complex commercial disputes.) The single arbitrator could design and administer pre-hearing procedures, such as admissibility, rules, scope and discovery. When it comes to deciding the merits, the parties could either continue to rely on the single arbitrator (and dismiss the wing arbitrators), or, on request of one, activate the wing arbitrators for adjudication.

- *Judicial Enforcement of Arbitral Awards.* An arbitrator's order (compelling some protective action) or award (awarding payment) will need to be enforced by a court having jurisdiction over the 'losing' party. Judicial enforcement involves additional costs, delays and risks.

Arbitrator's Valuation

Arbitration can be used as a valuation tool. Instead of having the parties agree to appoint a valuation expert, the parties could agree to appoint an arbitrator to listen to the different valuation theories presented by the divorcing shareholders. The arbitration would resemble a court hearing, not an expert's valuation. But it may achieve the same result.

'High-low' arbitration is a technique similar to Russian Roulette. Instead of having the shareholders alternately agree on a high or low price and on who will get to buy or sell at that price, the arbitrator makes the choice between two values presented by each of the two shareholders in dispute. Drama often imitates real life. In 'Russian Roulette' as played in nineteenth century 'cowboy western' movies, one cowboy holds the gun that is loaded with one bullet in six chambers. He points it to the other cowboy and pulls the trigger. If that fails to kill the other cowboy, then the gun holder spins the chambers again (or not) and then points the gun to the victim. This process may continue until someone dies, confesses or subordinates to this torture.

In a more humane adaptation for business divorce, one shareholder names a price, and the other shareholder agrees to either sell all his shares at that price or buy all the other shareholders' shares at that price. It's a forced exit. But any agreed 'Russian Roulette' buyout process still needs to define who gets to set the purchase price and who shall have the right to buy or sell. One solution involves the flip of a coin or the roll of the dice.

This process is usually unacceptable since negotiations can achieve a more reasoned price that is logical, justified and not excessively harsh. Still, some shareholder agreements may contain 'Russian Roulette' clauses exactly for this reason, to force each shareholder to be reasonable or suffer the risk of a lopsided price on exit.

Arbitrator's Choice of Party-Designated High-Low Values: 'Final Offer Arbitration' / 'Baseball'

High-Low 'Zone Management.' Normally, a court or an arbitrator decides the questions of liability (duty to pay) and the amount of damages. To present surprises in dispute resolution, the parties might agree upon upper and lower limits for a settlement, but allow a neutral third party (arbitrator, judge or potentially a mediator) discretion to select a value within such limits or at one of the limits. In a 'high-low' settlement process known as *'final offer' arbitration* ('FOA') or *'baseball' arbitration*, each party sets forth its top and bottom lines and accepts the decision of the finder of facts on liability and amount owed if it fits in the zone.[61] The parties agree not to change the limited offers until the arbitrator or court selects one or the other after the hearing.

---

[61] See Andrea M. Alsons and Kevin G. Faley, *'Settlement Techniques: High-Low Agreements,'* NY Law Journal (July 27, 2017), p. 3.

By narrowing the limits of liability, the parties reduce their dispute resolution risks within a zone of agreeable outcomes. The claimant is guaranteed a minimum amount, so long as the adjudicator finds some liability of the defendant to pay the claimant. The defendant is guaranteed not to be liable for more than the maximum amount, thus eliminating the risk of a 'run-away' jury voting on sympathy not on any realistic measure of damages. The defendant also benefits by not being liable for any award of pre-judgment interest expense, attorneys' fees or other expenses to the extent they might exceed the agreed maximum payout. The parties thus prevent the court or arbitrator from 'splitting the difference' between two numbers.

High-Low Settlements in Court. To be legally valid in a court, 'high-low' settlement agreements must meet certain procedural steps. (Your lawyer can advise you on your own state's rules). They must be expressly approved by each party and disclosed and filed in court, and available on the docket record. They must be submitted at any time prior to the announcement of the jury verdict. To avoid potential conflicting judicial rulings, they must also prohibit the parties from filing any motions for any inconsistent judicial ruling. In a sense, 'high-low' settlements do not solve the dispute. Both parties must still pursue all legal recourse and defenses. But, like a mediator's nudging toward final settlement, it's a start.

High-Low in Corporate Divorce. In a corporate divorce (especially in a 50-50 ownership), 'high-low,' 'FOA' or 'baseball arbitration' provides a possible solution for one party to offer a 'fair' price to sell but let a neutral third party choose between two proposals from the two parties. This process, which limits the arbitrator's discretion and encourages parties to make reasonable financial proposals, is sometimes referred to as an 'either/or' arbitration or final-offer arbitration. The neutral party could then be instructed to choose one of the two proposals (or to find a number between the two).

Day Baseball. In the 'day baseball' variation, the two co-owners each proposes a number and argues openly for the rationale for adopting it. The 'daylight' comes from the open argument as to the reasonableness of that party's number. 'Day baseball' valuations are fair when each party has equal access to information, equal understanding of the management of the business and equal capacity and time to actively manage the business after the sale. By contrast, 'night baseball' puts the arbitrator in the dark until the arbitrator decides on a number. Then the arbitrator must award that amount.[62]

Night Baseball. In 'night' baseball FOA, the parties' numbers are concealed from the other party or the arbitrator. This approach can have several variations. The parties might not disclose their numbers to each other, but the arbitrator would receive both numbers and select one. Or the parties would not share with the arbitrator but would agree separately to share with each other and agree to be bound by the number closed to the arbitrator's award. Or the parties might limit the arbitrator's role to identifying the winner, and the parties would agree that the winner's number would prevail.

Bracketed 'Zone Management.' If chosen by the parties, the arbitrator could also be bound by a middle number within a 'high-low' approach. Each party defines a target award amount. If the arbitrator's award amount is within the brackets, there is no change. If it is outside, then it is changed to the nearest number of the parties.

Appraisal (Formal or 'Drive-By' Valuation)

Appraisers skilled in business valuation face a difficult analytical process that can be costly, slow and possibly confusing. Even a well-crafted appraisal could be disputed because either party might say the appraisal fails to fully appreciate the uniqueness of the business or the steps necessary to identify factors that could make a 'comparables' valuation truly comparable.

Enter the 'drive-by' valuation process. In this process, an expert (or computer expert) identifies databases that are relevant and current and analyzes the data without inspection of the asset being valued. To avoid fraud, the failure to conduct an on-site inspection or do further investigation is disclosed. 'Drive-by' valuations, based on broker price opinions or online databases, have largely supplanted formal appraisals in large-scale financing of residential real estate.[63]

---

[62] See generally, Edna Sussman & Erin Gleason, *'Everyone Can Be a Winner in Baseball Arbitration: History and Practical Guidance,'* NY State Bar Assn, Journal (July/Aug. 2019), pp. 19-24.

[63] R. Dezember & P. Rudegeair, *'Investors Turn to 'Drive By' Home Appraisals, Adding Risk,'* Wall St. J., Jan. 22, 2018, p. 1, cols. 2–4 and p. 2.

Where the owners agree on an appraisal approach, they may wish to define both the process for selection of the appraiser(s), the roles of the appraiser(s) and applicable valuation principles.

- How many appraisers are needed? If there is only one, the appointment might be done by process of elimination from a list or requesting a third party (such as an arbitration institution) to appoint the appraiser. If there are two appraisers, the owners might each designate one and then agree on a valuation that is halfway between the two valuations. But to avoid favoritism, sometimes the divorcing shareholders each appoints a valuation specialist, and the two valuation specialists then appoint a third.

- What roles will the appraisers play? Are they merely consultants or arbitrators? A consultant must follow instructions under terms of appointment. An arbitrator decides definitively, and arbitration procedures can be *ad hoc* or administered by an arbitration institution.

- What valuation principles will apply? The parties might agree on applicable mandatory valuation principles, earnings multiples (for EBITDA cash-flow analysis) or reference to specific 'competitors.' The appraisers could apply the principles of valuation dictated by the divorcing shareholders, or they could apply their own approach.

Breaking Deadlocks

If the parties do not identify a 'zone of reason,' a deadlock will occur due to 'irreconcilable differences.' As the deadlock continues, each owner loses value as the joint enterprise spirals downward through indecision.

In anticipation of deadlocks, they can plan ahead to define deadlock-breaking terms for buying or selling their share in a business. Each deadlock breaker starts with a definition of deadlock (such as inability to agree on a major change), to trigger the method for its resolution. The deadlock flows from a scenario that neither party wanted to occur and that will cost in money, pride, control or other embarrassment to fix. The cost to fix by mutual future commitments is too high. There is no 'reasonable' solution for either party.

Fairness suffers. True, while draconian (forcing a buyout or a sale), the provisions have some degree of perceived fairness, separating control over the decision to sell/buy and the price, leaving both unhappy but divorced. But these solutions do not achieve fair value. The parties might not submit high offers because of financial constraints or other internal factors unrelated to fair value.

Worse, these draconian solutions do not permit 'productive cherry-picking.' As neither party can selectively purchase or sell employed talent, or particular assets or business opportunities, both lose the chance to deconstruct the enterprise and seek the highest value of its components. The deadlock prevents restructuring of ownership or control, innovation, release of value, and emotional and corporate freedom to refocus on other opportunities. By continuing the deadlock, the stalemated parties are inviting vulture investors to a feast in a bankruptcy sale.

Russian Roulette. In a buy-sell negotiation with 50–50 ownership, the parties can agree to allow one owner to set a price, and the other party could choose whether to buy out the other, or sell to the other, for that price. This approach offers some advantages. First, it puts both at risk of giving control to the other. Second, it encourages the first party to give a fair value, at a price where that party is indifferent to whether to buy or sell that party's ownership. Third, this approach encourages strategic valuation to induce the other party to take the 'problem' and accept the 'solution.' Thus, the other party has to decide whether the future challenges of operating the business will be palatable. If the party offering the price (the 'offeror') wants to get the future upside from running the business (and is willing to take the downside risks), the offer should make a price adjustment that increases the 'true' fair value to a point where the other owner will be happy to sell. Conversely, if the offeror does not want to run the business, then the offeror should offer a low price that communicates to the other owner that the other own can get a bargain, or 'fire sale.'

There could be some disadvantages. This approach encourages an economically stronger party to submit a low bid, anticipating that its partner cannot afford to pay full value to buy it out for cash. The one who would be the likely seller has no opportunity to run the business (or to restructure to take a part of the business) — so the recipient has no effective choice of a true 'fair market value.' This method prohibits access to earn-outs and third-party financing and creative restructuring. Hence, if there is unequal bargaining power, Russian Roulette might be better replaced by a 'baseball arbitration' that offers a semi-appraisal approach.

'Texas Shootout' or 'Shotgun' Buyout. The same quickie divorce can be planned under a 'sealed bid' 'Texas shootout' process. The parties agree a deadlock exists. Each submits to an umpire a sealed bid stating the all-

cash price at which it will agree to buy out the other party's share or sell its share. The party submitting the highest bid must buy out the other party. Like Russian Roulette, a 'shotgun' buyout may put one party at a serious disadvantage due to inequalities in wealth, liquidity and capacity to manage the business after a buyout.

Modified Dutch Auction. A true Dutch auction involves multiple bids starting at a high asking price. In a modified Dutch Auction, each submits a sealed bid stating the all-cash price at which it will agree to buy out the other party. The party submitting the higher bid must buy out the other.

Layered Choice Negotiations. The governing agreement can offer a list of possible reasonable resolutions to an anticipated scenario. Such layered choices may be incomplete and can result in delays and further joint downward spiral. Hence, incomplete solutions invite alternatives such as arbitration or litigation.

Tools to Manage Damage from a Hostile Business Divorce (Blackmail, Mutiny, False Claims, 'Stickups')

Special situations might trigger a buyout as a negotiating tool to eliminate a problem attributable to one or more co-owners. Some strategies might damage, but not eliminate it.

Incomplete Assignments of Rights by a Founder

Where an individual founder has the financial capacity to build, market and sell an innovative product or service, he or she might decide to retain ownership of some assets essential to the business before allowing others to invest. This incomplete assignment of essential rights creates risks for any co-owners, who normally would insist on a complete assignment to the company. An incomplete assignment might protect the founders against a new co-owner until the new co-owner's 'sweat-equity' value has been proven.

From the Case Files

I was consulted to stop an abuse by a do-nothing equity owner. After a year as a startup, the two founders agreed to admit a third co-founder for no capital contribution unconditionally to own a third of a startup. When the new owner failed to do his job, he demanded a buyout at an extraordinarily high value that the others could not afford. So the two others liquidated, distributed the digital assets and reformed a new company under the trademark owned by one of the two original founders. So the do-nothing got nothing, while the others could restart. In hindsight, the two founders should have contributed the trademark earlier and put conditions on the issuance of equity to the third 'co-founder.'

Stopping Employment-Based Claims by Employees

Today, business owners face employment-based claims that can be used for blackmail or damages. To safeguard, the company should ensure it has policies and procedures to limit risks and to defend against possible claims.

Hostile Work Environment

A worker cannot be expected to focus on doing the job if there is a 'hostile work environment' that denigrates the worker on account of some personal attribute. Bullying, yelling, cursing, obstruction, insults, needling and other aggressive or demeaning conduct can thus violate the employee's rights.

Business owners need to cut off all such misconduct immediately, or they could be deemed accomplices. More importantly, you, as owner, cannot go off the handle and create a hostile work environment. You might have to trade some real money for your right to terminate the employee, or you might just have to live with that employee as a protected employee under local law (with back pay, front pay and damages). Be nice and respectful. You can still be the boss, but drop the drama.

Age Discrimination

Similarly, a young business owner cannot discriminate against older business owners on the basis of age. Don't say anything about the older employee or owner's gray hair, age, wrinkles or age cohort.

Sexual Harassment

In today's publicity-driven business environment, any claim by a female executive of sexual abuse, sexual harassment, gender discrimination or hostile work environment can be devastating to the viability of any enterprise, large or small. Allegations alone can be fatal to a man's reputation. Since 2018, federal law prohibits a company from deducting payments of hush money in a confidential employment settlement for 'sexual abuse' or 'sexual harassment' (neither of which are defined). Some states adopt the same approach. So even the threat of such claims can imperil the loyalty of key customers who have adopted a 'zero tolerance' policy internally and for their suppliers.

From the Case Files

Employment law claims or a failed joint exit can trigger a corporate divorce.

Where two co-founders work together for several years and then fail in an effort at joint exit, one co-founder might artificially create a civil rights claim as a dispute-based exit strategy. They might dispute the adequacy of the best exit price offer (obtained after an informal auction by an investment banker). With hindsight, they might be unhappy over each other's perceived 'inadequate' preparation for sale or perceived 'unrealistic' price expectations. Then, one day, the minority owner incites an argument on a matter of business judgment. Knowing the majority owner's personality, the minority induces the majority owner to dramatically release pent-up frustrations in a staged yelling incident conveniently witnessed by others. Pointing to the 'open yelling,' the minority then threatens a civil rights lawsuit. In 'settlement,' the minority offers a choice: either the minority gets operational control or the minority gets bought out. With assistance of negotiating attorneys, the founders resolve their unhappy exit failure by agreeing to a complex financially engineered redemption agreement.

Stopping potentially extreme employment-based claims requires preparation. An employee manual, for which each employee acknowledges receipt, should create an open-door policy for reporting any employment-based claim to a neutral person such as HR Director, other senior officer, board member or company lawyer. Then an investigation should occur, and any corrective actions should be taken.

For a key owner-employee, deterrence can be effective. The employment agreement might include some governance-related provisions to promote timely disclosure of 'material adverse changes,' use of personal computers for business operations or risks that normally should be reported immediately to the board.

Further, to establish the facts, the manager might wish to have another person attend all meetings that are likely to be contentious and elicit some form of hostility by the management team.

In some jurisdictions, a false and malicious complaint of sexual harassment can subject the accuser to the same punishment of the person falsely accused.[64] While such laws are not universal, the complainant's good faith can always be an issue at trial, with possible counterclaims for defamation.

Employment-practices liability insurance should be considered a wise investment where the co-founders are of different sexes. EPLI policies generally have large deductibles for the company's initial legal fees, but insurers may be required to contribute to an exit plan and redemption even though the exiting co-founder contrived the alleged violation of such co-founder's employee rights.

Plan for Protection of Company's Brand, with Expulsion of CEO or Brand Leader

A 'business divorce' can occur when the individual representing the company is fired for social misconduct, not for failure to perform services. The company can limit reputational damage by preventive contractual clauses relating to employment, trademarks and by negotiating smart exit agreements when expelling a wrongdoer.

'Morals Clauses.' If a founder or CEO is accused of disregard for an employee's civil rights or some crime or other 'moral' impropriety, the company's brand value will be affected. If the accused controls the company, he or she might make cosmetic changes in roles of management to lessen his or her apparent involvement. If the accused is only a minority owner

---

[64] India, 'POSH Act': *Sexual Harassment of Women at Workplace (Prevention, Prohibition and Redressal) Act, 2013*, available at https://indiacode.nic.in/handle/123456789/2104?view_type=search&sam_handle=123456789/1362, accessed Nov. 12 2019.

with no veto, the other owners normally consider whether to expel him or her.

A 'morals clause' is a traditional risk management tool for companies hiring a Hollywood movie star or star athlete to endorse their products. Under a 'morals clause,' a key person ('brand messenger') agrees to avoid acting in a manner that brings social opprobrium on the individual and thus on the company. Such clauses can be set forth in agreements for employment, shareholder relationships, personal services and licensing of the individual's name and likeness. Since the consequences of socially offensive conduct and reputational damage are drastic, 'morals clauses' require careful definition of what conduct is not permitted, who decides, how the decision may be made, what evidence of misconduct must exist before termination, and the legal consequences of termination.

Given the new environment for civil rights protections, privately owned companies should consider requiring all founders and 'brand leaders' in the C-suite to include a 'morals clause' in their employment agreements and the shareholders' agreement.

Brand Protection Plan. In such situations, the board (not the majority owner) needs to take action to protect the company's goodwill. An action plan by the board might include several steps:

- adopt and update corporate governance policies, procedures and oversight so the company remains a safe and respectful environment for diverse employees;

- monitor your trademarks using monitoring service covering new trademark applications, new domain names (URL's) and social media for negative comments;

- in response to any claim, hire a law form to investigate the allegations against the founder, and, after internal review and due process, sever employment 'for cause' under a 'morals clause';

- adopt a succession plan to deal with the possibility of a future void left by a departing 'brand leader';

- structure a share buyout to reduce the ownership and thus the reputational influence of the departing key person;

- ensure that all employment agreements and your equity incentive plan allow the company to terminate employment, equity compensation and other incentive compensation for fraud, misappropriation, embezzlement, dishonesty, breach of fiduciary duty or willful acts or omissions by the employee that reflects adversely on the integrity and reputation of the company for honesty and fair dealing (a sort of generic 'morals clause');

- likewise permit the company to cancel any unvested incentive compensation and pay in cash (and not shares) upon a merger or other change of control, to give the board discretion in the exit transaction structure;

- consider various provisions in a settlement agreement such as a tapered exit period for services and ownership of shares, cooperation in defense of claims against the company, non-disparagement covenant, license to use the founder's family name (or to change the company name.

Stopping a Corporate Mutiny (Going 'On Strike')

In a mutiny, two or more subordinates take action to defeat the control of the superior individual in the chain of command. A mutiny can get results. Or it can backfire.

From the Case Files

A corporation had two shareholders. In a 'corporate mutiny,' the minority owner (acting as a senior corporate officer) and a key employee conspired to quit on the same day. They stated they wanted to protest the 'inhumane' neglect, control and poor business judgment by the majority owner who was also board chairman. The chairman was vulnerable because he depended on both mutineers to run the business. The mutiny succeeded in drawing attention to a disagreement on next steps towards a joint exit and on the rewards and changes demanded by the two mutineers to manage for a future joint exit in two or three years.

In response, the majority owner agreed to a restructuring of the key employee's incentive compensation structure (with new equity-flavored incentives and key performance indicators) but did not grant any new benefit to the minority owner. For financial and legal reasons, the minority owner lacked credible leverage. First, the harm to the company would have destroyed enterprise value, with a loss in share value for all owners. Second, without a negotiated resolution, the majority owner (or the company) could assert a claim for damages due to the minority's breach of fiduciary duty as officer (acting as employee, not as shareholder) not to collude with any employee to disrupt operations. As a result, the majority owner understood that he could negotiate with the key employee without any benefit to the minority.

Ironically, the mutiny generated mutual benefits over time. In declining to accept both resignations, the majority owner balanced the benefits of accepting one or both of the resignations against the harms. He adopted a long-term strategy. For the short term crisis, he partially acquiesced. For mid-term, he adopted plans for business continuity, risk management and resiliency and institutionalization of knowledge and customer/client relationships. For the long term, he developed plans for buying out the minority. Within two years, both mutineers were no longer associated with the company. When leaving, each was bound by a non-competition covenant.

Mutinies can be staged to have a catastrophic impact on both the superior 'officer' and the company. The company might be in a highly vulnerable condition, such as active fundraising from investors, planned sale of the business, pursuit of valuable prospective clients or strategic alliance negotiations.

Preventing corporate mutiny requires paying attention to the founder's personal relationships with all employees, particularly minority co-owners and key employees. Stopping a mutiny requires careful navigation between avoiding 'abusive' and 'retaliatory' employment discipline (no instinctive punishments). The best preventative is to have a succession plan at all times and anticipate all contingencies. Hopefully, leadership by example and effective listening skills can avoid the 'crew's' need for mutiny.

Stopping Corporate Blackmail, whether Internal or External

Blackmail is the extortion of money or some form of compliance in return for the blackmailer's silence about the victim's highly embarrassing non-public vulnerability.[65] The victim pays the blackmailer to remain silent and to not take any hostile action using the embarrassing information. When the blackmailer demands the ransom, the victim has no legal contractual right to ensure the blackmailer's future silence or that the blackmailer will not ask for an additional future ransom.

Corporate blackmail comes in various forms but is most egregious in employment. A co-owner's blackmail plan might be dressed up as a complaint about sex discrimination, loud voices and harassment of employees of the opposite sex, hostile work environment, sexual abuse or sexual harassment. In court, such a complaint will be impossible to dismiss as a frivolous claim, even if the parties have been negotiating terms of a buyout of the employee. So it's a winner for the complaining co-owner. Worse, the blackmailer might induce the alleged events by disputing a business decision and using personally derogatory words. The blackmailer then surreptitiously takes audio or video recordings on a personal electronic device. The blackmailer knows the claim will tarnish the company's brand goodwill as well as the accused co-founder's personal reputation.

A blackmailer abuses the personal information about co-owners or co-workers. In privately owned businesses, the co-owners become intimately familiar with each other's personal failings, foibles, medical conditions, emotional weaknesses, psychological dependencies, financial difficulties, tax frauds and other private personal vulnerabilities. Such personal information is protected under European Union law as a fundamental

---

[65] See N.Y. Penal Law, § 155.05(2)(e) (larceny by extortion).

right to privacy.[66] In the United States, common law protects against invasion of privacy, invasion of intrusion into a secluded private place, intentional inflection of emotional distress and defamation ('publication' about a 'non-public figure'). Filing a lawsuit or administrative complaint is legally protected by 'litigation privilege' that pre-empts such personal privacy rights. So personal privacy laws offer little protection to a business entity if the founder's name is vilified by 'staged' disputes and litigation blackmail.

Such blackmail in business divorce triggers a corporate governance crisis. The board of directors and majority owners seek to avoid or neutralize the potential reputational damage. To do so, they must defeat the blackmailer's ability to disclose the embarrassing personal information.

Preventive measures depend on good governance, compliance, transparency and ongoing reputation management showing a 'good' corporate culture.

Crisis resolution may justify a buyout and potentially payment of special compensation. The blackmailer will want to avoid bankrupting the company before all payments are made and may actually honor the usual restrictive covenants on non-competition, non-solicitation and non-disparagement.

Stopping a 'Stickup' Demand by a 'Highway Robber'

A 'stickup' demand is like a robbery. The shareholders dispute each other's goodwill and good and faithful performance of their roles and responsibilities. In short, they want to dissociate. Then the one shareholder accused of non-feasance (or other incompatibility) demands a buyout price so high that the others cannot find a way to pay, either through a redemption or a person-to-person buyout. The company is in growth mode, short of cash and cash flow, but with a promising technology and prospective customers.

---

[66] Regulation (EU) 2016/679 of the European Parliament and of the Council, of 27 April 2016, on the protection of natural persons with regard to the processing of personal data and on the free movement of such data, and repealing Directive 95/46/EC (General Data Protection Regulation), available at https://eur-lex.europa.eu/legal-content/EN/TXT/HTML/?uri=CELEX:32016R0679&from=EN.

What could the other shareholders do to stop this 'highway robbery'? Every 'robber' normally has some weaknesses that can be exploited to force a 'reasonable' outcome.

From the Case Files

We were asked to stop a co-owner's 'stickup' demand upon his termination of employment. The 'robber' was a young lawyer who had persuaded the two co-founders of an online B2C startup to receive fully vested one-third ownership in exchange for past services and future services as in-house legal counsel. An in-house attorney's includes intellectual property protection. This requires getting all individuals who create works of authorship for the company to assign their copyrights to the company. He failed to do so. As a result, when he was fired for laziness and sloppiness, he demanded an unaffordable $500,000 for his one-third ownership even though he had earned it. Rather than negotiate a ransom, the two co-founders decided to liquidate the company and distribute the assets pro rata to all owners. The lazy young lawyer received his pro rata share of the cash on hand and a copy of the copyrighted works but lacked the initiative and skills to reconstitute the business. In this case, one co-founder had retained the trademark rights as part of the shareholder agreement, with a royalty-free license to the company. This enabled the co-founder to contribute the trademark to the new company.

Having a 'secret file' or discovering such weaknesses can be crucial to defending against a 'robber.' For example, one can imagine other weaknesses beyond non-feasance, such as non-compliance with law or company policy, misrepresentation, or breach of fiduciary duty. Such weaknesses form the basis for a counterattack that turns the 'robber' 'stickup gun' around at the robber, forcing a reasonable resolution. The rules of civil procedure permit 'discovery' of admissible evidence of such weaknesses, which explains why litigation costs so much more than arbitration or mediation. Any 'discovery' in arbitration is a matter of the arbitration clause and the arbitrator's judgment. In short, know your partner and stay up to date on his or her personal weaknesses as much as you stay on top of your own.

Getting Your Money Back from an Embezzler: White-Collar Crime

White-collar crimes can occur in the typical business divorce situation where there is any embezzlement, securities fraud ordinary fraud or conspiracy to defraud. For victims, criminal prosecution does not guarantee restitution and may, indeed, incarcerate the malefactor instead of allowing the malefactor to remediate directly. Further, victims have no control over the discretion whether and how a prosecutor might prosecute the white-collar criminal. Criminal law punishes. So criminal prosecution is rarely pursued if alternative solutions are available.

From the Case Files

One of our clients was a 50-50 owner and unsecured lender of $13 million to a jointly owned company. One day, the CFO disclosed that he had 'borrowed' over $500,000. We adopted a strategy of confronting the CFO's entity that was the other co-owner. We demanded an immediate buy-sell exit agreement for both crisis management and restitution. Restitution was not feasible: neither the embezzler nor his co-owner entity could cover the $500,000 loss. Our client prevented further embezzlement by getting agreement to appoint a mutually trusted independent financial officer to take over the financial functions and report to all owners. The client made an agreement on the terms of a joint exit, with the embezzler's entity having the right to sell the entire company for a period, followed by a second period in which our client could sell the entire company. During this period, we helped our client clean up all messy documentation, rectify corporate housekeeping and enhanced internal policies to look attractive to a buyer.

This resolution did not compensate our client for the distraction, legal costs, or assumption of risk of liability for potential breach of representations and warranties. It was a 'fire sale' with a low price, but enough to allow our client to recover the full $13 million loan. The embezzler's entity received very little.

Preventing Ransom Demands

A business divorce could arise if the company failed to have adequate resources to resolve a ransom demand from a third party, such as a malware hacker. Such risks can be predicted and insured, with risk management policies to mitigate losses by redundancy, encryption and tighter access controls.

Tips to Prevent and Win in Litigation

If you are a good manager, you can avoid crises and minimize the damage of a possible business divorce by effective management.

- You can prevent employment-based blackmail by good governance, compliance and risk management practices. At a minimum, the board should adopt a code of conduct, a whistleblower protection policy, a quality policy and diversity policy. All employees need periodic training to combat discrimination and harassment in the workplace. The company should consider employment practices liability insurance as well as a risk management policy, a quality policy, a business ethics policy and a sustainability policy. Design and implementation will require consulting professional advisors.

- Your GCR practices should be reviewed and updated at least annually to identify and mitigate the material risks of running the company, including political, commercial, human resources and succession management risks.

- Finally, adopt a culture of compliance. Get rid of any autocratic or patriarchal attitudes. A culture of transparency, ostensible mutual respect and individual accountability of managers can protect shareholders from blackmail, attract employees wanting to work for an ethical organization and build long-term brand value by earning the customer's trust despite 'minor' setbacks. Such a culture can avoid the crisis that threatens shareholder value.

As an owner or director, you should hire your own separate personal attorney. Do not ask your company's attorney for how you will be impacted by succession or exit or other governance dispute. The company's attorney represents only the company. What you say must be shared with the entire board and maybe all shareholders, even if you are the majority owner!

If you are aggrieved, don't jump into litigation until all other avenues have failed. If you must, identify your grievances and notify the board and pursue negotiations. But once you file a lawsuit, you narrow the opportunities for a beneficial outcome. Then, if you want to put the litigation on hold, your attorney might warn that you are looking weak, so you cannot easily undo it. Early settlements offer the widest range of solutions, since huge attorneys' fees have not been incurred.

Your Professional Advisors

For crisis management and dispute resolution involving individual shareholders or separate stakeholders, you can get valuable assistance from attorneys in business, employment, compliance and dispute-resolution; mediators and/or arbitrators, appraisers, accountants, crisis public-relations advisers, insurance brokers and personal wealth advisers.

Your Self-Assessment

- Do you have an agreement with your co-owners that defines the method for resolving disputes in scenarios where one or more co-owners will cease to own any equity?

- Which exit scenarios are covered by the agreement? Which scenarios are not covered?

- Does the method cover the decision-making process, valuation principles, valuation procedures and the timing, conditions and amounts of payments?

- Since that owners' agreement was signed, have there been any changes in circumstances that suggest you and your co-owners should revisit and renegotiate 'the deal' on valuation upon exit?

- Does the documentation for future co-owners address the methods for resolving such disputes?

- What circumstances have changed since you entered into the agreement? How does such change affect the fairness, feasibility or 'politics' (relationships) among co-owners (and prospective co-owners)?

- What defenses does your company have to nullify any risk of litigation by a co-owner asserting rights other than as a co-owner? Could such litigation force a buyout on terms unfavorable to the remaining owners? What impact would such litigation have on your company's business reputation, client base, other employees, lenders, suppliers, service providers and financial condition?

PART III

Particular Business Types

5

Succession Planning in Family Businesses

Succession planning provides continuity of day-to-day management, without necessarily changing any ownership. Of course, ownership may change, but the founder may define how the new ownership structure integrates (or not) into the intergenerational wealth planning. Your succession planning should address several questions:

- What are the objectives and priorities of the founder and of the family? Who should control decisions?
- When should the founder leave?
- To whom should the business be transferred to?
- Do you have a family 'heir apparent' as successor? If so, what conditions are needed for transitioning?
- When do you want to transfer wealth to younger generations, how much, and under what conditions?
- How can you integrate personal planning with business succession planning?
- What levels of risk and complexity can the family tolerate?
- How can you increase the business value for a sale or partial sale?
- How much money can be taken from the business, when, and for whom?

Classic Succession Planning for Any Business

To survive, a company must maintain innovation in the core business, sustain growth, propose new lines of business and respond to the marketplace. Guided by the board, the CEO is responsible enterprise viability.

For any company, succession planning serves to define selection criteria, identify, train, evaluate, inculcate values, transfer enterprise leadership knowledge and transfer operational control of the business to a new CEO. In the earliest stages, several candidates are considered and given an opportunity for personal growth. Later, a 'succession plan' is announced, and one candidate is designated as the heir apparent to succeed the current CEO. (Sometimes co-CEOs are selected, with the goal of grooming one to win and the other to exit on good terms. Such internal competition can be divisive and self-destructive if continued too long. Or the two co-CEOs can allocate work between client relationships and administrative and accounting services, with the client services co-CEO usually winning out.) When active day-to-day management is passed to the new CEO, the replaced CEO remains on the board of directors for continuity in strategy, leadership and knowledge transfer.

Communications with employees are critical to successful successions. For a new in-house CEOs, the communications may be simplified. Employees already have seen the candidate's credibility and understand that new CEO knows the business, the people and the customers. For lateral CEOs hired from outside the organization, the senior founders need to enlist consensus, support the lateral CEOs new initiatives, confront potential mutinies with direct interactions and support a renewal of a defined corporate culture.

Most importantly, the succession plan should be set up years in advance. This will allow for training for a 'stretch' experience by those moving up the ranks, encourage teams to learn from each other and set deadlines for owners to exit before they reach the target exit age.

Special Succession Planning for Family Businesses

Family and business do not always mix well. Personal expectations of equality, loving kindness and loyalty are not always shared among spouses and family members. The same organizational challenges faced by startups are aggravated by unspoken personal expectations and later frustrations with the lack of success, incompetency, inexperience or poor decision-making, unilateral actions without consultation processes, and eventual personal divorce. Eventual participation by children poses significant challenges for control, tax planning, growth and scalability, capital investment and exit or succession planning. At the very least, a family-owned business needs all the psychological and emotional commitments and caring 'parenting skills' of a family plus savvy business leadership.

In *succession planning*, family-owned businesses face a series of hurdles where it is assumed that a family member will assume operational control.

- *Competency.* The family must produce at least one qualified new leader with interest and ability.

- *Harmony within Family.* If multiple family members could qualify, the shareholders should decide on roles and responsibilities for multiple members. Unless the family business is to be run by a council, one leader must be chosen. Then the role of the others must be decided.

- *Ownership: Buyout or Transfer?* The founder must decide whether company ownership be transferred to the new CEO or put into trust. What dregs will the other family members in the next generation ('G2') receive, select roles that are compatible and do not generate excessive conflicts.

- *Third Generation's Role.* Few enterprises (especially publicly traded companies) survive if they are controlled by the same family beyond two generations. At some point, professional managers must be hired. Some families might try to retain operating control by special voting shares (for example, Alphabet, Ford Motor Company, FaceBook, WeWork). Other families might decide that the third generation would be too numerous, and lack common agreement on operations, so they might adopt a family constitution to bar third generation members from senior management but establish a private foundation or trust for their welfare. Still other families designate one or two members of the next generation as 'heirs' of the family business, provided they have professional qualifications, and in such event the question of exclusion of future generations from active management gets deferred.

In *estate planning*, intergenerational wealth transfer involves many conflicting rubrics. Intestate succession, 'forced' heirship' (limiting a spouse's right to transfer the estate to others on death), a trust's fiduciary decision-making rules and decision-making participation by spouses, siblings and children. Further, gift and estate taxation play a key role in the design of the enterprise, structuring and funding of new opportunities to benefit the next generation, ownership, voting control.

Family law varies. If both spouses own a family business, the marital regime takes precedence over the business regime. In a 'community property' jurisdiction (including several U.S. states and European countries), both spouses share equally in the work product of the other. (In the U.S., the community property states are Arizona, California, Idaho, Louisiana, Nevada, New Mexico, Texas, Washington, and Wisconsin.) A pre-nuptial (or post-nuptial) agreement is needed to protect the spouses and possible other shareholders (such as employees or investors) in future marital disputes. And if the couple move from a non-community property state to a community-property state, they need to act like they just got married … and see a lawyer about the rules.

Third parties investing in a family-owned business face special challenges in governance and business divorce. If the family holds a majority, the family members might decide to restructure the operations, or incur liabilities, or fail to pursue opportunities, without the minority's consent. Even if the family holds a minority, the third-party investor faces the risk of loss of value if the family members divorce or fight. In a personal divorce, each divorcing spouse would likely lack control, leaving the business in crisis of management and ownership, unless the divorce settlement allocates ownership to one spouse.

Such marital and family issues are negotiable in a shareholders' agreement, but add complexity, cost and risk for the third-party owner. A shareholders' agreement can protect the other owners from having a deceased owner's estate, which might sell shares to a third party or force unwanted changes. Survivors can be required to sell back shares to the company at a predetermined price or at a price based on a pre-determined method of valuation. This prevents blackmail by the survivors, who might allow a buy-back only at an inflated price. It also ensures the survivors receive a fair price. As with any buyout, life insurance can provide liquidity for payment of the exiting owner.

Family Psychology

While the business might have been organized for profit, it creates a family. Managing a family evokes all the fears, hopes and dreams of childhood, parenthood, empty-nesting and grand-parenthood. This chapter focuses on psychological barriers to effective succession and transition to the next generation (whether the successor is a family member or employee). Similar emotional stresses occur in startups, though the financial focus of investors reduces the psychological barriers to planning for a change of control.

Common Fears. Founders of family businesses face a host of emotional fears, ambitions, misbeliefs and confusions when dealing with issues involving succession and transition to a next-generation manager or owner. Similar confusion arises for individuals who are founders but have no family and must 'adopt' friends as quasi-family. Such emotions run a full range:

- fear of being seen as 'unfair' to family;
- fear of losing control during the pre-succession planning and testing period before transfer of control;
- fear that the successor will make major mistakes, or 'betray' the founder's trust, such as pursuing a major change in business direction;
- fear of change, with nothing to do after retirement;
- fear that transitioning to a family heir will create less sustainable value than a sale to an acquirer;
- fear that the succession process will spiral out of control;
- inexperience at adapting to change of management style and roles;
- inability to conduct an iterative and adaptive testing program;
- guilt at forcing the next generation to take over the family business.

Families and 'quasi-family' friends can face significant costs, hurdles, unnecessary publicity and conflicts due to errors in structuring at inception.

Common Mistakes. The founder may emotionally deny the importance of planning and managing transition. Transitions to a new generation or a new owner do not occur magically, without effort.

Like a parent, the controlling founder normally wants to be fair and equitable to all his or her children. In corporate succession planning, the founder might define fairness as giving each child an equal ownership stake and maybe even a seat on the board. Such equality ignores the demands, difficulties and diligence need for developing, training and testing new leadership. Ironically, the same definition of fairness in family matters contradicts the fairness that should protect all in the 'company family.'

Any transition of control demands huge effort, usually done at the same time as 'ordinary business' goes on. Exhaustion, inability to absorb complexity and poor judgment may result from doing 'succession planning' in a rush. Prudence suggests consulting with professional advisors.

Common Solutions. To deal with your family and your business, first follow the rules of good housekeeping: document your plans for ownership and transfers of ownership, as well as capital contributions, dividends and shareholder approval of transactions that could be arguably characterized as self-dealing or breach of fiduciary duty.

Second, decide who should be an owner? Minor children should not be named directly as owners. They are legally incompetent to make their own decisions. A parent as guardian might not be approved by the court if the parent has a potential conflict of interest, such as owning shares directly or being a contingent owner upon the death of the other parent.

Third, decide what happens if an owner dies. There should be some mandatory buyout of the estate of an owner who dies. Otherwise, any remaining owner will be working for the estate of the decedent, without receiving the benefits of work inputs from the now-deceased owner. The deceased owner's heirs will want to exercise their rights, creating conflicts. Death insurance can cover the purchase price, and soft payment terms can ease the burden of the remaining owners.

Fourth, consider what happens if the owners no longer agree? Small businesses need other supports for continuity in the face of scenarios for possible disputes. Such scenarios include the possible incompetency or disability (temporary or permanent) of a key owner, or a change of business focus that is not unanimously supported.

Finally, consider conflicts and rules for resolution. Conflicts may arise between individuals or between individuals, directors and fiduciaries.

Family Members as Employees

Several possible advantages arise from putting children on the company payroll. They can learn the business and prepare for possible eventual succession to the role of CEO or COO. The company can pay salaries (subject to wage taxation), provide retirement plans and offer stock or stock options for future capital gains. The family member might solve an immediate need for talent in an entrepreneurial or growth venture.

But pitfalls are predictable when employing family members. Tough and disciplined decisions taken for business purposes can easily impair family harmony and trust. Due to family relations, a family member might abuse a managerial position or, alternatively, be too reticent to use necessary discipline. Family-based employment could trigger scenarios governed by special family-based laws that could adversely impact the company in tax compliance, succession planning (community property, inheritance rights and divorce).

In family companies, the founder faces a conflict of loyalties that can destroy family relationships or the business, or both. Nepotism is the granting of favors or employment to relatives or friends, without regard to qualifications. Imprudent decisions, negligent supervision or vicarious liability by a founder or employed family member can be expected to result in litigation, white collar crime, class action lawsuits, punitive damages, reputational damage, family strife, resentment and hostility by other family members and lost opportunities.

The conflicting loyalties collide in the decision to hire a family member and the practical 'impossibility' of firing a family member. A family member might be unsuitable for the business due to lack of minimal competency, lack of dedication or low standards of performance. Worse, unsuitability can result in illegal conduct such as sexual abuse of non-family employees, civil rights violations, hostile workplace from abusive language, embezzlement and other illegality in employment. Even without any illegal misconduct, hiring a family member can lead to irreconcilable differences in good-faith conflicting beliefs and management styles, leading to conflicts in the boardroom.

For business design and planning, such conflicting loyalties must be resolved in advance. Before hiring a family member, the founder should design some form of family constitution or other tool for family relationship governance and family-based share ownership. The founder thus makes clear the family has no right to be employed or to counteract the founder's judgment. In addition, the company's 'code of conduct' should treat family members no differently to others.

Family Governance: Do You Want a Family Constitution?

Where family personal relationships and family business intertwine, a family constitution (or family charter) can set guiding principles for adults without 'parental supervision.' Family constitutions may be more common in second generation (G2) and later generations. While the founder (G1) is still manager, a family constitution can provide useful guiding principles and procedures for management transition and harmony. Above all, the family constitution can help the family 'self-regulate' and achieve shared emotional commitment, tempering the harshness of business leadership tasks with community-building frameworks for mutual respect, empathy, intimacy, appreciation, coaching, and emotional support.

As a tool for family governance, a family constitution first identifies the principles and values of success, growth and succession: the need for future growth, dependency on employees, and mutual moral commitments by family shareholders (who are admitted to ownership only upon passing performance hurdles). A key function is to limit any automatic privileges of family members. Since it is not adopted by the company, a family constitution is not a corporate obligation and should not be the basis for litigation. Rather, it serves as a framework for families to resolve disputes behind closed doors in a family way. Like companies, family members may need professional advisors to help achieve the lofty goals of the family constitution.

In a smartly designed family constitution, the family's guiding principles combine the constitutional rigor of a corporate charter, by-laws and policies with the self-disciplines of married life. On the business side, a family constitution can be designed to overcome the asymmetries of access to information and conflicting objectives of business managers and owners. On the family side, the family constitution can facilitate personal cohesion across generations establishing an ethic-based framework for training and transitioning to new family leaders over time.

- *Flexibility and Adaptation.* The format should be as simple principles, not hard rules. The charter should be easily modifiable. After working under version one, the family should regularly evaluate how to improve the constitution, reflecting 'lessons learned' from the evolving interactions. Amendments can be triggered by schedule review, changes in tenure of the current leader of the business or pre-defined events such as health, age or business decline or growth.

- *Multi-Forums for Multi-Functions.* Create and support different forums across functions. A family council can identify generational transitions and choices. A business council can evaluate business plans in the context of what's best for the family as a whole and how to allocate talents and rewards as a family business. An owner's council can elicit and study opinions on what is in the best interests of the owners. A family office can manage wealth, charity, personal hobbies, travel, and other projects to allow each family member to get the advice and support necessary for personal activities.

- *Transparency.* While a family business needs to maintain trade secrets, the family constitution can forestall certain family conflicts by encouraging the founder to share business information and concerns. A little openness can create and maintain trust.

- *Family Cohesion.* To build cohesion, adopt facilitated 'family retreats' that bridge the gap in business operating information and business sophistication. Include trainings for the next generation, both in business and wealth management. Initiate teams for family participation in projects that create cohesion and a shared 'family brand' and 'family identity.'

- *Family Decision-making.* The family charter supports cohesive decision-making, encouraging dialogue, investigation of alternatives for smart risk-taking and avoiding regrets. To promote consensus, serious decisions may require general unanimity or due consideration of 'minority' recommendations. Autocratic patriarchal founders might disagree with any challenge to authority in the business decisions. A founder's dominating personality may explain why the first family charter might be limited to principles on corporate human resources and not corporate governance. So, you should institute a decision-making process that is fair to all.

- *Conditions for Hiring Family Members.* Family members should not be eligible to be hired in the family business without adequate training and skills. Children should get real-world experience, preferably in other companies, before considering participation in the family business. Children should start in operations, not management. How else can a manager know whether the staff (or suppliers and contractors) are performing their jobs, if the manager has never performed that task, witnessed both good and bad outcomes and learned the lessons?

- *Business Cohesion.* To avoid spillage of family conflicts, family members working in the same field should resolve their disputes in private. Then they can adopt one voice to the world, without exposing rifts.

- *Family Code of Conduct.* All family members should be guided by a family code of conduct. Even if not directly involved in the business, they are stakeholders and can affect the business value and operations. The family code of conduct can resemble the corporate one, with duties to avoid waste, squandering resources or diversion from the business scope without adequate consultations.

- *Dispute Resolution.* A family charter succeeds best when family or business disputes do not spill over into each other. To identify and remediate a concern and its 'root cause,' the complainer should be required to address it directly with the source and not whine to others. A robust dispute resolution process can include an ombudsman to listen and investigate facts, mediators to resolve deadlocks, 'satisfaction surveys' and trainings in negotiation principles and amicable conflict resolution.

To serve such needs, the family constitution anticipates conflict and establishes tools for durable resolution.

Family Divorce: Avoiding Harm to the Business

A family divorce between two spouses, who are major owners, can destabilize corporate governance in a closely held business. In community property states and other jurisdictions applying similar rules for splitting the assets created during the marriage, a pure 50–50 split could defeat the majority control or veto rights that the two spouses held jointly before the family divorce. Where one spouse's role is so fundamental, indeed indispensable, to the continuity and success of the closely held business, it may be reasonable for the non-indispensable spouse to not insist on a 50–

50 split. Such an unbalanced split works in favor of the non-indispensable spouse, who will continue to reap the benefits of the indispensable spouse's efforts in continuing and growing the business after the divorce. Without such an accommodation, the indispensable spouse could abandon (or diminish the level of effort for) the closely held business and pursue a new venture with 100 percent control. However, such a 'restructuring' might come with the risk of possible liability to the non-indispensable spouse for self-dealing and misappropriating corporate opportunities of the jointly-owned business existing before the family divorce.

From the News Files: Family Divorce Affects Company Ownership and Control

The divorce settlement of Jeff and MacKenzie Bezos illustrates this principle. Before the family divorce, Jeff owned 12.04 percent and MacKenzie owned 4.01 percent of Amazon.com, the third largest U.S. company behind Apple Inc. and Microsoft Corp. Subject to judicial approval, the spouses entered into a voting agreement and proxy that continues during Jeff's lifetime or until a determination of his legal incapacity. He is authorized to exercise sole voting control over all Amazon shares that either of them owns (and any additional shares issued to MacKenzie in a stock split, stock dividend, recapitalization, reorganization or the like). Such voting control will not apply to any shares that MacKenzie might sell in the open market or that she donates to a non-profit organization (as a tax plan for her) with the belief the non-profit intends to sell such shares in the open market.[67] As she tweeted, MacKenzie also agreed to transfer to Jeff all her ownership in The Washington Post and the rocket company Blue Origin LLC, which Jeff had founded, to 'support his continued contributions with the teams of these incredible companies.'[68] Ms. Bezos's advisors may have considered the deal reasonable, given the length of the marriage, other personal commitments and that the divorce would not affect her lifestyle as a multibillionaire.

---

[67] Form 8-K, Amazon Inc., on file with Sec. & Exch. Comm'n, filed Apr. 4, 2019.
[68] J. Greene and V. Dagher, *Bezos Divorce Deal Settles Amazon Shares,* Wall St. J. (Apr. 5, 2019).

Succession Planning for Controlling Founder's Exit

Business exit (or business succession planning) sometimes takes ten to twenty or more years. For family businesses, succession planning involves both family estate planning and corporate succession planning.

A succession plan identifies candidates to step into leadership positions when an incumbent leader retires or otherwise leaves the company. The plan requires clear job descriptions including required skills and knowledge base. It may involve training via assignments to different areas of the company's operations. It may also include participation in leadership decision-making processes as a prelude. Most importantly, the planning should identify various contingencies and possible back-filling and interim solutions in case of emergency. As new opportunities arise, adaptability becomes an important attribute, beyond core competencies. And the ladders of leadership succession should be updated periodically for optimization and adaptation. Succession planning is a critical element to business continuity planning and disaster recovery planning as well.

Family Wealth Plan

No plan for management transition or sale of your business is complete without a family wealth plan. You should consider the possibilities of death, disability, divorce or other disaster for each family member. Key issues involve 'control' (governance by you individually or by a third-party fiduciary), insurance (see chapter 8), taxes, succession and family harmony across your business lifecycle and your family lifecycle. For good corporate governance, you should not allow your family wealth planning to impair your private company's enterprise value.

Control before your Exit

Profit Sharing Plan

You and your family members (as employees of your business) can reap significant tax benefits under a profit-sharing plan. This enables all employees (not just owner-employees) to contribute to a personal retirement account where appreciation is not taxed until retirement.

Trusts and the Shareholders' Agreement

Trusts can be useful in lifetime asset management. The trustee(s) must administer the assets for the purposes stated in the trust agreement. A family trust is formed by contract where the grantor transfers assets to a trustee for the benefit of one or more family beneficiaries for a period of time. For tax purposes, the transfer is not subject to gift tax if the grantor retains the right to revoke the trust.

In succession planning for closely held businesses, grantor trusts are useful to enable the founder to select, interact with and train his or her co-trustee, who may be a business professional who knows the founder's family and almost acts like a surrogate parent. Without such a trust, the transfer of ownership at the founder's death would lack continuity of management. Upon the founder's death, the remaining co-trustee(s) could make business decisions (exercising the rights of a controlling shareholder), such as to promote replacement management. If successful, the trust structure could keep the business well managed for a generation. If unsuccessful, the trust structure could lead to a sale of the business to the junior managers upon the founder's death, subject to negotiated terms.

Family trusts can serve as a disincentive for employees to serve in senior management positions. Corporate governance where a founder's trustees exercise majority control effectively precludes non-family members from any future opportunity to grow and assume control, except through a management buyout. As a result, non-family managers might negotiate protections such as stock options, buyout rights and some veto over major changes in corporate policy. Most founders would refuse or restrict such protections. Thus, if a founder wants to continue to 'control from the grave,' the business enterprise might suffer from a lack of independent professional management after the founder's death.

Trusts can be vehicles for intergenerational wealth transfers and delegation and training of next generation. Under a trust agreement, the grantor (such as a founding shareholder) transfers property (such as shares) to a trustee who agrees to hold, invest and transfer it after a period to designated beneficiaries. A trust must terminate at some point, usually after a period of named lives in being plus 21 years plus a period of gestation (if the measuring life is a new child).

Many shareholders' agreements permit a corporate founder or key owner to assign all shares to a trust for that owner and his or her family. Such trusts can be abused where the corporate founder creates a trust that lasts long beyond death. Shareholder agreements should authorize a buy-back by the company or remaining shareholders upon the death, disability or termination of employment of the key owner.

Corporate Governance Rules for Personal Trusts before Owner's Exit

Corporate shareholder agreements normally anticipate the need for family wealth planning. To avoid potential marital dispute spillover in any exit scenario, your spouse should sign the shareholder agreement and waive any objections to the manner in which your shares will be bought or sold by the company in a buy-sell, drag-along, or tag-along scenario. Your co-owners take business risks, not risks that your spouse will blackmail you and them later in a joint exit scenario.

Plan Your Exit

Your exit from control and/or ownership of a family business should fit into a tax-focused estate and gift plan. For example, if you own control of the business, and you want to transfer your shares to your children, you could make a gift of some shares and sell the other shares, with the sales being subject to an installment promissory note. This approach uses your lifetime estate tax exemption and defers taxable income to you.

Control after your Exit

After a founder's exit from day-to-day management, the founder might continue to exercise some control as shareholder and board chairman. There are various legal solutions to such continuation, since ownership can be put into the hands of a trustee or other family members. Your decision on post-exit controls will be reflected in several areas.

Wealth Management Tax Planning

For taxes, you should get professional advice on the usual personal individual and married income, gift, estate and inheritance taxes. Your advisor will suggest various key events and possible vehicles for asset ownership, risk management and mitigation and wealth transfer. You can discuss family limited partnerships or other entities as holding companies for investments, marital gifts, educational expenses, charitable giving, timing of gifts to your descendants and the impact of your possible divorce and remarriage.

Some wealth transfer practitioners propose plans to 'freeze' and 'squeeze' the founder's assets and estate, so that it can be transferred at lower taxable valuations. Timing is critical. Such plans are best implement using a business valuation made long before any particular buyer is identified or a specific price is negotiated.

Your current and future places of 'residence' and 'domicile' will affect family wealth planning. You might reside in a 'community property' jurisdiction that may give automatic equitable ownership rights to your spouse and children. In that case, work-based assets are community property. If the company bears your name, it's community property if you build it. But it may be separate property if you inherited it from your parent and it is merely a passive investment or one where you just get a salary. In a non-community property jurisdiction, the result might be similar upon divorce under equitable distribution principles. So your spouse is an automatic business partner in waiting, until your death or divorce.

Governance Planning for Family-Owned Shares

For governance of family wealth, you may consider who should be making decisions on pre- and post-exit investments. You can delegate wealth management to investment advisors who act under your supervision, or you can transfer your assets to a fiduciary (trustee or executor) for prudent investments. Your fiduciary could be an individual or an institution, or a combination. If you trust an individual but want an institutional trustee, you might appoint an institutional trustee and authorize a trusted individual to act as 'trust protector' with power to remove and replace a trustee who has become insensitive, imprudent or unprofessional in your protector's eyes.

Trusts can serve several purposes. A trust can minimize estate taxes. Some trusts can protect assets from creditors of the founder and family members (who might be spendthrifts),, legal claims and divorce. Generally, trusts also serve as a substitute for a will. Depending on the particular family configuration and any special needs, your wealth management plan might include one or more trusts or other entities.

- Asset management and transmission tools, such as:
    - o grantor (revocable) trust for yourself and incidentally for your family succession and wealth devolution;
    - o spousal lifetime access trust (to adapt to changing estate tax exemptions over time);
    - o marital trust for your spouse;
    - o family limited partnership for holding investments;
    - o dynasty trust for your descendants for multiple generations (but get advice on durational limits, letters of wishes, trust protectors, trustee advisors and adaptation to future uncertainties)
- Asset protection entities, such as a trust or holding company (subject to fraudulent conveyance laws);
- Special needs trust for medical and personal care for an individual;
- Irrevocable insurance trust (to receive life insurance for distribution to your beneficiary free of estate taxes, depending on the size of the taxable estate and the applicable tax-exempt amount);
- Sale of shares to an 'intentionally defective grantor trust' to produce wealth for the next generation using loans and interest rate arbitrage (actual return vs. adjusted federal rate);
- Charitable trusts (such as charitable lead annuity trust, charitable remainder annuity trust or charitable remainder unitrust), charitable foundation, or donor-advised charitable fund.

To substitute for the grantor, a trust protector could be appointed with authority to change the trustee, restructure the gifting formulas as beneficiaries' needs change

For foreigners building a business with U.S. operations, additional angles need a plan. How can you or your family own a business, travel freely and comply with political sanctions, national security investment reviews by the Committee on Foreign Investment in the United States ('CFIUS') of cross-border sales and ever-changing visa conditions? What steps have you taken to limit overall estate taxation in different countries?

Trusts can invite tax audits,[69] so consult a professional advisor.

Spouse as Co-Owner and Co-Manager

In a family business, your spouse might be a co-owner and co-manager. Spousal ownership invites analysis and structuring for control. Otherwise, a 50–50 ownership model is an invitation for disaster (i.e. liquidation and loss of brand value and ongoing clientele) upon a personal divorce. By contrast, if your family business is a professional services firm, professional ethical rules normally nullify the value of such goodwill (and thus valuation for a liquidation sale) by nullifying any non-competition covenants after a business exit.

Family Holding Company

Founders of family businesses frequently establish a 'veil of tiers' with holding companies owning a key operating company, which in turn might own a series of foreign subsidiaries. Such structures allow for the usual benefits of such structures, such as consolidated income taxation (at least for U.S. operations), offshore tax deferral, opportunities to make tax-free acquisitions and even tax-free divestitures. For families, holding companies can include shareholder agreements, or be owned by a family succession trust, to implement transition and succession goals.

Family LLC or Limited Partnership

Business owners can contribute assets (such as family business shares) to an entity that allows the founder to retain operating control while transferring future appreciation to family members. Such arrangements must have a valid business purpose, such as portfolio management for the entire family. The transfer of assets needs a current valuation, which may be discounted depending on ownership percentages. Your attorney can advise on details.

---

[69] See IRS, *Abusive Trust Tax Evasion Schemes - Special Types of Trusts*, https://www.irs.gov/businesses/small-businesses-self-employed/abusive-trust-tax-evasion-schemes-special-types-of-trusts, accessed Nov. 12, 2019.

Family Office

A family office can also be established as a business enterprise to pursue family wealth management. It can hire specialized investment managers to pursue investment strategies defined by the family scions and family decision-makers. It can provide clerical support to the family for investment related activity. When properly structured as a for-profit business, the family office can deduct operating expenses, which would not be deductible if the individual family members made their investments directly.[70] A family office can help achieve effective and efficient wealth management and transmission, operating efficiency, accounting and tax transparency and deductibility of ordinary and necessary business expenses of the family's wealth management activities.[71]

Some Tax-Advantaged Strategies for a Founder's Exit through Succession

Prior to a family business founder's exit by sale of company, some strategies might yield benefits upon sale or afterwards.

Private Equity's Dream #1: New Company for New Ventures

Some successful family business owners establish new companies for each new venture, giving the shares to a trust for an infant or for multiple children. Such transactions allow the parents to work for the benefit of the children's company, and to enter into transactions between affiliates that provide mutual benefits. For example, a child's company could provide R&D support to the founder parent's company, allowing that child to provide earn profits from the relationship. Care must be taken, however, to ensure intercompany transactions are justified as being on 'arm's length' terms, so that income tax authorities do not attempt to reallocate profits to reflect economic reality.[72]

---

[70] Code, § 212, as amended through 2025 by the Tax Cuts and Jobs Act of 2017.

[71] See generally, Thomas J. Handler, 'Global Virtual Family Offices,' in Barbara R. Hauser (ed.), FAMILY OFFICES: THE STEP HANDBOOK FOR ADVISERS. (Globe Law & Business Ltd 2019, 2nd ed.).

[72] See Code, Section 482 and regulations thereunder. Income tax treaties also provide for reallocation of revenues to avoid abusive profit shifting between international affiliates.

Private Equity's Dream #2: Strategies by Child to Optimize Self-Driven Value Creation

In distributing family assets, fairness is judged at a particular moment in time. A child wishing to work in the family business has a choice. He or she may work directly as an employee, thus benefiting the remaining family members. Or he or she might establish a series of ventures, one for management, one for R&D, another for distribution, that belong 100 percent to that child. Thus, after the 'succession' moment in time, the child reaps the future growth in his or her companies, which are interconnected with the family company. And the child can choose a tax-favored residence to conduct the child's businesses. This variation as family planning evokes the private equity's dream of an ecosystem of interconnected companies under common control.

From the Case Files

I assisted structuring a family succession with early distribution of family assets and new personal business opportunities for the chosen successor. The father, in his 70s, wanted to continue managing the entire business while encouraging a business-oriented son to become successor. The father distributed non-business assets to other heirs to satisfy statutory heirship rules while agreeing in a trust agreement to distribute company shares to the business-oriented son. The son moved to a nearby tax-advantaged jurisdiction, where he established a product development company to serve the father's family business. (There was no usurpation of corporate opportunity since the son offered talents and R&D skills not available or accessible to the family company and the business scope of the father's business did not include the particular product development.) The intercompany dealings were on commercially reasonable terms. There was full disclosure and no self-dealing. For risk management, all family members agreed to the reasonableness of the succession plan.

Asset-Stripping by Founder before Exit

Some creative planning can augment the value derived from the sole owner's sale of the company. New vehicles can be bought for the company just weeks before the closing, and the selling owner can buy them at depreciated value when the acquirer closes the purchase. While they might accept asset stripping, buyers will require that the company, as purchased, has all necessary operational assets for its continuing operations.

Tips on Succession in Family Business

When starting your business, sign your will (or trust). Otherwise, your intestate heirs will own your interest the business.

By working at an unrelated business first, your children and other family members can get valuable training, credibility, self-confidence, personal insights and enthusiasm if they choose to join your family business. Your first job as parent is to teach your children how to fly on their own. Your second job is to let them come back for family gatherings. Third and last, your job is to welcome them and help them share your business if they want to, but judge them like any outsider as to skills and temperament.

Be aware of disparities in expectations as to timing. You should continuously assess and communicate your expectations and listen to your family on theirs. Whether your children or employees take over, the transition requires careful design and implementation under a clear strategic business plan.

For those children with no capability or interest in being your successor, you can provide for their inheritance without including them in the business. So your game plan might change from succession to sale.

Your Professional Advisors

For family-owned businesses, you can get valuable assistance from consultants, attorneys, accountants, appraisers, accountants, tax advisors, insurance brokers, real estate brokers, private bankers and personal wealth advisers. A trusted family advisor, friend of long duration and/or family therapist can help with intergenerational relationships. Depending on the circumstances, you might also wish to consult an investment banker (for possible sale to a third party) and/or business broker.

Your Self-Assessment

- How can you transfer your shares under conditions most favorable to your family?

- Do you have the right team?

- Is the business ready for a succession or sale?

- Which factors affect your timing to plan and complete a succession or sale?

- In your family business, how have operational, investment (and re-investment), strategic alliance and succession planning decisions been made in the past? Who has ultimate decision-making authority? How does the decision-maker evaluate and respond to suggestions by those who are consulted? Who has a veto?

- Which family members are interested in becoming members of the family business, both for operational and ownership purposes? What is your strategy and toolkit for training and promoting such family members? How does this strategy impact your HR decisions? What is your strategy for your family wealth planning (creation, growth, accumulation, preservation, 'decumulation' and succession to the next generation?

- Have you explored with your professional advisors legal, tax and financial strategies for corporate governance of your family business, with reference to significant future changes in life-style, health, competitive advantage of your business, sustainability under present and future management, and disruptions such as startups, digital transformation, political and economic trends?

- Have you established any holding company or trust(s) to limit potential liabilities across your different lines of business, across risks of sudden changes in your personal condition and the needs of each member of your family as they progress over time?

- How have you balanced family relationships with business relationships, in respect of decision-making authority, control, vetoes and transition (transfer to a family member vs. transfer to an unrelated buyer)?

- Have you balanced risks and obligations that will continue after the transfer?

6

Exit Strategies in Startups and Other Multi-Owner Companies

Special Exit Issues for Startups and other Multi-owner Companies

Startup companies are in a hurry to grow. They seek market share by disrupting traditional business channels while complying with existing legal regulations. They live on the Internet as 'direct to consumer' retail, e-commerce, fintech, insurtech, medtech, legaltech, edutech, cleantech, govtech, energytech and 'anytech.'. Startups can build tools for artificial intelligence, virtual reality, augmented reality and robotic process automation. Startups depend on investors unless they can bootstrap till they are profitable.

While startups have many unique benefits, they regularly invite business exit because startup business models pressure the founders and team to experiment, build and scale rapidly. Such pressure invites excesses such as bold overspending, spending on wasteful operations, running out of steam and pivoting towards new solutions that demand new capital and new dilution of founders and employees.

Startups depend on a reward system of deferred compensation. Stock options in lieu of a 'regular' salary can create great wealth, but also can burn out founders and employees, leading to attrition. Where securities are issued for services, poor choices for structuring deferred compensation can be harmful to personnel. Those who receive securities are subject to a substantial risk of forfeiture in a diabolical deal: you can make a tax election that converts ordinary income to capital gains, but you must first pay taxes on receipt of the securities and you might never live to realize a growth exit.[73]

Thus, the tools for rewards, tax optimization, and totally 'immersive' time commitments come at the cost of intrinsic conflicts among the various stakeholders.

While not exhaustive, this chapter invites you into the realm of 'lessons learned.' Your mentors and professional advisors can shepherd you through the most egregious risks for your personal risk management and resiliency.

Unwanted Baggage from Prior Startup(s)

If you or your co-founder made some mistakes in a prior startup, learn from your mistakes. Make a list of lessons learned. Adopt this learning to never make the same mistake twice.

If your prior startup ended in bankruptcy, insolvency, liquidation or abandonment, do not try to make up in venture #2 what you messed up in venture #1. Do not succumb to your venture #1 investors to give them any free or discounted shares in venture #2. While the venture #1 investors might hold you in higher esteem (and maybe not sue you for some earlier misconduct), you lose in venture #2 by dilution of your ownership and control. In turn, this will narrow your room for error, leading to fewer opportunities to obtain VC funding at favorable conditions. You look stupid by not learning.

Likewise, do not feel it is your moral or legal obligation to refund any capital lost by a venture #1 investor. Such refunds are non-deductible. But, you can try your luck and get a tax deduction from your other income if you can prove (i) your primary purpose is to protect your personal business

---

[73] 26 U.S.C. § 83(b).

reputation in an unrelated business (like being a rock star singer), (ii) your venture #1 investors were acquainted with you based on that unrelated business industry and (iii) the insolvent venture #1 business bears your name and goodwill.[74]

Planning for Multiple Potential Exit Scenarios

For a startup, the optimal plan for a business exit is normally a joint exit. But startups bear risk, so many alternative exits need to be considered. The typical exit planning occurs at each of several predictable growth phases.

At launch, the founders create the entity and receive equity for their contribution of cash or past services, pre-owed technology or other assets. Sometimes a portion of such equity is put at risk of forfeiture if the 'founder' is just an under-compensated senior manager who has yet to demonstrate value by achieving some key performance indicators under an employment contract. This structure facilitates bootstrapping for rapid growth, assuming the prime founder can solicit enough co-founders to 'invest' by sweat-equity for little or no compensation during launch phase.

In the first funding round, investors contribute cash to enable payments of operating expenses. Soliciting investors requires compliance with securities laws. In turn, presentation of the investment opportunity to investors in a 'pitch' depends on your leadership team and well-crafted business plan, budget, unique selling proposition and schedule for completing a minimally viable product. At the funding stage, you allocate ownership interests to the investors, either based on an early defined value or on some future valuation when additional investors are invited in order to scale the operations as expenses grow to sell to customers. The first investors receive a minority ownership but insist that the founders be solely responsible for any subsequent ownership dilution (such as from stock options or new investment). In subsequent funding rounds, the founders and employees are diluted further.

At each stage, investors and founders jockey for advantage in possible scenarios of exit. The investors' term sheets define several exit scenarios. The suitability of various methods of rewarding founders, employees and investors depends on the phase and value of the company as it considers

---

[74] See *Jenkins v. Comm'r, 47 T.C.M. 238 (*1983) and T.C. Memo. 1983-667.

issuing new equity to others. As dilution occurs during startup growth, tensions mount between founders and investors about viability and timing of an exit, and the tools for an investor's early exit if there are irreconcilable conflicts. Also, employees and founders may conflict about the wisdom of pursuing risky commercial choices. So a founder who is both employee and subordinate to the primary founder might pursue employment-based pressures to obtain advantages. Any exit plan thus needs to define each growth phase and its relationship to a potential exit. Each new stage must anticipate further dilution to get to the next growth phase and risk and rewards for achieving the next growth phase or actual joint exit.

Founders' Agreements, Capitalization and Vesting Conditions

As a best practice, three basic elements should be ready and agreed at the start of the business: a founders' or shareholders' agreement, the capitalization table, and vesting conditions for all but the top founder. Delays can distort the terms by giving leverage to one or more founders and thus create tensions.

A founder's agreement defines the rights, roles and responsibilities of multiple founders who wish to start and run a business together. While it can be signed before the formation of the business entity, it usually is signed as shareholders' agreement or LLC operating agreement after formation. Such agreements cover many subjects discussed in the next chapter.

Scenario #1: Founders Only

Upon entity formation with founders only, the capitalization table must have at least one owner with fully vested equity with voting rights. Typically, this means one class of common voting shares (corporation), membership interests (LLC) or partnership interests (limited or general partnership). The entity's capital structure can invite disputes almost immediately, just as soon as one founder perceives an inequality in burdens of management and contributions to enterprise growth.

For protection against a majority's later issuing additional shares, the entity's charter may include pre-emptive rights allowing each shareholder an option to purchase a proportional number of newly issued additional shares. Without pre-emptive rights, the majority owners could issue new shares to themselves or their cronies, and in that case the minority owner may have a claim for breach of fiduciary duty for issuing ownership interests at too small an amount. But the minority owner would still be subject to dilution where there is no dispute about valuation at the time of future issuance of equity interests.

Shareholder disputes can also be driven by an 'unfair' capital structure that rewards each owner regardless of actual contributions of effort, assuming each partner is fully vested and cannot be diluted. Once you have vested shares, you have no further incentive to do a better job in order to acquire the reward of equity. You already have the equity.

Scenario #2: Founders with 'Friends and Family' Investors

Investors who are 'friends and family' are usually motivated by personal philanthropy as much as greed for future profit. Consequently, 'F&F' investors normally take on greater risk than professional investors in new companies. Even though an F&F investor might be treated by the SEC as sufficiently sophisticated as an accredited investor, the tendency is not to insist on shareholder rights that might hold the founders accountable for failure to achieve the business plan's goals and targets. In return, however, such investors should benefit by obtaining a large percentage of equity at a relatively modest pre-money valuation of the enterprise.

Scenario #3: Venture Capital Investors plus Others

Venture capitalists are professional investors. They invest other people's money (from a venture fund they created). They seek to build and sell a fledgling business, targeting a 100 to one return on investment since many investments might fail. They impose a number of minimum conditions. For regulatory reasons, the venture capital ('VC') fund must have contractual rights directly with a startup or other operating company to substantially participate in, or substantially influence the conduct of, the management of the operating company.[75]

A normal term sheet would include the following:

---

[75]   25 C.F.R. §§ 2510.3-101(d)(1)(ii) and 2510.3-101(d)(3)(ii)

- Preferred shares, with a preference that might include a guaranteed dividend rate, a preference in liquidation and a preferential payment of proceeds of sale;

- The right to participate in proceeds of sale on a pro rata basis in addition to a preference payment (which might be considered 'double dipping');

- Management rights such as a board seat or board observer seat for the VC or the VC's designee, the right to examine books and records of the operating company and the right to consult or advise management;

- Covenants granting greater rights than are typically found in covenants in debt instruments.

- Prohibitions on sale and other transactions, except under specific conditions or with the VC's approval;

- A right of first refusal for the VC to fund all future loans and equity;

- Reduction in founders' percentage ownership, not VC's ownership, for the issuance of any stock options or other form of equity as incentive compensation;

- Registration rights to piggyback on an IPO;

- Deferred Equity as Compensation for Services; and

- Qualifying Incentive Stock Options.

When soliciting funding, startup founders should ask not only for the term sheet, but for the VC investor's attitudes and needs for the future. For startups, the VC investor's exit strategy should align with management's decision-making. For example, management-friendly VC's can streamline the investment documentation with simple drag-along and tag-along clauses, clear rights on additional fundraising, limited exits, open-ended liquidity targets and limited veto rights.

Deferred Vesting of Ownership Rights

Qualified Incentive Stock Options

Under a qualified incentive stock option plan,[76] a corporation's employee can be eligible for incentive compensation where the stock purchased upon exercise of the option is not taxable until sale of the stock after a two-year holding period. Independent contractors are not eligible. The employer must design the plan to comply with basic rules.

- First, the stock option must be granted by the employer corporation or its parent or subsidiary corporation. (An LLC can issue similar options, but with less advantageous tax consequences.)

- Second, the option plan must specify the aggregate number of shares which may be issued under options and the employees (or class of employees) eligible to receive options. Typically, option pools are between ten percent and twenty percent of the total authorized capital. Any larger pool could impair the company's ability to attract investors and likewise impair the ability to the founders and existing shareholders to control the common stock.

- Third, the option must be granted within ten years from the date such plan is adopted, or the date such plan is approved by the stockholders, whichever is earlier. The grant of the option must state, by its terms, that it is not exercisable after the expiration of ten years from the date such option is granted. Finally, for U.S. income tax purposes, the QISO plan must be approved by the Board of Directors and ratified by the stockholders of the granting corporation within 12 months before or after the date such plan is adopted.

Other rules apply. As a result, in a business exit involving a single employee's exit, the availability of QISO tax advantages depends on timing of sales of option shares not only by the 'divorced' employee-owner, but also by other employee-owners.

---

[76] 26 U.S.C. § 422.

Vested Equity subject to Substantial Risk of Forfeiture (Section 83(b))

For LLCs and partnerships, Code Section 83(b) elections may allow some incentive compensation, but without the deferral of income taxation on the employee's receipt of equity.

When any person receives property (including corporate shares, LLC membership interests or partnership interests) in consideration of services, such property is ordinarily taxable as ordinary income. Worse, such property is an 'ordinary' asset and generates 'ordinary' income upon eventual sale.

To give incentives for individuals to render services to startups and other entities on an 'at risk' basis, Code Section 83(b) permits an election by such an individual to pay tax on the property received, pay tax on it currently and convert the property to a 'capital asset' for future capital gains taxation. There's only one 'catch.' The individual's rights must be subject to substantial risk of forfeiture.[77] Yet the individual must pay the full tax on the full value of the 'property' without regard to the fact that the individual's ownership is subject to a 'substantial risk of forfeiture.

If such an election is made, the individual must pay current tax on difference between (1) the fair market value of such property at the time of transfer (determined without regard to any restriction other than a restriction which by its terms will never lapse), over (2) the amount (if any) paid for such property.

Once such election is made, no further tax on the receipt of the property is owed. However, if such property is subsequently forfeited, no deduction shall be allowed in respect of such forfeiture.

A Section 83(b) election offers a big tax benefit: it converts the property to a capital asset (and thus generates lower tax rates on sale). The holding period starts at the earlier of when the owner first has the right to transfer such 'property' (shares), or when the risk of forfeiture ceases.

---

[77] Code, § 83(c)(1): 'The rights of a person in property are subject to a substantial risk of forfeiture if such person's rights to full enjoyment of such property are conditioned upon the future performance of substantial services by any individual.'

Deferral Stock (Options or Restricted Stock; 80 percent Participation) (Section 83(i))

'Deferral stock' is a new concept for promoting broad stock ownership among ordinary employees. With a suitable drag-along clause, deferral stock options or grants can promote support for a joint exit.

Under Code Section 83(i), an employer whose shares are not publicly listed for sale can adopt a restricted stock plan or stock option plan that gives more than a *'de minimis'* number of 'deferral stock' shares to at least eighty percent of the U.S. situated employees. (Current or former one percent owners, CEOs, CFOs and the four highest compensated employees cannot participate). Under such a plan, an employee receiving restricted stock can defer taxation on the value of such stock in a later year. The delayed timing of taxation of receipt of 'deferral stock' as taxable income depends on five possible events.[78] Generally, the tax must be paid when the restrictions on transfer lapse or when the stock could be sold on a securities market.

The employee must file a Section 83(i) election within thirty days after the first date when the rights of the employee in the deferral stock become transferable or are not subject to a substantial risk of forfeiture. Unlike an 83(b) election, 'deferral stock' treatment is available only to U.S.-based employees. To avoid possible favoritism for some employees of operations conducted by multiple affiliated entities, all affiliated entities are counted for purposes of the eighty percent coverage test.

Two Classes of Common Stock: Voting and Non-Voting

Some founders prefer to retain control by splitting the share capital into voting class A and non-voting class B common shares, with all other rights and privileges being equal. Or Class A might have, for example, ten votes per share and equal rights in liquidation, with the holders of both Class A and Class B voting as a single class.

Either approach may lull the founders into thinking (falsely) that they never have to obtain the affirmative vote of the non-voting class B common shares. Founders should be careful to control all classes of shares (if not prohibited by VCs or other investors), to avoid two situations where each class of stock

---

[78] Code, § 83(i)(1)(B).

is entitled to vote separately. Adversely-affected classes of stock are required to vote separately as a class, under Delaware law where either:

- the company seeks to amend its certificate of incorporation to increase the authorized number of shares of a class of stock, or to increase or decrease the par value of a class of stock; or

- the company were to seek to amend its certificate of incorporation to alter or change the powers, preferences or special rights of a class of stock in a manner that affected its holders adversely.

Contingent Incentive Compensation (Not Equity)

Stock Appreciation Rights

Sometimes it's too costly taxwise or not possible to reward a key employee with stock options or restricted stock. For this, 'share equivalents' were designed to allocate to such employees a fractional share of the purchase price on joint exit.

Stock appreciation rights ('SARs') are an obligation to pay the holder an amount equal to the appreciation in the share value from the date of grant to the date of sale of the company. As a variation, phantom stock is the right to get paid the equivalent on the purchase price of one share upon sale to a third party. The SAR only gets appreciation in value, but phantom stock is treated as a share, like any other share. The measuring period for the appreciation in value can be a fixed term (such as a period of months or years) or measured and payable only upon exit (sale or restructuring).

As equity equivalents, such accounting fictions are not equity, give no stock ownership or voting rights and are not paid directly by the buyer. Rather, they are contractual liabilities of an employer to pay to such fortunate employees an amount as if they owned shares. The company pays from its own cash on hand at the closing of sale. Such depletion of cash reduces the enterprise value to the buyer, who in turn reduces the purchase price to the selling shareholders. In turn, the price per share of actual shares is reduced to reflect the cash payments for SARs and phantom stock.

The legal rights of holders of SARs and phantom stock are limited to a claim for payment of a contractual obligation. They are unsecured creditors. Like holders of stock options, restricted stock or restricted stock 'units' where the employer may pay off in stock, their rights may be subject to future vesting upon satisfaction of contractual vesting requirements. In short, holders of SARs and phantom stock cannot assert claims of mismanagement, but they can assert claims for fraud in inducement. This distinction limits litigation over fiduciary duties of owners and directors.

SARs are convenient because they constitute deferred compensation and thus also defer the recipient's payment of income taxes. As a debt of the company, the SARs must be paid off in due course. So the structure of an exit with substantial SARs will need some adjustment in purchase price to reflect this liability of the 'target company.' f

Phantom Stock

Phantom stock is identical to SARs except for one element. The base valuation (from which future appreciation is measured) starts at zero (or, for purists, par value). Phantom stock thus includes built-in appreciation from periods prior to the date of employment of the employee who receives them. Phantom stock can be useful to provide future value accretion to a departed owner, without giving any owner's rights that normal shares might entail. For example, a redemption agreement might convert some common stock to 'phantom shares' where the company pays value in a future change of control (sale of company) as equity equivalents.

Deferred Compensation (Unvested) (Section 409A)

The federal tax code (Section 409A) allows employers to adopt plans that allow deferral of ordinary compensation until some future date at least six months ahead. Under the plan, the employee would be guaranteed the payment, but the date of payment would not be in the year when the deferred compensation is issued. Like Section 83(b) (property received for services) and QISOs, the employee's right to receive the deferred compensation must be at substantial risk of forfeiture. In this case, such a 'substantial risk of forfeiture' will exist if the individual's rights to such compensation are conditioned upon the future performance of substantial services by any individual.'[79]

---

[79] 26 U.S.C. 409A(d)(iv).

Deferred compensation plans are helpful in stretching out the payments of compensation, permitting the company and employee to avoid volatility in amount and thus maintain lower base income tax rates.

Preferred Stock

Basic Preferences: Dividends and Liquidation

Sophisticated investors demand preferred stock to give them assured exits on favorable terms. Through such preferences, they can exit with a multiple of their investment (on a joint exit) or can recover the company's assets if there is a liquidation. Such 'preferences' are defined in the certificate of incorporation and give holders of preferred stock an absolute priority over the payment of dividends to other classes of shares and/or the payment of proceeds of liquidation.

In real estate partnerships or startups, the preference structure can cascade in a manner that allows one investor to receive 100 percent of profits up to a certain point, then shift to pay another investor 100 percent of the next slice of profits, and thereafter allocate profits based on a formula that relates to ownership percentages. (Special tax-avoidance rules apply where the distributions have no relationship to ownership rights.)

Preferences upon Sale (maybe deemed liquidation)

In startups, venture capitalists may require preferences upon a sale. By defining 'liquidation' to include a sale of a control or a sale of a majority of the asset value, the VC gets to collect resale proceeds ahead of the common stockholders (founders, employees with exercised options and friends and family). Generally, VCs require priority payment of an agreed multiple of their capital investment before the common stockholders receive any payments. The multiple (or 'hurdle rate') may be adjusted to reflect timing, so that the annual 'internal rate of return' ('IRR') on invested capital achieves the hurdle rate necessary for the VC fund managers to earn their 'carried interest' in the funds (around twenty percent) in addition to their management fee (around one or two percent) which is guaranteed.

Startup founders may be able to bargain for reduced preferences where the VC fund managers can use third-party borrowed funds (rather than capital called from VC fund limited partners) to make an investment in the startup. Typically, if the startup has valuable assets (such as patents, long-term contracts or any annuity cash flow), the VC fund managers might be able to leverage such assets as collateral for a loan. In this case, the VC fund managers escape having to issue a call on capital from limited partners, who, having contributed less capital, get a disproportionately high IRR, boosting the VC fund manager's carried interest.

Participating vs. Non-Participating Preference

Startup founders should understand whether the VC's preferential distribution will be 'participating.' If so, the VC is entitled to collect 100 percent of the preference distribution upon the sale of its preferred shares and, in addition, the VC participates (on a 'fully diluted' basis) in the remaining proceeds of sale. Thus, a VC might be entitled to 4X its capital investment plus thirty percent of the remaining proceeds of sale as if its preferred shares had been converted to common shares (thirty percent, in this example).

Voting Rights

The voting rights of preferred shares are defined in the Certificate of Incorporation. In many VC-backed ventures, the preferred shares have such voting power as would apply if their shares had been converted to common shares.

From the Case Files

Our client, a VC-funded startup, developed software that offered innovations for makers of video games. During the pre-exit phase, the team faced internal conflicts over nepotism and divestiture of a line of business. With board approval and without consulting me, the company's CEO hired his brother to manage key technologies that would extend the company's core business from video games to telecom and smartphone tech. The new lines of business would be funded by profits from operations with one strategic customer in video games. This growth strategy highlighted the company's dependency on one customer. As that dependency grew, the strategic customer offered to purchase the entire company.

This offer precipitated internal conflicts shortly before a joint sale to the strategic customer. The CEO's brother and the technology team wanted to split off their development into a separate company. The technical team leader begged the VC's board member to override a sale of the entire company. The strategic customer acquired the entire company. Lesson: Hiring a family member creates huge stresses and risks, especially in a multi-owner company. If the company had split up, the value for the non-technical founders (including the CEO) would have been greatly reduced. Then the technical team would probably have usurped the corporate opportunities that were offered to the acquirer for financial value. And other co-owners might have sued the directors, CEO and his brother for nepotism. As a family, CEO and his brother would have 'divorced' without reconciliation. Interviewed in hindsight, the CEO advises 'never hire a family member in your business.'

Succession Planning for Multi-Owner Companies

The board of directors is responsible for developing risk management and contingency plans for foreseeable business risks. To ensure the company's survival upon the death, incapacity or sudden resignation of a founder or other key person, the board and owners should have backup plans. A business continuity plan should normally include several key tools:

- institutionalization of essential operational knowledge;
- multiple points of contact with key clients and influencers;

- a program for cross-training of key persons so they understand each other's jobs;

- identification of candidates for a possible emergency appointment of a successor (whether interim or permanent) to the affected key person; and

- development, training and cross-pollination of a pool of potential successors.

Succession plans can be defeated by a key person's controlling personality. In such cases, the other co-owners and the family of the key person should lobby to persuade the controlling personality of the benefits to all stakeholders of planning when there is no emergency. The key person's refusal to participate in such planning could affect not only family and co-owners, but also employees, clients, customers, suppliers, lenders and service providers. The company might shut down, and someone might set up a new business that builds on the defunct company's team. In short, controlling personalities can protect their loved ones – and the company's team and ecosystem – by planning for emergency succession, disaster recovery and business continuity.

Tips for Multi-Owner Companies

At launch, do not rely blindly on template agreements governing buyouts and vesting. There are risks and disadvantages that could prove unfair later. Certain buyout provisions may be unfair to the exiting owner. Get advice on how your equity agreements (and employment terms) might be unfair to you or others over time.

Your co-owners need to huddle before board meetings. Are you still in agreement on liquidity timing? If not, work it out so the founders can collaborate on joint exit strategy. That might require an early exit for a dissident.

Your financial investors have a time frame for a liquidity event. You might have negotiated it when they provided their first funding round. But they might change their mind if they become disenchanted with how the founders are building the business. Be sure you understand the conditions and timing so you do not get forced into conflicts. At your board meetings, be sure you continuously set expectations on conditions, preparations and timing of exit. It will be on their agenda!

Your Professional Advisors

For designing and advising on alternative structures and documentation of governance documents, you can get valuable assistance from attorneys in business and corporate finance. For tracking values over time to 'mark to market' and decide whether to revise exit planning documents based on new developments affecting valuation or finances, you can consult appraisers, accountants, crisis public-relations advisers, insurance brokers and personal wealth advisers.

Your Self-Assessment

- Define your company's business twice. First, define it narrowly. Then define it broadly. What financial, management and operational scenarios and constraints make the difference between the two definitions?

- Have you formalized the ownership, decision-making, governance, roles, responsibilities, business plan (unique selling proposition, strengths, weaknesses, opportunities, threats)?

- Does your corporate governance documentation (such as shareholder agreements) treat the respective interests of the original founder(s), add-on founder(s), financial investors, future potential financial investors and potential strategic investors? Would the veto by anyone with veto rights prevent the startup from achieving its existing goals? What types of 'unfair' decisions might occur that are not addressed in the governance documentation?

- What exit scenarios does your corporate governance documentation address specifically? What is missing?

- How would dilution of ownership equity be applied in case of departure (such as termination of employment, death or disability) of any founder, employee-shareholder, employee-option-holder?

- Do the founders have any rights to buyout any financial investors? Do the financial investors have rights to force the company to buy out the investors?

PART IV

Toolkits for Smarter Business Exits

7

Toolkit for Business Startup and Normal Operations

About Toolkits

Surprisingly, you can select from many methods to achieve your corporate succession or business exit. For succession planning, you have the usual process of selection, evaluation, training, testing and cultural acclimation of the successor manager after you have extracted your liquid 'next egg' for your retirement.

For business divorce where a founder or key owner exits your existing business, there are basically three tools: purchase or redemption of shares, joint exit, or reorganization. In each case, you must negotiate pre- and post-transaction relationships and contingencies. In amicable business divorces, the parties might restructure to permit some ongoing relationship such as commission sales, brokerage, sales agency or other arrangement that does not impinge on your company's freedom of movement and control by the remaining owners.

Co-Owner Selection Process

Commonality and companionship are not sufficient for placing your future in someone else's hands. Your selection of co-owners should not depend on trust derived solely from childhood friendship, kinship, community, common religion or direction. Yes, such commonalities can help support a durable 'partnership.'

Instead, the selection process should involve deliberate evaluation tools. It should start with vetting of personality, prior history (including prior disputes with others), education, financial condition, ability to absorb disappointments maturely and without hostility. After vetting, you should test your prospective co-owners for skills, aptitude, analytical skills, initiative, energy level, attitude, humor and fit for the proposed task of building a successful business. Finally, you should verify your co-owners' willingness to operate under the rules that govern contributions, rewards and exits.

This need for discipline explains why, in professional service companies, the selection partner process for those without prior ownership experience may take months or years. In startups, the process can be shorter so long as it is disciplined as to personality, capabilities, performance and wise judgment.

Ownership 'Vehicles': Personal Holding Companies and Trusts

Why should you directly own shares in your operating company? Consider layering up for insulation and personal warmth! Professional investors normally engage in 'layering up' or a 'veil of tiers' by using legal entities as holding companies. You can transfer your ownership to a holding company or trust that you control, but this would add additional layers of cost and compliance. [80]

Without a personal ownership 'vehicle,' a business owner is exposed to personal liability to the company's creditors upon insolvency. Such liability

---

[80] Personal holding companies require ongoing administration for legal and tax compliance. If it is a C corporation collecting passive income, the holding company might be subject to a special tax. See 26 U.S.C. §§ 542-543.

may be imposed under common law theories of thin capitalization, fraudulent use of insolvent entities, fraudulent conveyances and piercing the corporate veil and under bankruptcy clawbacks of preferential transfers.

Ownership through a personal holding company or trust can limit such direct liability during your control of the business and after you sell it.

Like a personal holding company, a trust can also be useful to hold your shares in a private business. Both a holding company and a trust support business governance continuity upon your death or disability or divorce. As with a holding company, your co-founders and investors will want to ensure such ownership structure does not impair your personal accountability for decision-making (as a board member).

Ownership Governance: Basic Agreements

Before launching or relaunching your firm, you should have agreements that limit the capacity of stakeholders to harm the enterprise. Intertwining stakeholder rights thus can be woven for the benefit of all.

Equity Owners' Agreements

Typical governance mechanisms are set forth in a founders,' stockholders' or LLC members' agreement. If the owners cannot get along, a buyout, redemption, joint exit, asset sale[81] or judicial liquidation[82] may follow. To get along, the owners may enter into agreements on how to manage the company without disputes. Several employment-focused provisions in a shareholders' agreement may be designed to trump employee rights and thus help preserve enterprise value from certain employment disputes. A shareholders' agreement might cover some or all of the following terms:

- a definition of the company's business and purpose;
- capital contributions, timing and associated rights for each class of shares;
- loans to or by a co-owner;

---

[81] See Del. Gen. Corp. Law, § 271 (asset sales are permitted by decision of a majority of shares and the board of directors).

[82] See Del. Gen. Corp. Law, § 273 (50–50 ownership).

- a prohibition on sales or transfers of shares except as permitted by the agreement;

- the management positions and responsibilities of the shareholders;

- special voting rights, proxies or voting trust agreements, as to special scenarios;

- the method for valuing the shares of the corporation in a buyout or redemption;

- the method for adding or removing shareholders for misconduct, death or inability to function in the management of the business;

- the mechanism for valuation and sale of the whole business of the corporation;

- the method(s) for determining management salaries, bonuses and dividends;

- non-competition and non-solicitation clauses to prevent a departing shareholder from taking a key part of the corporation's business and thereby damaging the corporation and its remaining shareholders;

- a buy-sell provision for individual exits, such as rights of first refusal, call options, put options and possible repricing depending on 'good leaver' or 'bad leaver' classification;

- drag-along and tag-along provisions for joint exit, including the percentages of each class of shares whose approval is needed to authorize a joint exit, waivers of appraisal rights and financial terms;

- succession arrangements to spouses or the next generation upon death or disability of a shareholder;

- life insurance on key management employees and shareholders (and deciding whether the buyout will be a 'buy-sell' or 'cross-purchase');

- voting rules for any special majority or unanimity, or veto by a defined class of shareholders, required for certain types of corporate decisions such as the sale, lease or exchange of the whole enterprise of the corporation or substantially all assets, including goodwill, commencing a new enterprise or pivoting to a new business, borrowing or mortgaging assets[83];

---

[83]   See Del. Gen. Corp. Law, § 271.

- voting agreement to define the size and composition of the board and its observers, including the expulsion of board members who violate certain agreed principles;

- dispute resolution including arbitration and choice of law provisions; and

- spousal consents.

Investor-Specific Governance for Exit

Professional investors will normally reserve some special rights to exit earlier than you might. Your investors will want several alternative exits.

Put Option. In the shareholders' agreement, your investors will want the right to force you to buy them out for some price after a long period. This put option is risky for the investor, who will not get paid if the company's lacks liquidity.

Joint or Separate Exit: Registration Rights and VC Sell-Downs. Your investors will therefore insist on the opportunity to sell out at their convenience, subject to whatever limitations you negotiate.

Investors in closely held, high-growth businesses inevitably want the right to sell out and gain liquidity. In anticipation of an initial public offering ('IPO') in the distant future, VCs and PEs insist on a registration rights agreement giving them the right to sell their shares in an initial public offering. Such right would be in preference to any right of the founders to sell their shares in the IPO, since a walk-away by the founders would render the IPO press unpalatable to public investors. Registration rights agreements normally give the maximum rights to the investors but authorize the lead underwriter to decide not to allow any right of co-sale upon the company's issuance of new shares in the IPO.

In some cases, your professional investors will want to extract their invested funds in a 'sell-down' to reduce equity ownership. Such sell-downs typically involve an initial public offering where the public investors buy-down some of the professional investors' equity.

Exit to Public Market: Piggyback Registration Rights and Straight Registration Rights. If the company completes the IPO, the VCs and PEs will generally require the right to have the company file (at company expense) a registration statement for the sale of the VCs or PEs shares to the public, if and when the company conducts a secondary offering. The registration rights agreement will normally include such a 'piggyback' right but may limit the number of times, and the timing, when the VCs and PEs can require the company to provide such a liquidity event.

In late-stage equity investments by VCs, PEs and institutional investors making 'alternative investments' in privately owned businesses, the investors might demand registration rights unconditionally, depending on timing or some scenario such as a positive cash flow or new product development. 'Straight' registration rights are less customary but can be part of the overall exit plan for professionally managed investment funds.

Employment Documentation

Since employees may become shareholders, all employment documentation should be reviewed from the perspective of strategies for individual exits, joint exits and succession planning.

Employment agreements set parameters for roles, responsibilities and, with employee manuals, discipline of owner-employees. For employees who are co-owners, the shareholders' agreement should define special overriding conditions relating to ownership changes if the employee leaves employment for any reason. Executives typically negotiate special incentive compensation and protections against abusive termination by the company without cause. In return, the company may withhold incentives upon the employee's departure without good reason.

Your company's *employee manual or handbook* is a critical tool for limiting the company's liability (and thus any residual liability of its selling owners) to employees. The manual will define procedures on employee activities, protected status, sexual harassment and other civil rights. Before exit, you should update the employee manual and conduct the training required for ongoing HR compliance.

Separate agreements on intellectual property, arbitration of certain employment disputes and post-termination covenants may be used instead of putting everything into an offer letter or employment agreement. Many lawyers prefer to put non-competition, non-solicitation and non-disparagement covenants into separate agreements to make them stand alone.

Your employee stock option and incentive plans and *restricted stock agreements* grant equity to 'employees.' Such plans and agreements should adopt restrictions and conditions on vesting of rights over time or upon achievement of particular milestones, or both. By granting restricted stock, the company can put a key person on a leash, with full vesting only on delivery of performance goals. Include a warning on the rules governing 'golden parachutes' so that a change of control does not trigger the penalties where key employees receive 300 percent of normal compensation on a merger.[84] The rules for key employees may be different from those for other employees.

Intellectual Property Rights Assignments

In a service economy, intellectual property, trade secrets and confidential information are coveted assets. Relevant service agreements should be signed with all individuals and companies providing services, to ensure your firm owns such rights. And relevant procedures for continuing the confidentiality of trade secrets should be adopted.

Delegation of Voting Rights

To minimize governance disputes, shareholders sometimes agree to delegate their voting rights. A voting agreement or voting trust lends predictability and credibility to companies where the co-owners have suffered a personal divorce or past personal dispute. Corporation laws generally permit shareholders to agree on how they will vote under certain circumstances. Voting agreements can have different flavors, depending on the number of shareholders, the maturity of the business and the need for quick actions.[85]

Proxies

A proxy is a form of delegation of voting authority and can be set forth in an agreement. It is a type of limited power of attorney. By giving someone (such as the CEO) an irrevocable proxy, certain shareholders (such as the early founders and early VCs) can designate a key decision-maker to

---

[84] 26 U.S.C. § 280G.
[85] See Calif. Corp. Code §§ 705-706; Del. Gen. Corp. Law, § 212; NY Bus. Corp. Law, § 609.

express common interests over a long period. Or the proxy might be only for a single shareholder meeting.

Voting Agreements

In a voting agreement, shareholders can agree to vote in a certain manner (such as to elect certain individuals to certain offices) or to delegate voting authority to a designee by 'proxy.' By agreement, the shareholders delegate voting discretion to someone else. The agreement should specify whether the delegation is revocable or irrevocable, the duration of the agreement, whether it covers all possible voting issues or only certain votes, and what happens upon death or disability of a shareholder.

The advantages include forming a block with common financial interests that assembles a large number of small stockholders, giving leverage to achieve shared goals in corporate governance (election of directors and maybe amending the charter).

The disadvantages are the loss of actual control of voting if the agreement is irrevocable for a long time. Voting agreements can be enforced judicially to compel a particular vote. But they are not enforceable if the agreement authorizes one class of shareholders to remove an officer (such as the founding CEO) unless the voting provisions are also mirrored in the certificate of incorporation or by-laws.[86]

Voting Trust Agreements

In a voting trust agreement, the shareholders transfer their shares to a 'voting trustee,' who then has authority to exercise share voting rights. The transfer makes it harder for the parties to argue about voting. The voting trustee must follow the principles agreed by the co-owners jointly.

---

[86] 'Appointing the CEO is thus a core board function that only can be limited in the certificate of incorporation (pursuant to Section 141(a) of the DGCL) or bylaws (pursuant to Section 142(b) of the DGCL).' *Schroeder v. Buhannic*, C.A. No. 2017-0746-JTL (Del. Ch. Jan. 10, 2018) (Order), available at https://www.delawarecounselgroup.com/wp-content/uploads/2018/02/pierre-schroeder-et-al.-v.-Philippe-Buhannic.pdf.

Code of Conduct

A code of conduct sets company policy for compliance with law, ethics and prudent management. When vetting your business, your customers will want to see your code of conduct to ensure it covers conflicts of interest with your customers and suppliers, anti-bribery, anti-money laundering, personal privacy, improper personal relationships and mechanisms for reporting for instances of suspicious, unethical, fraudulent or discriminatory behavior. While targeting your company's eligibility as a 'good corporate citizen' protecting the good name of your customers, a code of conduct can be even more critical to protecting your company from blackmail, class actions, fraudulent claims and perverse demands by individuals who are co-owners or employees.

Operations Governance: Risk Management and Resiliency Planning

Risk management and resiliency planning is reflected in your shareholder agreements, your governance structures and all your company's business dealings. There are serious risks other than shareholder disputes.

In *risk management*, the company identifies threats and risks with the goal of avoiding, mitigating or insuring against losses. In *resiliency planning*, the company adopts an ongoing contingency planning program to evaluate and prepare for the impact of significant events that may adversely affect customers, assets, employees and the business generally. Resiliency planning focuses on continuity of operations to reduce the risk of a service interruption to customers.

Supply Chain Management Plan

Supply chain management ('SCM') risks involve the risk to the upstream enterprise customer from a failure or delay by a supplier at any level in the extended supply chain. SCM requires constant adjustments in logistics, for integration of outsourcing, insourcing (self-provisioning) and shared sourcing among related enterprises.

Business Continuity Plan

Business continuity plans ('BCPs') identify possible internal and external risks to normal operations and planning responsive to the business impact analysis. Such plans involve training of employees, conducting and updating *business impact analysis* exploring risks and threats, redundancies of technologies and facilities, program management with value metrics that are reported to the board of directors. BCPs should include objectives for recovery time, sequence and recovery points. The board must be vigilant on identifying and mitigating known vulnerabilities, and on updating the internal rule book for continuing operations. With large penalties for cybersecurity breaches, the risk of bankruptcy can now be anticipated as a consequence of non-compliance with regulations. In short, risk analysis requires probability assessment of multiple risks and the possibility of combinations of risks with potentially catastrophic consequences to the firm.

Disaster Recovery Plan and Crisis Management Plan

The business continuity plan lays the roadmap for the disaster recovery ('DR') plan. Part of the DRP, a crisis management plan can identify risks and threats at each phase in the corporate lifecycle. As with any crisis management plan, you will need to identify the largest 'values at risk,' the probability of occurrence and the cost of alternative backup and recovery measures. For each phase in your company's development, you can create your own DR Plan and crisis management scenario analysis, identifying both external and internal threats. Consider whether you or your co-owners might pose any threats to your business if anyone had an opportunity to gain unfair leverage.

Cyber-Security Risk Management Plan

Cyber-risk management should be implemented as part of normal risk management. Cyber-risk insurance policies should be considered for potentially catastrophic events.

Succession Plan

Every company needs some form of succession plan for senior executives. As observed in Chapter 5, succession plans define the conditions for replacement of current key persons. The plan should include identification of successor managers and successor owners, a 'training' period with job performance goals and timing factors for starting and completion. Such plans require constant updating by the board of directors.

Your Adaptive Organization: Midstream Restructuring and Recapitalization

Long before exit, business owners can restructure the business to adapt to the marketplace or changes in opportunities, without necessarily exiting the business. By midstream restructuring, you can enhance value, eliminate disputes, eliminate waste, sell unproductive operations or assets. By midstream recapitalization, you can swap out owners, add new lines of business and expand both ownership and the business.

Restructuring can involve a variety of strategies, including recapitalization, divestitures, small acquisitions, new minority owners, bankruptcy and reorganization, mergers of equals and conversion to a public company or a new jurisdiction of incorporation. In any event, a restructuring typically brings in new people into ownership and management and may include reorganization into different businesses.

Restructuring your business might dilute your ownership. But perhaps such dilution would be a small price to pay for the benefits of relief from distress and possible total loss.

Sample restructuring and recapitalizations may include:

- *Partial sale to an ESOP.* By transferring some shares to an Employee Stock Ownership plan, the owners can get some cash without losing all control.

- *Buy-in by a New Co-Owner.* Ownership capital is normally diluted by a new co-owner. While this is a classic restructuring for a professional services firm, it poses challenges for multi-owner entities and family businesses.

- *Spin-off, Split-off or Split-up.* The owners can divide the enterprise into separate entities and distribute them to different owners as a form of business divorce. Such transactions involve lengthy, costly and substantial planning. This restructuring exit is not clean because of possible disputes on corporate opportunities, the allocation of key persons among different entities, and continuing interdependencies that can cause ongoing friction.

Such transactions also risk loss of value where some assets must be sold or abandoned.

- *Self-Rollup.* Your company could become the platform to acquire other businesses under a new holding company. The acquisitions would dilute your ownership unless you could borrow the purchase price. But perhaps you would be happy to dilute ownership in a tax-free recapitalization to achieve synergies in costs, revenues, volume purchase discounts, standardization of operations and geographical expansion.

- *Restructuring to Change Jurisdiction.* Political and fiscal changes may force owners to consider relocation of the jurisdiction of formation to a more 'stable' environment. Such restructurings can arise in international family businesses.

- *Restructuring in Distress: Liquidation or Bankruptcy.* For companies in financial distress or deadlock, the courts can resolve disputes of ownership and other claims.[87]

Restructuring and recapitalization tools can permit your company to pursue new opportunities or to stabilize before a future joint exit.

Tips for the Co-Owner upon Launch

The most divisive issues arise from valuation. At company launch, you and your co-owners should agree on as many key elements of valuation. The goal is to adopt rules that are fair and reciprocal.

Upon company funding by investors, the investors may impose one-sided exit terms. The new owner might insist on some special exit preferences that are duplicative, oppressive or capable of forcing a liquidation or forced exits of founders. Hence, you must choose: identify and align with the goals of your investors, or not accept their investment. Hence, finding the right investors is more important than just inviting new capital.

You should adopt policies for compliance, like a code of conduct and specific compliance rules. This will help prevent spurious claims by co-owners that you engaged in mismanagement or violated laws favoring the co-owner.

---

[87] Del. Gen. Corp. Law, § 273.

As you evolve, the founders might pull each other in different directions. Voting agreements might be useful to align the founders as a team so they can avoid being divided by one or more investors.

Tips for the Sole Owner upon Launch

If you are the sole owner, before selling you have a last chance to organize your corporate affairs as lifestyle tools after the sale.

Captivating Captives. If it's not too late, you can still set up a captive affiliated services company for post-exit wealth management, assuming there is enough time for building some value in it before the exit sale.

Family Office. A 'family office' is a business with employees helping family members manage their wealth, health and happiness. After selling your primary company, you will no longer be able to get such help. So you might hire an individual as 'family office administrator' to quarterback a team of independent service providers. Or you could set up a business to serve as your 'single-family office' ('SFO'). Maybe you join an existing team of professionals existing under the umbrella of a 'multi-family office' ('MFO'). Or maybe you hire an outsourced 'virtual family office' where your affairs get part-time attention from a team helping many families.

Your Professional Advisors

For single owner exits, you can get valuable assistance from attorneys in business, employment, compliance and dispute-resolution; mediators and/or arbitrators, appraisers, accountants, crisis public-relations advisers, insurance brokers and personal wealth advisers.

Your Self-Assessment

- How robust are your toolkits for corporate governance and legal compliance? Are they designed to help avoid, minimize or resolve amicably any irreconcilable major disputes with another co-owner?
- Do your toolkits cover the highest risk and highest value scenarios?
- Do your toolkits handle an existing or persisting tension that could erupt into a crisis?

- Based on the current situation, how fair and equitable are your toolkits in resolving disputes on control, decision-making deadlock (such as on major changes in business operations), valuation, payment and terms of change of ownership?

- Are you unhappy with the current corporate governance and compliance toolkits? Why?

8

Insurance Tools for Smarter Business Exits

Many different types of insurance policies can facilitate your business divorce, individual and joint exits and succession plans. For example, life insurance can finance a buyout so that you do not go into business with your co-owner's spouse, if your co-owner dies. Coverages that protect directors, owners and employees during your ownership can continue to protect after a change of control, if you add 'tail' coverage. And special policies protect sellers and buyers from losses due to breach of the acquisition agreement in a joint exit.

A review of some classic insurance policies highlights the problems of a hostile business divorce. Insurance is designed to cover negligence or poor judgment of an owner-manager. (Some polices do cover employee defalcations.) In a hostile business divorce, the relevant insurance might not cover your intentional misconduct as a manager, fiduciary or owner. In short, insurers underwrite accidental risks, not intentional self-inflicted wounds. So read the fine print.

Insurance for Owners and Managers

Life Insurance. Life insurance offers many opportunities to provide liquidity in a closely held company. While an owner or the company cannot normally deduct the premiums, the proceeds are generally not taxable. The shareholders' agreement should define the intended uses and payees of life insurance proceeds. Insurance strategies help solve different problems.

- Under a restrictive endorsement split dollar insurance policy, the company insures the key co-owners, endorses the death benefits to a family beneficiary (such as spouse) and thus funds liquidity for the entity, the family and succession of ownership. This requires an IRS filing on Form 8925.

- Under a survivorship life insurance policy, the proceeds can fund estate tax liability on the death of key owners.

- Under a 'warehouse' term life policy, the proceeds on death of a key owner can ensure both preservation and operation of the company upon the key owner's death.

Liquidity for a Buyout. In a buy-sell agreement, life insurance can fund the buyout price, so that surviving co-owners can avoid sharing ownership with a deceased owner's family members. In a 'cross-purchase,' where there are only two owners, each co-owner might buy a policy on the life of the other, to pay for a buyout upon death. Alternatively, corporate ownership of the life insurance policy on the lives of owners can provide liquidity for both a buyout (by redemption or by a dividend to remaining partners) and for continuing operations.

Equalization of Distributions to Family Members. In family-owned companies, life insurance can serve to equalize the value of assets of a deceased owner to be paid to his family. Assume that shares in a family-owned company are the major part of the value of the founder's estate, and that the estate has multiple beneficiaries. If the founder's will gave the company to heirs who are working in the business, then the remaining estate assets would be insufficient to provide equal distributions to non-working family members. The business owning a policy on the founder's life could use the proceeds to pay a dividend to the founder's estate to cover estate taxes and then permit equalized payouts to all heirs.

Key-Person Death. To provide your business with cash flow after the death of a key executive, life insurance can provide the cash flow needed to cover fixed expenses, pay debts or hire and train a replacement.

Key-Person Disability. If the business were to collapse due to disability of a key person, a disability insurance policy could make up for the lost value in the business. Such policies provide effective risk management where no existing partner would be required to buy out the disabled partner at fair market value, or where the business could not be sold without some continuity of the owner's wisdom and experience.

Loan Protection. In a privately-owned business, lenders often demand personal guarantees by the owners. Life insurance can fund repayment of the loan if the company cannot pay it.

Fiduciary liability insurance, also known as *management liability insurance,* is intended to protect businesses and employers against claims resulting from a breach in fiduciary duty. Essentially, the policy protects parties against liability for managing or administering employee benefits plans under the Employee Retirement Income Security Act of 1974 ('ERISA'). The fiduciary's role requires prudent selection of advisors and investments for such plan, minimization of expenses and following plan documents exactly. In a sale of your company, the buyer will insist on your indemnification for breach of such liabilities. A fiduciary liability insurance policy can cover or limit this sellers' liability.

Errors and omissions insurance protects owners, managers and employees from liabilities to third parties, such as customers, clients, suppliers and service providers. This may give comfort to your eventual acquirer.

Directors and officers liability insurance ('D&O') covers the liabilities of corporate directors and officers (or managers of an LLC) for alleged failure to perform their duties under corporate law. The policy pays off if an employee, creditor or other shareholder wins a lawsuit holding directors and/or officers liable for losses incurred by the claimant. Such insurance protects minorities (particularly VCs and friends and family) who choose to become directors or officers.

Such D&O liability policies are distinguished by several 'flavors' to define different types of coverage. Such policies are used primarily to induce and indemnify directors and officers of public companies to take the risks of being sued by customers, regulators and others. 'Traditional' D&O policies do ordinarily cover losses from self-dealing and breach of fiduciary duty to minority shareholders. Special policies will cover such losses but only after careful examination of risk by underwriters. The scope of coverage and exemptions can be complex. It helps to check with your insurance broker.

Insurance for Operational Risks

Comprehensive Liability Insurance ('CGL') is a broad liability policy protecting the business entity and is managers against general liabilities customary in most businesses. It protects the enterprise from liability claims related to products, completed operations, landlord and premises owners' liability and operations, as well as liability caused by the enterprise's independent contractors. The policy does not cover vehicle liability or injury to the company from a breach of duty by its managers.[88] Rather, such policies cover damages when the company causes injury to third parties.

Employment practices liability insurance ('EPLI') is a type of liability insurance covering an employer's wrongful acts arising from the employment process. Such liability may arise from alleged discrimination, sexual harassment, wrongful termination and retaliation by the employer against the employee's assertion of statutory rights. EPLI policies also cover other claims of inappropriate workplace conduct such as employment-related defamation and invasion of privacy. The policies cover directors and officers, management personnel, and employees as insureds, but not necessarily any non-managing shareholders. To avoid intentional misconduct, EPLI policies may exclude claims for bodily injury, property damage and intentional or dishonest acts.

Cybersecurity insurance policies generally cover your company's liability for unauthorized access to someone's private data. Given the expansion of privacy laws since 2016, such policies have become standard for any business that collects, processes or stores personally identifiable information ('PII'). Such policies are relatively new, so underwriters are playing with the exclusions. You might be surprised if your policy excludes hacks enabled by your employees' 'social engineering' mistakes, such as giving out confidential access to a 'phishing' hacker or a rogue website. Cyber-risk insurance can also sustain a strong joint exit sale price if it covers a change in control.

Business Overhead Insurance covers your normal operating expenses until a disabled owner returns to work after disability or illness or until the

---

[88] See, for example, *Lloyd Farr v. Farm Bureau Insurance of Nebraska*, 61 F3d 677 (8th Cir. 1995), cited in Martin O'Leary, DIRECTORS' AND OFFICERS' LIABILITY INSURANCE DESKBOOK (2nd edition) (2007), at p. 125.

disabled partner's share in the business can be sold. The company can deduct such premiums as a reasonable and necessary business expense.[89]

Business Interruption policies cover a business's lost income upon an interruption caused by some fortuitous external event, such as fire or hurricane. Generally, governmental actions such as regulatory prohibitions are not covered.

You should consult your insurance broker and corporate lawyer about other insurance policies for operating risks. These may include coverages for business automobile insurance, employee dishonesty (fidelity) insurance, errors and omissions and completed acts.

'Captive Insurance' Tools for Smarter Business Exits

Your smarter business exit might start with either an 'independent' captive insurance company separately owned by your co-owners or an insurance program in a pooled captive insurance program. Each approach can be tax-advantaged solutions for wealth accumulation through prudent risk management.

For best timing and internal harmony, captive insurance alternatives work best if you achieve a joint exit. Upon a co-owner's individual's exit, special restructuring might be needed to unwind the unrealized accrued value on an equitable basis. In either case, all equity holders should be included in the arrangements, either by consent or co-ownership. It's advisable to consult insurance and legal advisors on captive insurance tools.

Your Captive Insurance Program

Captive insurance programs consist of insurance policies tailored to your business's particular risk profile. Your policy would be pooled with policies of other businesses. Your premiums are normally deductible but may generate added value if there are no claims against the covered policies. Premiums may accumulate tax-free pending payment of premiums or liquidation of the policies and/or the insurance pools. Remotely contingent liabilities could be capped under a 'stop-loss' arrangement.

---

[89] Rev. Rul. 55-264, 1955-1 C.B. 11 (1955).

Your Captive Insurance Company

If your company pays substantial insurance premiums, you might wish to establish your own captive insurance company. A captive insurer is an insurer that accepts the risk to pay for the insured loss. However, it may limit is liability by re-insuring with a re-insurance company.

If your captive generates profits, from collecting more in premiums than it pays to re-insurers, the captive could become a private investment vehicle after your liquidity event in selling your shares. On sale or liquidation of the captive, the retained net profits from insurance operations could be taxable as capital gains.

Captives have been abused by companies disregarding the rules on risk selection, underwriting, investment of proceeds, reporting and bona fide business activities.[90] Your captive insurance structure should be carefully planned and managed.

Insurance for Post-Exit Liabilities

Insurance of Exit Transactional Liabilities: 'Representations and Warranties' Coverage

In any purchase of shares or assets, the buyer will normally seek to reduce the 'agreed' term-sheet price after discovering, upon pre-closing investigation, some surprises that could impair the value to the buyer. Such surprises are normally handled by restructuring the pricing for a hold-back, an escrow pending delay of a year or more, earn-out under special conditions or a parent company guarantee.

Such buyer-oriented risk structures worry sellers. The seller cannot freely use the sale proceeds until the expiration of the buyers' contractual risks. The buyer assumes risk of loss, which can be material depending on the risk and the cap on seller's liability. The buyer's constraints tie up seller's capital for a potentially long time, preventing immediate reinvestment for new ventures or investments. The amount at risk might be higher than the

---

[90] See IRS, *'Notice 2016-66, Micro-Captive Transactions,'* I.R.B. 2016-47 (2016), referring to Treas. Reg. § 6011-4(b)(6) and 26 U.S.C. §§ 6111 – 6112.

seller's comfort level. In short, sellers want a 'clean exit' with peace of mind after the closing.

As an alternative risk allocation method, since the early 2010s insurance companies have offered transactional liability insurance policies for acquisition-related liabilities. Such policies come in different flavors. In 'representations and warranties' coverage, the policy covers losses from inaccurate (but non-fraudulent) reps and warranties. Other policies may cover tax liabilities for 'open' tax years subject to tax audit. Environmental liability covers regulatory compliance risks. A 'litigation buyout' policy covers potential liability under pending or threatened litigation claims. More broadly, a 'contingent liability' policy could cover general liabilities such as potential breach of contract, products liability, completed operations and the like.

Who Should Buy Transactional Liability Insurance?

Both buyers and sellers can obtain coverage. However, the buyer might find such insurance more enticing because the buyer gets 100 percent coverage on representations and warranties, regardless of seller's fraud, and the buyer has no worries about the future solvency of the seller. In contrast, the sellers get coverage only for risks unknown (and undisclosed) to them.

For this reason, buyers' premiums are generally higher than sellers' premiums because the coverage is broader. If the seller has substantial bargaining power, the buyer might require a policy. If the buyer has negotiating leverage to impose the traditional post-closing risk allocation methods, then the sellers might get the policy.

Transaction liability insurance policies generally priced based on a percentage of the policy limit. The underwriter weighs both the probability and amount of the loss. Hence, an 'insured' will get a better deal by demonstrating (with extensive due diligence) the probability and potential loss amount are both low. The premium may also be affected by a high or low retention of risk (the 'deductible') by the insured.

The underwriting process has up-front costs for the insurance purchaser. Even before the closing, the party buying the policy must usually pay various non-refundable fees to the insurance broker and the underwriter. Such fees cover the costs of review and structuring of the policy and may include a break-up fee in case the transaction fails to close.

For all policies, the carrier may exclude risks that are not adequately defined or investigated. A coverage gap may also occur where the insurance carrier normally excludes coverage of certain risks. In this case, the buyer will want the seller to give the usual indemnities and risk allocation protections. The seller will have to assume liability for the coverage gaps. For transaction liability insurance, such exclusions can include known risks, punitive damages, consequential damages, and breach of undertakings and covenants. For reps and warranty policies, the carrier might exclude future-oriented statements, pension underfunding or particular taxes or tax entitlements (refunds, tax credits, tax losses).

The process of obtaining transactional liability insurance involves several players and steps. The insured hires a broker to advise on structure and strategy and to auction the placement of the policy to the 'best' carrier. The insured gets non-disclosure agreements from the broker and the target carrier. The broker and target carrier require the insured to sign an agreement for unconditional payment of legal review expenses and break-up fees. The broker invites carriers to bid, and the carriers would respond with non-binding indicative terms of coverage. Based on such responses, the insured then requests the broker to pursue a possible deal with one carrier. The insured and the carrier then negotiate the coverage terms, including what is an insured 'loss,' policy limits, deductible, warranties by the insured, policy duration, broker's commission, whether litigation defense costs are included in the policy limits and exclusions.

Viability and Suitability of Insurance in Exit Transactions

The economic viability and suitability of transaction liability insurance remain uncertain. As to viability, as with any insurance product, underwriters are guessing about probabilities, scenarios, loss valuations, and the variables affecting risks of the particular policy coverage, as well as how to write a one-off 'manuscript' insurance policy. And underwriters must negotiate exclusions and conditions of coverage. So the pricing may be underweighted as new market entrants seek market share.

As to suitability, from the insured's standpoint, the policy offers no adequate economic value and should not be purchased because of the uncertainties of the underwriting process. Thus, there is no justification for buying a policy if the exclusions are too broad (which won't be known until after the insured has made the investment in the legal review costs and break-up fee), and gaps need to be plugged by traditional personal liability and escrows. Further, as the market matures, concessionary pricing will wither, premiums will rise, and the insured will self-insure when the premium is somewhat close to the percentage of the seller's holdback or escrow at risk in a traditional M&A transaction.

Tips for Insurance Coverage

The insurance company's underwriter looks at the probability of one or more events causing the maximum damage for a total loss. As the insured business, you can reduce the underwriter's fears by demonstrating you have policies and processes that manage or mitigate risks that you will want the insurance company to insure. GRC and good housekeeping will make your business more insurable, for higher coverage limits and faster turnaround.

Insurance policies can be creative. Transactional liability insurance is a 'micro-policy' with limited time frames and limited covered risks. You might need some special micro-policy for some other identified risk (hypothetically called 'pothole' liability insurance, for fun). Ask your broker about how to optimize your risk profile through insurance.

Your Professional Advisors

For 'tricks of the trade' for optimizing risk management strategies in an exit or succession plan, you should start with a sophisticated insurance broker. To implement such planning with relevant documentation and legal structures, you should get advice from an attorney in business. Where insurance is used to protect some asset such as your business for buy-sell purposes, you should consult with appraisers, accountants, estate and trust planners and personal wealth advisers.

Your Self-Assessment

- Where can you access copies of your company's insurance policies?
- Have you recently consulted your insurance broker on policies targeting shareholder disputes, buyouts, buy-ins, restructuring and stakeholder claims?
- Have you discussed personal liability and insurance coverages with your spouse? Your co-owners?

- What insurance-based strategies have you implemented to address liquidity needs relating to individual and/or joint exits by the current and future co-owners? What scenarios are covered? What scenarios are not covered?

- What insurance-based products have you considered that would build up cash value for you (as owner) and/or your business over time, prior to any exit? How do such products optimize your cash flow and asset value in pre-exit and exit scenarios?

- When did you last discuss your exit-related insurance coverage with your financial, legal, tax and insurance advisors? Is your existing insurance program out of date or otherwise not responsive to your current risk profile relating to co-owners, de-equitization and exits?

9

Tax Tools for Smarter Business Exits

Every business divorce or restructuring entails some tax planning. What might be advantageous for taxation might also be unfavorable for personal, family, trust, estate or corporate operational reasons. Tax strategies should be balanced and weighted against other aspects of the transaction structure. The best time for tax planning starts before you establish your business.

Ownership Design for Tax Efficiency

Your tax residency defines the law governing your taxability. You are free to change tax residency. Over time, you might want to move your office and residence from a high-tax jurisdiction to a low-tax jurisdiction. If you transfer your ownership to trust or personal holding company, the same rules apply to the taxability of the registered owner.

So, in considering a tax plan that might take ten or twenty years to finalize, choose your business, residential and holding vehicles for their known tax efficiency for allocation and taxability of entity income and personal income. Be ready to move your family and your business to a low tax jurisdiction such as Florida, Texas, Nevada or New Hampshire.

Operational and Transactional Design for Tax Efficiency

In a business exit, there are many ways to structure transaction for tax benefits. Here are a few examples.

- *Choose the Right Legal Entity for Tax-Efficient Exit.* While every situation requires individual evaluation, corporations may offer the most tax-efficient exit for all founders and employees. Corporations can grant qualified incentive stock options and 'deferral stock'[91] to employees, but LLCs cannot.[92] A corporate stock option plan can create a capital asset and defer payment of capital gains until actual sale of the shares. No tax is payable on issuance of the stock option. Prior to any sale, a corporation can restructure tax-free to spin-off unwanted operations or make small acquisitions. Affiliated corporations can file one consolidated income tax return. n contrast, for incentive compensation in the form of ownership interests, the employee (or contractor) of an LLC must pay tax immediately on the fair market value of the LLC's membership units when issued, and suffer total loss of the value of such payments if the units are later forfeited before vesting.[93] As incentive compensation, an LLC's 'profits interests' do not share in enterprise value and cannot qualify as capital gains.

- *Defer Gains.* By delaying your receipt of capital gains to be held for at least a year, you convert a short-term capital gain to a long-term capital gain. This can cut your tax bill nearly in half. Using an installment sale,[94] with payments over several years, you delay payment of taxes and maybe reduce your marginal tax rates too. Puts and calls can be used to defer gain while retaining controls over the event of change of ownership. (Puts and calls can also serve as a 'collar' to preserve value of marketable equities from market volatility.) If your company owns real estate, you might defer gains by a like-kind exchange of one property for another of similar tax nature.[95]

---

[91] 26 U.S.C. § 83(i).
[92] 26 U.S.C. §§ 421-422.
[93] 26 U.S.C. § 83(b).
[94] 26 U.S.C. § 483.
[95] 26 U.S.C. § 1031.

From the Case Files

Our client was one of several operating companies that wanted to do a self-rollup across several countries under a new holding company and new common trademark. In the U.S., this could be done by simple tax-free reorganization without realizing any capital gains. In one foreign country, the transaction would be taxable. So the foreign company structured a purchase and sale agreement with puts and calls. Upon a future joint exit, the foreign owners could exercise a put option (to sell), while the holding company could execute a call option (to acquire the shares). This put-call structure deferred gains until a future liquidity event.

- *Defer Ordinary Income.* By negotiating a deferred payment plan (such as under a 401(k) plan for retirement or a 409A plan for delayed payment of incentive compensation, you can defer ordinary income.

- *Convert Ordinary Income to Capital Gains.* If you receive equity payments for your services, you can convert the equity from ordinary income to a capital asset by paying immediately the tax on the value received. This only works if your vested rights are deferred and subject to substantial risk of forfeiture.[96]

- *Convert Capital Loss to Ordinary Loss.* If your company makes an election at inception, you may be able to convert your personal capital loss to ordinary loss if it goes out of business. Individually, you can then deduct up to $50,000 of the loss against other income.[97]

- *Split the Pie using Tax-Free Reorganizations in a Business Divorce.* If you cannot agree on a buyout, redemption or joint sale, you can agree to divide your company into multiple entities in a tax-free reorganization. Your co-owner can receive shares in a new or existing company in exchange for shares in your business. You can spin off a line of business as a separate company, to be owned by yourself or a co-owner. Similarly, a 'split-up' or 'split-off' can divide and distribute company assets among different owners, with no

---

[96] 26 U.S.C. § 83(b).
[97] 26 U.S.C. § 1244.

tax. If you have to pay each other some money to equalize the value distributed, amounts received will be taxable.[98]

- *Tax-Loss Harvesting.* This tax strategy is useful for investors with a portfolio of marketable securities where some have declined in value. The harvesting of a capital loss is advantageous since it allows the taxpayer to offset taxable capital gains. In an undiversified portfolio such as a startup or family-owned business, the absence of diversification prevents any tax-loss harvesting. Exceptionally, owners of an LLC may use the LLC's operating losses to offset taxable income from unrelated sources, assuming such owners have unrelated income.

- *Do Not Throw away your Tax Deductions.* Normally, a C corporation can use the losses in one year to reduce taxable income in another tax year. In an LLC taxable as a partnership, such losses flow through to the members, but if the member is a 'passive investor,' it cannot use its portion of the loss to reduce income from other sources. Similarly, a non-resident alien (or foreign entity with no U.S. trade or business) cannot use an LLC's losses to set off U.S. taxes on other income, where the LLC is the only U.S. business owned.[99]

- *Avoid Double Taxation of the Same Income.* If you have multiple offices in the U.S., speak with your accountant about how states sometimes tax the same income twice. If you have international customers, or if you have foreign subsidiaries or branches, you should be familiar with how income tax treaties can help you avoid having two countries tax the same income twice. If you are a non-resident alien of the U.S., you should consult an advisor on avoiding U.S. gift and estate taxation by holding your U.S. assets in offshore entities.

- *Don't Get Caught in 'Tax Avoidance' by Poor Tax Planning for Related-Party Transactions.* You can avoid surprises in tax audits by properly documenting all dealings between the company and every stakeholder. The tax authorities have the discretion to avoid abuses from artificial profit-shifting transactions between related parties. On audit, tax authorities may recharacterize your business transactions between your related entities for what they 'really' are.[100] The IRS may also recharacterize related-party loans if the

---

[98] 26 U.S.C. §§ 354, 355, 356 and 368(a)(1)(D).
[99] 26 U.S.C. §§ 861 – 864.
[100] 26 U.S.C. § 482.

interest rate is below current benchmarks.[101] For international businesses (including foreign 'startups'), ownership, control and intercompany transactions with controlled foreign corporations must be reported to ensure they are not part of a plan a principal purpose of which is the avoidance of federal income taxation.[102] Post-sale payments by a buyer to a selling shareholder could be recharacterized as ordinary income for post-closing services, unless your documentation speaks clearly.

• *Avoiding Penalties.* Certain business exits can cause the company (and thus the buyer after change of control) to incur tax penalties.

     o *Parachute Payments to Individuals on a Sale.* A twenty percent federal income tax penalty is imposed on private companies that pay 'parachute payments' within a year of a change of control of ownership or transfer of a substantial portion of the company's assets. Caught by this penalty are 'parachute payments' to employees, independent contractors, and other individuals providing personal services, where they are also either an officer, shareholder, or highly-compensated individual. A 'parachute payment' is one whose aggregate discounted present value exceeds 300 percent of the base compensation in the prior five years. In addition, the company cannot deduct the expense to the extent it exceeds such 300 percent. The rule does not apply to S corporations whose shareholders have authorized the payments.[103]

     o *Depreciation Recapture.* If you took depreciation deductions on your personal property or real property, you normally pay a tax on phantom income in the amount of prior depreciation. You may avoid any such phantom income by not structuring the transaction as a sale of the assets.[104]

---

[101] 26 U.S.C. § 1274.

[102] See 26 U.S.C. §§ 78, 861, 951 951A, 1502 and 6038; IRS Forms 5471 (Dec. 2018) available at https://www.irs.gov/pub/irs-pdf/i5471.pdf; Final, Temporary and Proposed Regulations under Tax Cuts and Jobs Act, P.L. 115-97 (Dec. 22, 2017) rules on controlled foreign corporations, global intangible low-taxed income ('GILTI') and foreign-derived intangible income ('FDII') from low-taxed foreign countries, 84 Fed. Reg. 29288 (June 21, 2019).

[103] 26 U.S.C. §§ 280G and 4999.

[104] See 26 U.S.C. §§ 1245 (personal property) and 1250 (real property).

Tips for Balancing Risks and Taxes

Tax planning must be counterbalanced by assessment and limitation of economic risks. Private company equity involves valuation volatility, over-concentration, vulnerability to external market and political shocks and illiquidity. In an individual exit by redemption or buyout, a deferred payment might never transpire if the company goes bankrupt before the final payment. So personal guarantees and collateralization might work, assuming the enhancement of credit risk does not cause the guarantor or the company to become insolvent. In a joint exit by reorganization, you might trade your company's securities for those of the acquirer, in a trade of one risk profile for another.

In short, while gains deferral might be the simple and popular template for business exit, you should balance tax efficiency against illiquidity and the risk of future loss in value. You should consult a tax advisor at startup and on anyone's exit for a tailored balance between tax, risk management and your appetite for volatility in value.

Your Professional Advisors

Tax planning is not self-taught. For optimizing retained value in your exit strategy or succession plan, your first advisors should be your business and personal accountants and your business lawyer. Some fancy insurance planning takes advantage of niches in the tax law, so be sure to confer with your insurance broker and seek a specialist in captive programs. Don't forget the adviser left to manage the proceeds of sale: your personal wealth adviser, trustee(s) and estate planners.

Your Self-Assessment

- Since forming your business, have you discussed with your financial planner, tax and/or legal advisors how your 'exit strategies' or 'succession plan' might be taxed under current tax law?
- Have you had any such discussions since the latest tax legislation?
- Are you aware of any tax reporting errors or items that may be challenged? Do you have a plan to remediate the past or improve for the future?

- What would be the worst and the best tax outcomes for your exit strategy? For your succession plan? Have such expected outcomes changed recently?

- What concessions would you be willing to make in the selling price for your business in order to optimize your tax situation? Conversely, what concessions would you be willing to make as to your tax objectives in order to achieve the best selling price?

10

Toolkit for Buyout or Redemption of Individual Owners

Timing of an Individual Exit

As owners and/or managers, individuals leave a business for several reasons: death, disability, retirement or dispute. Typically, disputes among co-owners involve employment, but can also come from a pivot in business strategy or the marketplace, personality friction, failure to meet personal or business goals (and resulting financial stresses) or misconduct. Events precipitating a buyout or redemption may depend on internal triggers – such as personal emotional or financial exhaustion, a health scare, a new conflict of interest, an impending date for vesting of equity interests or a co-owner's project failure that exposes your company to liability, embarrassment or loss of momentum or reputation. External triggers might include loss of a key customer or supplier or a merger or acquisition among strategic partners.

The key point in timing is to constantly review individual relationships and to act promptly to terminate incipient crises. If the majority owners want to squeeze out a minority owner involuntarily, litigation can ensue if there is no reason other than to take advantage of a new corporate opportunity.

Cohesion Issues

Buyouts or redemptions of individual owners can be divisive for the remaining co-owners. Some might disagree with the reasons, pricing, timing or terms. Others might want to leave under the same conditions but cannot. Cohesion may suffer unless all remaining co-owners are persuaded of the need for the individual exit. Loss of cohesion could impair your company's well-being.

Deal Structures for Agreed Individual Exits

Generally, the enterprise and stakeholders benefit when an owner no longer 'belongs' in the organization and the shares are bought out. The shareholders' agreement normally defines the conditions for individual exits by any shareholder. An individual can transfer ownership in return for money or assets in various ways. Possible non-cash exits such as spin-offs and division of assets are discussed in Chapter 12. Here, we consider purely cash-based exits.

Redemption or Cross-Purchase (Sale to Company or Insiders)

In a buyout, the departing owner sells all equity ownership interests, usually with no future relationship. This single-exit deal comes in two variations, both of which are glibly called a 'buyout.' In a redemption, the business entity buys back the equity ownership. In a 'buyout' by 'cross-purchase,' one or more shareholders buy the equity interests of other shareholders. In either variation, the remaining co-owners are freed from the fiduciary duties to the former owner, whether as controlling shareholders, directors or officers. In a buyout, the selling shareholders agree to sell their equity (and usually any other rights) to other shareholders.

In choosing a sale to co-owners or a redemption, various factors come into play. Redemptions offer some advantages. First, the payment comes from the company, not the co-owner's personal assets. Second, the co-owners might or might not personally guarantee the redemption payments. Third, in a redemption, the redeemed shares can be put into 'treasury stock' that is held on the accounting books as 'issued but not outstanding' shares. Treasury shares can then be re-issued by the company to new investors or added to the pool of shares authorized for issuance under a qualified incentive stock option plan or a restricted stock plan. A redemption is not available when the corporation is (or would become) insolvent by the transaction.

Where an investor might not have a right to force a redemption, it might have a right to demand a cash dividend. This might resolve a dispute as to financial compensation, but the dividend would normally be taxable at the highest income tax rates.

Redemption by the Company

A share buyout by the company is called redemption. In a complete redemption, the company pays the shareholder for the shares and any other rights to acquire shares. If the company cancels the shares, the redemption reduces issued share capital. If the company chooses to maintain the shares as 'issued shares,' they are treated as being put into the company's 'treasury' and are available for future issuance. A redemption imposes costs on the company: repurchase costs, legal fees and accounting fees. These costs can be controversial.

- First, there might be self-dealing. If the redemption was triggered by a controlling owner and was not desired by the other owners, the remaining minority owners might deplore the redemption as an abuse of authority and self-dealing by the majority owner.

- Second, redemptions deplete corporate capital and reduce the company's creditworthiness and ability to borrow for essential growth needs such as new hiring, purchasing essential equipment or inventory, R&D costs and maybe a strategic acquisition. To avoid such resource depletion, shareholder agreements may be fashioned to give the company an opportunity to pay the purchase price over a period of years. Under such a deferred payment plan, the company can pay from future revenues, and the selling owner can get a higher price to reflect the risk of non-payment due to bankruptcy. In drafting shareholder agreements, founders might therefore wish to include the terms of such a deferred payout plan under a company redemption, such as upon a right of first refusal for fully vested shares (not subject to buy-back at a discounted price).

- Third, redemptions may alter the balance of strategic power among the remaining shareholders who lack pre-emptive rights as to the sale of treasury shares. In such cases, the redeemed shares might be reissued to a third party, such as a new investor or a new manager hired to replace the departing owner-manager.

Accordingly, redemptions to resolve business divorce should generally be approved by most, if not all, of the remaining shareholders.

'Buy-Sell': Purchase by One or All Other Owners

Given the relative ease of a redemption to pay an exiting owner, when should one owner (or the other owners pro rata) buy out the departing owner? In a multi-owner context, a buyout of one owner by another might be ideal where the company's value is so high and its financial condition so weak that the company could not reasonably be expected to pay off the exiting owner. In such cases, ownership is restructured to give greater control to the purchaser, who might decide to invest additional capital (and perhaps buy out the remaining minority to consolidate control).

In a two-owner context, a buyout of one owner by the other might be preferable where the company's financial condition and covenants under a loan agreement might trigger a financial crisis for the company.

Right of First Refusal (Sale to Outsider)

To enable some form of liquidity, typical shareholder agreements permit a shareholder to sell all of the shareholder's shares to a third party, but only if the corporation and the other shareholders have first decided not to purchase such shares at the same price and terms under a 'right of first refusal' ('ROFR').

A right of first refusal is normally triggered by the seller's decision to sell and the seller's negotiation of a deal with a third party that might be matched by the holder of the right of first refusal. Since founders and majority owners of business ventures generally do not agree to pricing for a future sale as they build value, the call option solution might work for a short time. A right of first refusal is more customary for the longer term.

Right of First Refusal (Call Option or Redemption Option)

Shareholders' and founders' agreements normally enable the company or other shareholders to acquire the shares of a shareholder that wishes to exit.

A right of first refusal empowers the company (or the other shareholders, depending on your choice) to buy out the exiting owner. In turn, the exiting owner agrees not to sell the shares to a third party if the price and terms offered by the third party are matched by the holder of the right.

A 'right of refusal' can be built into cascading rights, with prioritization among potential buyers. If one option holder (such as the company) elects not to exercise the right of first refusal, a second group (the remaining shareholders pro rata) can have a 'right of second refusal.' You can even structure for a 'right of third refusal,' where any existing shareholder willing to pay can buy up the dregs not sold off under the first and second rights.

In a right of first refusal, one owner agrees not to sell equity to a third party without first offering it to the other owner(s) or the company at the same price and for the same terms and conditions. This protects the other owners and the company from being forced to admit a new third party who might have intentions and expectations that do not fit with those of the other owners. Without a right of first refusal, the remaining owners could become exposed to a hostile proxy fight to take control of the company and split it up, merge it with a company under the new owner's control, or otherwise face the risk of being sued for breach of fiduciary duty or loyalty.

In structuring the right of first refusal, the parties and the company need to select who will have the first preference to exercise the right. If the company has the right of first refusal ahead of any such right of the remaining owners, its exercise of such right will benefit all other owners proportionately. Further, the company might be best suited to finance a buyout, by borrowing against future cash flow or as secured by company assets. However, buying out a large shareholder could strain the company's financial capacity for growth, so it might be advantageous to allow another large shareholder to exercise such right.

Conversely, if the other shareholders have the right, each other owner could buy a proportionate share of the selling owner's equity in the business. However, due to lack of adequate capital, in a two-step scenario, the right of first refusal might be attractive only to the next largest shareholder, with the smaller owners electing not to purchase. In a second step, once the smaller owners have waived their right of first refusal, the other principal owner can step in and buy out the entire selling owner's equity. Hence, by giving the shareholders the first preference in exercising a right of first refusal, the odds are stacked against the smaller owners when, later, one of the larger owners seeks to exit.

A right of first refusal has negative consequences for the minority owner by depressing the demand for closely held company ownership. Unrelated third parties are deterred from investing when they become aware that a 'fair market' offer will be matched by the other owners or the company. If aware of the ROFR, the unrelated third-party buyer would likely give a lowball price to reflect the risk that its investment in due diligence and negotiations will be lost by the preferential ROFR buyer. To offer a 'market' price, unrelated buyers would need some inducement to invest in due diligence and accept some recompense if the deal were lost due to a ROFR.

Put and Call Options (Sale to Insider(s))

Given the advantages for the inside buyer, the minority owner as prospective seller might negotiate a put and call in lieu of a right of first refusal. The minority owner would have a duty to give the preferred 'buyer' a notice period (such as 90 or 120 days) to formulate a purchase offer. The 'seller' would have a put option to sell at this price if the buyer could find no other buyer during a notice period. In one scenario, if the 'seller' found another buyer at a higher price, the buyer could accept that offer. In an alternative scenario, the 'seller' could elect (or be required) to conduct an auction between the insider co-owner and the unrelated buyer. Such an arrangement, while not common and not liked by financial investors, allocates the risks and costs of developing a buyout to the co-owner, not the prospective third-party buyer.

Individual Exit by Financial Investor

Every investor in a startup should have a contingency plan in case of the company's failure.

Put Option by Investor

Professional investors buy shares based on a story. If that story crumbles, they want the right to put their shares to the founders or the company. Such a put option can force the founders to buy out an investor, force the company to obtain third-party financing of any type, and can prevent other investors from entering until the buyout of the investor has been settled. Accordingly, the investor's term sheet may include such put options upon events that demonstrate the venture will fail. Each investor will have a separate list of such events, but one could start with the death of a key founder, a key failure to respect warranties, representations or covenants or some other event linked to the other owners and managers. In return, such other owners should reject such a put option if it is based on externally driven scenarios, such as a change in law or a force majeure event.

Recalibration upon 'Down Round'

In lieu of a put option, the financial investor might acquire the right to increase the investor's percentage ownership upon a less threatening event. Thus, as preferred shareholder, an investor might insist on the right to the issuance of additional shares to the investor upon any issuance by the company of shares to another shareholder at a per-share price lower than the preferred shareholder's original investment price.

Such further dilution of other founders could trigger other scenarios leading to an unhappy future business divorce. For example, by agreement, a preferred shareholder investor might be entitled to participate preferentially in liquidation, defined to include both bankruptcy and a change of control. Such preferences dilute the other founders.

Deal Structures for Forced Individual Exits

Squeeze-Out Merger ('Cash-Out' Merger)

A 'squeeze-out' merger offers a possible solution kicking out a disgruntled minority shareholder. However, the majority must take great care to avoid unfairness in the merger process. And the merger might be invalid if tainted by prior unfairness or misconduct of the majority.

What is a Squeeze-Out / Cash-Out Merger?

In a 'squeeze-out' merger, one company is merged into another pursuant to approval by the owners of each of the constituent companies in the merger.[105] The surviving company could be either of the two. (For continuity of contracts and tax compliance, the original company typically is the survivor.) Under the plan of merger, a minority's ownership is canceled in exchange for a payment, while the majority's ownership of the original company is converted into shares of the surviving or resulting company. At the majority-owners' choice, the shareholders being cashed out might be holders of small stock interests or they could be the entire minority.

'Quickie' 'Short-Form Merger' of a Subsidiary into Parent

Where a corporation owns ninety percent or more of a subsidiary, Delaware corporate law permits a squeeze-out merger of the subsidiary into the parent, or the parent into the subsidiary. If there are minority shareholders, the parent's board of directors must disclose to the minority 'the terms and conditions of the merger, including the securities, cash, property, or rights to be issued, paid, delivered or granted by the surviving corporation upon surrender of each share of the subsidiary corporation or corporations not owned by the parent corporation, or the cancellation of some or all of such shares.'[106]

Planning and Implementation

To minimize risks and costs of a dispute, careful attention is needed to plan for the merger. Valuation of being cancelled in a merger must have some financial justification. Otherwise the board of directors is acting in in breach of fiduciary duty of 'entire fairness.'

In a Delaware corporation, the directors have a fiduciary duty to shareholders and are personally liable to shareholders if they fail to inform themselves of all relevant and reasonably available information and if they fail to disclose to shareholders all material information that reasonable shareholders would consider important in deciding whether to approve a merger. Thus, if the merger price is less than the fair value of the shares being cancelled in the merger, the directors are liable.

In a Delaware corporation, the board of directors must disclose to shareholders the objective reasons why they believed the merger would

---

[105] See, e.g., Del. Gen. Corp. Law, §251.
[106] Del. Gen. Corp. Law, § 253(a).

be in the best interests of the company and is shareholders. Such reasons might validly identify the need for additional capital contributions and the unwillingness of a minority to do so, assuming they have pre-emptive rights or other anti-dilution protections. In addition, the board must disclose the terms of the squeeze-out. If any shares are to be cancelled, the notice must identify 'the cash, property, rights or securities of any other corporation or entity which the holders of such shares are to receive in exchange for, or upon conversion of, such shares.'[107]

Since validity depends on procedural formalities, the notices of meeting of shareholders must meet the minimum delays under statute.

To effect a squeeze-out merger, the corporation must give each shareholder of record adequate notice of the shareholders' meeting at which the merger is proposed. In Delaware, the prior notice must be twenty days. In one Delaware case, the minority complained that it received notice fewer than twenty days before the meeting, but the court validated the notice since it was sent more than twenty days before the meeting.[108] However, no prior notice is required if the majority owners' consent. After the majority's action, the corporation must still notify the minority to trigger the possible judicial appraisal.

Legal Validity of Squeeze-Out Merger

Generally, in a squeeze-out merger, dissenting minority shareholders cannot enjoin a merger, even if it merges the corporation into a subsidiary of the majority shareholder formed solely for purposes of the merger, so long as the merger has a valid business purpose and the minority has appraisal rights for judicial valuation of the canceled shares.[109]

Invalidity may arise from lack of valid business purpose or from lack of resolution of prior breach of fiduciary duty.

Thus, where the purpose of a cash-out merger between interested parties is to freeze out the minority interest, some courts may find the merger is void.

---

[107] Del. Gen. Corp. Law, § 262(b)(5).

[108] *Ince Co. v. Silgan Corp.*, No. 10941 (Del. Ch. Jan. 7, 1991) cited in CSC, DELAWARE CORPORATION LAW, 2004, at p. 228-A

[109] *Grimes v. Donaldson Lufkin & Jenrette, Inc.*, 392 F. Supp. 1393 (N.D. Florida 1975).

The use of corporate power to eliminate a minority, absent a valid business purpose, breaches fiduciary duty of the majority to the minority.[110] A court, applying principles of equity, could disregard the validity and impose a trust on all parties to treat the squeeze-out as if it never happened.

Such invalidations occur because, once a corporate opportunity has been presented to the company, the board and majority shareholders cannot simply decide to let the opportunity be pursued by a separate company that does not include the company's minority shareholders. At this stage, it is generally too late to then use a squeeze-out to defeat the minority shareholders' claim to diversion of corporate opportunity. Rather than be a clean merger under 'entire fairness' and in compliance with fiduciary duty, the board's cash-out merger could be held to be an artifice to conceal and deprive the minority of rights already violated by fraud, looting or other prior misconduct.

'Appraisal Rights': Judicial Valuation

Dissenting shareholders may have statutory appraisal rights so that valuation is determined by a judge, not by the majority stockholder(s). Since corporation laws vary by state, you should refer to the laws of the state where the entity was organized.

In California, local law protects minority shareholders by requiring the majority to identify the process for judicial valuation under statutory appraisal rights.

In Delaware, both statute and common law require disclosure to the minority owners of their appraisal rights and the information necessary for them to make an informed decision whether to accept the cash-out merger offer or demand judicial valuation under statutory appraisal rights. Generally, such disclosures should include the kind of information one normally finds in any private or public offering:

- Current and historical financial statements or comparable reports that will allow shareholders to calculate basic financial ratios;
- A description of the company's current business and operations;
- Projection as to future business revenues;

---

[110]   *Singer v. Magnavox Co.,* 367 A.2nd 1349 (Del. 1977).

- Substantive valuation data, and background information supporting the valuation information;
- If relevant, information relating to industry-specific valuation metrics (or where to obtain such information if available in the public domain).

To exercise judicial appraisal rights, the dissenting minority owner must not have voted in favor of the merger nor consented in writing.[111] In Delaware, the dissenter must seek judicial appraisal within twenty days after the notice of the squeeze-out shareholder vote. No appraisal rights are available for publicly traded Delaware corporations or where there are more than 2,000 shareholders in a Delaware corporation, but federal and state securities laws may provide equivalent protection.

Minority shareholders can ensure appraisal rights by choice of governing law, in the certificate of incorporation or in a shareholders' agreement. The certificate of incorporation can guarantee appraisal rights for sale of substantially all assets or a change of the rights under the certificate of incorporation, even if there is no merger.[112]

Relative Benefits of a Squeeze-out Merger

Normally, a squeeze-out merger benefits the minority owner more than in a negotiated price or an appraised valuation, assuming the merger is either valid or its validity is not challenged. In a judicial valuation, the court would normally determine enterprise value and award payment to the minority of a fractional share of that value corresponding to the fraction of total ownership. In a negotiated buyout (or appraised buyout valuation), the majority owner might validly claim a lower payment is owed because certain valuation discounts. Such discounts might apply to (i) minority ownership (lack of control), (ii) unmarketability and illiquidity of the minority owner's shares and (iii) if the minority wants to get cashed out at a difficult moment in the company's cash flow cycle, a 'fire sale' discount.

---

[111] Del. Gen. Corp. Law, § 262.
[112] See, e.g., Del. Gen. Corp. Law, § 262(c).

Variations on Squeeze-Out Mergers

Cross-Border Squeeze-Outs. Certain state corporation laws permit a squeeze-out merger to serve as a tool for moving corporate domicile from one state or country to another. In that case, the process can give the corporation new flexibility by escaping local laws that might impose personal liability on shareholders.[113]

Converting from Corporation to LLC. In addition, a squeeze-out merger might also be used to convert from a corporation to an LLC, or from an LLC to a corporation. While such a conversion could result in a large income tax in the year of the merger, it could save taxes in the future.

Converting Voting to Non-Voting Shares. If the majority owners merely want to prevent the minority from voting rights, a merger could convert all minority shares to non-voting shares. The minority would not be eliminated and could always assert claims of breach of fiduciary duty or breach of loyalty. Hence, such transactions are rare.

---

[113] For example, New York's Business Corporation Law, Sec. 620, holds liable for employee wages the ten largest shareholders, but Delaware's corporation law does not.

From the Case Files

A squeeze-out merger does not insulate a majority owner from liability for self-dealing and usurpation of corporate opportunity. In one case we were involved in, a foreign private equity firm had acquired a U.S. operating company from an American founder who retained a minority stake. The majority owner wanted to purchase another company through a separate acquisition subsidiary, without sharing the opportunity with the American founder who had introduced the foreign owner to the target. Rather than delay the acquisition or negotiate a buyout or other settlement to keep the American from participating in a future acquisition, the foreign investor did a squeeze-out merger to judicially liquidate the claims of the American shareholder. The American minority shareholder sued to invalidate the squeeze-out merger, arguing that the merger was a tool abused by the majority owner as a breach of fiduciary duty. In response, the foreign majority owner claimed that the jointly owned company could never complete the acquisition without another $50+ million that the foreign investor would have to pay. It argued that the jointly owned company's insufficient capitalization meant there could be no diversion of a corporate opportunity by the squeeze-out merger. The dispute settled out of court.

No dispute would have arisen if the foreign investor had bought out the U.S. founder at inception, limited the business purpose of the jointly owned company or otherwise taken precautions.

Preparation for a Buyout or Redemption

Financing Issues in an Individual Buyout

The biggest hurdle in a buyout is paying a significant price. Where will the funds come from? Deferred payment may offer some benefits to all parties.

In principle, payment in cash yields a full 'fair market value' under 'agreed' valuation principles. Payment over time with interest is the more customary solution. With 'seller' financing, the 'buyer' (the company or other owner) pays in installments under a promissory note. With 'bank' financing, the 'buyer' pays in full at closing, using money borrowed from a lender.

Financing benefits the remaining owners by enabling a complete exit, deferring payment and using future revenues to pay the purchase price. If payments are deferred over time, the financing also creates the opportunity to stop future payments if the departed owner breaches a non-competition covenant.

Financing likewise benefits the selling owner by allowing for a higher valuation. The risk of non-payment could be mitigated by securing the loan with collateralized assets or by a personal guarantee by remaining owners, who take the risk of an unpredictable decline in the business.

Human Capital Issues: Transitional Management; Interim Executives

Ideally, in a well-managed business, any business exit will have minimal adverse effect upon the human capital. If properly planned, the exit of a co-owner or key employee with equity interest should not materially impair the remaining personnel or operations.

In a buyout, the business loses the benefits and entanglements of the selling shareholders. Where co-owners have been disputing who should be in control, or management strategies and policies, elimination of one shareholder can be beneficial. The enterprise (and the remaining shareholders) can focus on executing an agreed strategy.

To replace the selling shareholder, the remaining shareholders should identify and allocate roles and responsibilities for those persons who can replace the role of the departing shareholder. If necessary, some skills can be outsourced to a service provider. Where leadership is required, an interim executive can replace the departing shareholder. Interim employment could transform into permanent replacement, and the interim executive might seek to some equity ownership.

Protection of the Company's Brand Value

When one co-founder or key executive leaves the company, the company's brand and goodwill could be impaired, assuming the individual has been popular with customers, key advisors, influencers, employees, suppliers or the press. Accordingly, care must be taken to avoid loss of this goodwill, as well as protection of the company from the departing individual's potential for competing with the company. Non-disclosure, non-solicitation and non-competition covenants should be included in the buyout documentation.

Special Consideration for Minority Protection in Individual Buyouts

Beyond drag-along and tag-along rights and the general corporate legal principles of fiduciary duty and duty of loyalty, minority owners can negotiate strong protections against certain foreseeable risks. The most common protection for minorities is to grant a veto or allow a potentially adverse governance or operational decision to be made only by a super-majority in interest of all owners. Shareholder and LLC Operating Agreements usually include such protections as to increase in capitalization (and thus dilution of the minority owner), payment of dividends, major borrowing, securitization of assets for a loan and mergers and acquisitions.

On occasion, a key minority owner might retain title (and grant a license or lease) to certain key assets that are necessary for the business's operations. Or the minority might retain certain assets as collateral to secure a loan to the business. Such exceptional protections might apply where such assets might also be used by others without impairing the business's competitive position.

A departing minority owner might justify receiving a premium payment, beyond a simple agreed share price, if the company is sold within a few years after the minority's individual exit. As a percentage of the ultimate sale price, the premium might decline over time. Such a premium would give the minority an option to share in the upside if the agreed valuation in a redemption or buyout proves to be too low. Such a bonus could be legally useful as additional consideration to the minority to justify a non-competition covenant with a long duration.

Tips for Individual Exits

No business should have to endure a dispute over an individual's exit. Any such dispute can rob all parties of valuable opportunities elsewhere, encourage the departures of key employees who are solicited to take opposing sides, prevent a smooth transition of client relationships and operational skills and knowledge. So, if you do not have an agreement on the valuation and terms of exit, you should negotiate reasonably and fairly.

For individuals forced out with no hope of litigating (due to cost and emotional distress), you can perhaps negotiate a fair price with payment over a period of time and a security interest in the company's assets in case of payment default.

Your Professional Advisors

For redemption or buyout of an individual owner, the project should be relatively simple if you have already planned via governance documentation. You should get advice, documentation and negotiating assistance from your attorneys in business, with assistance from your accountant and financial advisers on feasibility of the payment plans. An insurance broker might also have some tools to cover risks of non-payment or non-performance.

Your Self-Assessment

- Does your corporate governance 'toolkit' handle an existing or persisting tension or disagreement among owners that could erupt into an ownership crisis?

- Considering vulnerabilities and threats to company ownership or operations, who is most probably the most difficult person to deal with you and your business? What roles do they play as stakeholders? Consider roles as owner, option-holder, employee, financial investor, strategic alliance 'partner,' supplier, customer/client, whistleblower, or regulator)? How will such threat profiles and scenarios change in the next few years?

- Does your toolkit reward behaviors that preserve enterprise value upon the individual exit of key stakeholders? Does the toolkit punish 'bad' behaviors?

11

Toolkit for Joint Exit by All Owners

Timing of a Joint Exit

For a joint exit, many issues affect timing. Triggers may be a crisis in governance, new commercial challenges or new opportunities.

Merger to Avoid New Capital Expenses. Every startup reaches the point where it must choose between being acquired or going for unicorn status. At that point, the startup must either invest to compete with new emerging technologies or be acquired. Typically, a global enterprise acquirer will want to acquire the startup as a replacement for R&D that the acquirer never made, or made poorly. At this point, the startup needs to market itself as the solution to the acquirer's gaps. To get to this point, the startup must have already identified that gap in the marketplace.

Merger to Go Global. Smaller companies should always be aware of their competitors in foreign countries. Such competitors could be merger partners as an alternative to establishing one's own foreign offices. A more financially advantageous merger might be achieved by first establishing one's own foreign offices, generating name recognition in the foreign local markets and then finding a merger partner.

Merger to Go Public. Professional service firms face challenges of illiquidity to pay departing partners for their equity contributions and any post-termination compensation for contributions to the firm's intellectual property or clientele. Instead of taking from operating capital or borrowing against future revenues, a professional service firm might choose to issue shares to investors. Such shares could be used to pay departing 'partners' and to give them the choice of timing of when to sell. This solution is limited to unregulated professions such as business consulting, information technology services, and specialized technical services, since third-party investment in law firms and accounting firms remains legally prohibited or limited to 25 percent of all equity (in the District of Columbia).

Going public can provide not only liquidity for exit, but an effective merger strategy for different professional service companies. Where a number of small consulting companies with the same industry focus face reduced work, the leaders of each firm might decide to sell to a new public company in return for shares.[114]

Cohesion Issues

When can the majority owner decide upon selling the entire company? If the shareholders' agreement includes a drag-along clause, the majority owner is granted the right to force all other owners to sell to the same owner.

Unless carefully drafted, a 'drag-along' clause could jeopardize and disenfranchise the minority owners who would be required to sign the same representations and warranties as the controlling owner. Usually, the minority has no ability to judge the fairness or accuracy of such terms, and certainly has no bargaining power to limit their potential post-sale liability in case of a breach. Accordingly, minority owners should negotiate the terms of the drag-along clause to limit their obligations at closing to covenants as to their ownership of equity and their exoneration from having to make any covenants relating to the business. Such exonerations

---

[114] See e.g., Information Services Group, Inc., a NASDAQ-listed corporation resulting from the 'acquisitions' of various consulting service companies in the field of outsourcing and business process management. See http://ir.isg-one.com/about-the-company/Index?KeyGenPage=206643.

can depress the buyer's price offer because they limit the buyer's right of recovery in damages and right of rescission for fraud.

As a compromise, or fallback position, in making representations and warranties, the minority owners might limit their potential liability to only those matters within their actual knowledge. Even without any actual knowledge of a breach of rep or warranty, the mere threat or filing of a claim of breach would embroil them in costly litigation where they win but lose attorneys' fees, time and focus.

In a *'drag-along'* clause, the majority owner gets the right to force the minority owners to sell their equity investment if the majority sells out. Usually, this right is limited to a sale of all ownership interests, not merely a minority of ownership or a sale of control. Such clauses are fair so long as the minority has the right to the same pro rata percentage of proceeds and is not required to personally guarantee any warranties or indemnities other than those relating to title and capacity to sell. (There may be escrows and earn-outs to accommodate such limitation on the liability of the minority owners upon a sale of the entire company).

The 'drag-along' clause can generate litigation by the minority being dragged along. An allegation of breach of governance duties can be used to leverage a sweeter deal for the minority. The majority may be blackmailed to paying a premium to avoid having the buyer balk at an incomplete acquisition.

'Drag-along' and 'tag-along clauses' should be carefully drawn to ensure that the minority sellers have no duty other than to deliver their shares. The selling majority might want to have the minority share some of the post-sale liability that might arise from breach of warranties. Where the minority owner is not active in the business, it would be unfair to force a sharing in such liability.

What if the majority owner wants to sell all ownership interests without negotiating a deal for the minority owners? Under a *'tag-along'* clause, the minority owners are granted the right to force the buyer to buy 100 percent of the equity, if the majority owner sells the majority interest, for the same price under the same terms and conditions as negotiated by the majority owner. (The minority must take care to avoid being dragged into making representations on matters they are not aware of, or do not control).

Pricing Expectations

To sell at a high price in a joint exit, you need to demonstrate value to your buyer. But you might not get your best price due to bad timing or circumstances.

'Fire Sale'

By definition, in a 'fire sale,' some of the intrinsic value of the private company being sold goes up in smoke. Remember the definition of a fair market price! The fire sale price fails to achieve the fair market price because one of the parties is under a time limitation and 'must get out fast.'

So, why would anyone want a 'fire sale'? Usually, a fire sale occurs for a very good reason: the value has been crushed and there is no perceived alternative.

In one case I helped resolve without litigation, a co-owner sold its shares in a fire sale about four or five months after it was discovered that a co-owner had embezzled a large amount. My client wanted to escape the risk of further defalcations and frauds, as well as reputational damage.

A fire sale may be necessary to escape seizure of assets by tax authorities. The buyer was told that the seller owed payroll taxes, which were a quantified liability, but the company lacked capital (and borrowing capacity) to pay. So the IRS shut the company down but the buyer agreed to pay off the IRS and reduce the purchase price.

A fire sale might be necessary to pay off (or forgive) a debt by one of two co-owners to the company, where the borrower cannot repay and just wants to leave and let a new owner 'resolve' the problem. In this case, the company would have to pay tax on phantom income from forgiveness of debt. A consulting agreement with payments to the exiting co-owner may establish payments to set off consulting fees against loan debt. Both sellers agreed to a low price so long as the buyer took over the mess.

Fire sales occur, and each reflects a failure to manage a clean operation. The discount gives the buyer some maneuverability for investing to clean up someone else's mess, or to just buy a company that does not fit perfectly but can be restructured or split up to get the fair value of the buyer's efforts.

Sale 'AS IS'

How can co-owners seeking a joint exit maximize the sale price of a private company without special preparation for sale? If selling 'AS IS,' how can they avoid a 'fire sale'? In this sale, the buyer takes the target company with all its strengths and weaknesses. Buyers are 'strategic' buyers only if the acquisition fits within the buyer's strategic plan for expansion. The highest price should normally be paid by the buyer who can derive the most value by integrating the target company into its own operations, whether as a platform company or a 'tack-on' to an existing platform company. Hence, investment bankers and business brokers earn their living by identifying trends in business, learning what each player's roles and goals are, and being available to introduce a privately held company to a strategic buyer that can gain the highest value from the acquisition.

'Clean' SaleFor a 'clean' company, the buyer pays full price. The purchase agreement will contain many pages of representation and warranties about the condition of the company, subject only to specific disclosed particular warnings in a disclosure statement. Sellers who fail to do their internal housekeeping before opening the door to a buyer's due diligence (inspection of records and information) could regret it later if the buyer sues for a reduced price or to cancel the acquisition due to a breach of representation. Sellers might consider the relative advantages of an 'earn out' or putting a percentage of the purchase price into escrow and negotiating a cap on liability in case of a breach of representations.

Impact of an Earn-out

A company's sale price may be higher (or lower) if the sellers accept a lower base price and get a percentage of post-sale revenues earned later. Earn-outs require the sellers to devote more effort after the sale but reward the sellers for post-closing success. Buyers may like an earn-out as a hedge against hidden problems that surface only after closing. Typically, the term of the earn-out is between one and five years. Defining the terms of an earn-out can be tricky. The buyer can defeat the seller's expectations by changing methods of accounting, accelerating expenses, deferring income, changing tax elections, parking revenues with friends, and incurring new expenses that build for the future and thus depress net revenue during the earn-out period. The seller should define revenue and expense items, as well as other factors determining future cash flow, to achieve predictable comparability.

Optimistic High-Ball Offers as an 'Anchor' Value

Your price expectations should not be anchored to some unsolicited offer to buy 'subject to a term sheet and due diligence.' A buyer who has not knowledge of your confidential information on finances, operations or compliance is just seducing you (or your co-owners) to get a 'quick peek' under the hood. Such tactics invite heartache when the 'due diligence' report predictably shows the proposed price was excessive and unjustified, and the offered price slumps. No serious bid can start with a bare price first. So don't be beguiled.

Preparation for Sale

To maximize value for all shareholders, the company can adopt several strategies. These focus on *financial improvement, clean housekeeping* and solidifying the *management team* and *operational excellence.*

Clean-up Your Corporate Housekeeping

Internal Audits of Operations and Compliance

In any joint exit, a buyer will insist on detailed due diligence to identify possible reasons to reduce the purchase price or even walk away from a merger or acquisition. You can pre-empt loss of value by doing your own internal due diligence and rectifying any anomalies before you offer your documents to the buyer for buyer due diligence. This process will not only allow cleanup of minor messes, but give you confidence to address any issues raised during the acquirer's due diligence.

Internal Audits of Financial Accounting

Buyers want to know that the financial accounting and tax accounting are done in compliance with 'generally accepted accounting principles' (or international financial accounting principles) that are applied consistently from year to year. If not consistent over time, then aberrations must be described in footnotes. As a matter of good practice, business owners should ensure some level of accounting consistency, whether by audit or by financial review. In general, audited financial statements help sell and justify a higher price and EBITDA multiple.

Internal Audit of Human Capital

Acquirers have a heightened concern about potential liability for mismanagement of employees. Human capital management ('HCM') has been in turmoil in the last few years. Employee civil rights protections have been expanded to include freedom from sex harassment. Payments of damages and legal fees for sexual harassment are not deductible. The business design for compliance should include employee confidentiality and non-disclosure agreements (or accept written employee policies) to protect against claims of customers, clients, strategic alliance partners, licensors and suppliers. Hence, compliance with HCM procedures should be verified and documented.

If your company uses the services of independent contractors, your pre-sale internal audit should identify and resolve questions of misclassification. Proper classification for employment, unemployment insurance, worker's compensation insurance, disability insurance and employment tax laws has become more challenging under emerging legislation that imperils the 'gig economy' and criminalizes classification errors.[115]

Notices to employees and local officials may be required before closing. A U.S. employer with over 100 full-time employees is liable for failure to give workers sixty days' notice of termination of employment or a mass layoff. Exceptions may apply where the termination of employment was caused by business circumstances that were not reasonably foreseeable or the employer was seeking capital to forestall a mass layoff.[116] Foreign labor laws can provide more substantial employee protections upon a change of control.

Pending or Threatened Litigation

The existence of litigation creates a question of liability and damages that your company might owe. A buyer will want to reserve judgment (and money) for any pending or threatened litigation involving your company or any of its key employees. Pre-exit preparation includes resolution (or

---

[115] See California's law on the gig economy adopting an 'ABC' test. Assembly Bill 5, *Worker Status: Employees and Independent Contractors* (signed Sept. 18, 2019), available at https://leginfo.legislature.ca.gov/faces/billNavClient.xhtml?bill_id=201920200AB5.
[116] 29 U.S.C. §§ 2101-2109.

reduction of risk) for such unknown liabilities that any buyer would be assuming in a merger or acquisition.

Brand Protection: The Morals Clause in Key Employee Contracts

As noted above, your key persons could expose the company to embarrassment and loss of brand goodwill by violating a 'morals clause.' Keep it clean and hold individuals accountable for tarnishing your company's reputation.

Clean-up Your Personal Housekeeping

Individual sellers should ensure they have completed their personal financial, estate, wealth and family housekeeping to minimize potential post-sale liabilities, taxes and family disputes. Such plans are primordial for family-owned companies, but the same lessons apply to all sellers.

Get Third-Party Consents

Examine all your contracts, consumer protection notices, privacy policies and regulatory obligations. If you must get a third-party consent or governmental approval, get such consents or get ready to ask for them.

Sellers' Intermediate-Term Strategies

Assuming the sale can be planned for a year in advance, intermediate-term steps can be adopted to generate greater value. The company might open new offices in foreign countries to demonstrate global footprint (viability, brand value) and increased sales (for a higher earnings multiple upon sale). The company might develop new distribution channels for existing products. The company might expand online sales and services, particularly if this can be done rapidly with minimal marginal cost and easy integration with existing supply chains and value chains. Similarly, one could add new brands (registered trademarks) and gain name recognition in new markets through online sales and minimum other advertising costs.

In taking any step to 'look' better, exiting owners must balance the risks against the potential for intermediate-term 'growth' plans. A small acquisition might be considered to demonstrate thought leadership and add bulk that might justify a higher EBITDA multiple as the purchase price. But any acquisition is fraught with risk of poor choice, poor execution and post-merger integration, delayed benefits and lost value due to lack of synergies and wasted diversion of management resources. A similar risk-benefit analysis would apply to any intermediate-term joint venturing to enter a new business line that neither you nor your joint venture partner could pursue alone.

Sellers' Short-Term Strategies

Improve Financial Outcomes

If feuding owners can find peaceful co-existence for a year or two, they might be able to implement strategies for maximizing corporate value before a sale. Before doing so, they must find a modus vivendi that eliminates the distractions raised by intramural fighting, dominating and avoiding domination. Typically, this can best be achieved by hiring a coach for guidance both on the internal governance but more importantly on the key steps that add to corporate value. This means a 'turnaround' or 'transformation.' Let us live in peace (if we can)!

Since valuation depends on financial analysis, short-term actions to improve financial condition can be classified according to the impact on gross revenues, expenses, free cash flow and increasing assets while decreasing liabilities. These are accounting metrics for improving valuation. Manipulation of accounting will not work. In the purchase agreement, buyers normally insist that the sellers represent that the company complies with generally accepted accounting principles ('GAAP'), consistently applied and with no material accounting changes (for example, conversion from cash-basis to accrual-basis) in the one to three years before the sale. Much can be done by finding third parties willing to provide resources to the private company engaged in pre-sale 'spruce up' of its operations. However, in any agreement with a third party to tweak the accounting and increase cash flow or net asset value, the private company should be careful to avoid contract terms that give the supplier the right to terminate the agreement, or change prices or scope of work, upon the change of control of the enterprise customer.

Increase Revenues

Revenues can be increased honestly or by accounting artifices. Honest increases come from extending sales outlets using distributors (for sales of goods), channel partners (for software licensing and accompanying hardware sales and technical support) or 'low-cost' sales personnel with a modest salary and substantial commissions. In each business model, the seller gets a commission to reward sales growth. In negotiating such deals, the privately held company preparing a sale in the near future will not be able to induce third parties to risk sharing if the set-up costs for a distributor, sales agent, channel partner or commission-based employees must invest substantially to start up the relationship.

Where do you find such eager sales channels? Basically, the privately held company's managers should look for third parties who have already invested in their sales and sales support capabilities and for whom the private company's goods or services would fit without substantial additional capital investment.

Aggressive accounting practices could increase revenues artificially. A basic principle of accounting requires that income and expenses relating to the same accounting period be matched. Any acceleration of income or deferral of expenses could be considered excessive and fraudulent to a buyer. Gaming the accounting system could be achieved by not respecting GAAP. Manipulating revenue growth could invite a buyer's claim of fraud.

Decrease Expenses

Expenses can be decreased, but the company must watch its money. 'Quick wins' in expense management can be achieved across the company but should not eviscerate its dynamism. Excessive inventories should be reduced to minimize interest on loans from banks or factors.

Efficient purchasing and procurement practices can lower costs of purchasing necessities. The challenge is not merely to find low-cost suppliers, but also to induce them to bid on a Request for Proposals ('RFP') or Request for Information ('RFI') and get immediate reduction in procurement costs sufficient to make a big difference on sale of the company.

Capital expenses can be avoided by adopting a program of paying by the month or by the use. In outsourcing, the supplier or service provider pays the capital expenses of establishing and maintain equipment, technologies and hiring and managing people.

Increase Cash Flow

'Free cash flow' measures net revenues from core operations. Thus, 'earnings before interests, taxes, depreciation and amortization' ('EBITDA') concerns sales and costs of goods sold. To increase EBITDA, the company must either increase revenues or reduce cost of goods sold. Having discussed revenue increases, consider how to reduce cost of goods sold. This really applies to companies selling products which need to reduce product costs or negotiate advantageous pricing from suppliers.

For companies selling services or e-commerce subscription services to anything 'as a service' increasing net cash flow requires increasing sales at a faster rate than the increases in costs of software development or infrastructure acquisition. Welcome to 'Cloud Computing,' which allows small companies to rapidly scale sales and thus generate enterprise value.

Update Your Intellectual Property Rights and Policies

Intellectual property has its own separate value, apart from the enterprise. You should maximize its value by updating both the legal rights and the policies for protecting those rights.

If you have not adopted employment agreements and policies protecting trade secrets, you should do so before a joint exit, as well as before any termination or resignation of a key knowledge worker.

Pre-exit patent planning should include filing for all patents potentially available, keeping in mind that a patent application will be rejected for lapse of time if you used or disclosed freely the novel, useful and non-obvious invention. Collection of process information, legal evaluation for patentability and regular filings for patents should be a normal management policy.

Copyright registrations are not as valuable as patents since they protect only the expression of an idea, not the idea itself. But copyright registrations can be valuable in protecting against theft of software. To avoid your software becoming public knowledge, you may apply for a copyright under trade secrecy rules of the U.S. Copyright Office.

Transition Plan (Post-Merger Integration)

Before designing a transition plan for 'post-merger integration,' the sellers should conduct a feasibility study to identify all affected stakeholders, potential roadblocks and compliance obligations for notices to workers,[117] governments, lenders, suppliers and customers, among others. This feasibility study will also identify how the company's business model, human resources, clientele, financial structure and intellectual property could integrate into a strategic acquirer or a financial investor's platform. For example, anticipating a term sheet for a price based on no cash, no debt and no undisclosed liabilities, the sellers can anticipate and potentially design how each type of potential acquirer might find synergies and retain the maximum amount of the company's resources.

Terms of Sale (or Merger)

The joint exit can take the form of a sale of shares (or other equity) by the shareholders. Or your business entity (as 'target') might merge with the acquirer's entity (or a special purpose acquisition company, 'SPAC'). The risk allocations and other key terms relate to both forms.

How to Avoid a Failed Deal: The 'Material Adverse Change' Clause

Buyers often ask for protection against loss of value by the target, and thus the right to reduce the price or walk away, due to events occurring after the contract is signed but before the closing. A 'material adverse change' clause

---

[117] Worker Adjustment and Retraining Notification Act, 29 U.S.C. §2101 et seq. (60-day prior notice requirement). In Europe, see the 'Acquired Rights' Directive and related national laws (Council *Directive* 2001/23/*EC* of 12 March 2001 on the approximation of the laws of the Member States relating to the safeguarding of employees' rights in the event of transfers of undertakings, businesses or parts of businesses), available at https://eur-lex.europa.eu/legal-content/EN/TXT/?uri=celex:32001L0023 (accessed Sept. 14, 2019), implemented in the United Kingdom at the Transfer of Undertakings – Protection of Employment Act ('TUPE').

('MAC') addresses this risk. MAC clauses may be fair where an adverse change arises from misconduct or inadequate performance by the sellers or your company. But a MAC should not apply where marketplace changes beyond your control result in a reduction in value.

How to Avoid the Risk of Termination or Break-Up Fees

Both sellers and buyer might negotiate to protect against the risks of a delayed or failed closing due to non-satisfaction of some condition required for the closing. Typically, the sellers might need to obtain third-party consents (to avoid loss of valuable ongoing business). The buyer might need to get financing. If either condition fails, a 'break-up' fee ('termination' fee) might be owed by either, depending on the contract provisions.

How can you avoid the risk of a break-up fee? Start with eliminating the circumstances where a governmental agency, key customer or internal politics might delay or prevent a closing. Risk prevention involves organizational design (a clean house), organizational behavior (governance), contract compliance and customer relationship management. You should have updated your internal corporate housekeeping before going to the bargaining table. Be clean, be ready.

How to Minimize and Allocate Post-Closing Liabilities among Sellers

Every buyer wants a clean house. Some liabilities will not be known until long after the closing. This includes current and potential litigation, tax audits for past and future returns pre-closing, pension contributions, contracts and compliance. Sellers should be aware of the statutes of limitation for each of these liabilities and negotiate to exclude or reduce liability based on the passage of time, the future settlement of a claim and unchanged current laws.

Buyers prefer to have all sellers be jointly and severally liable for all post-closing liabilities. Sellers should seek to limit their individual liability to their pro-rata share of the purchase price received. However, by virtue of actual or imputed knowledge, sellers active in management (such as directors, CEO, COO and CFO) probably should be liable for the entire amount of certain liabilities. Where they have made personal representations and warranties based on their own personal knowledge, such seller-managers cannot usually avoid full liability.

How to Structure Your Earn-out

In a sale with an 'earn-out,' the key seller agrees to accept a 'low' sales price in return for a future payment upon satisfaction of specified conditions.

Where the earn-out is designed merely to verify certain conditions before closing, the contract of sale would note the earn-out is just a post-closing recomputation of the sales price contingent on achieving agreed value drivers. Such value drivers might be key performance indicators for post-sale services by the seller under a consulting agreement. Or the drivers might be computations of the company's net revenues. A well-drafted sale agreement would help minimize the risk of tax reallocation of the earn-out amount as ordinary income. The terms should clarify that any services are merely ancillary and not to create any new post-sale value.

You might structure the earn-out as a share of future net revenues.

Whenever the sale price is adjustable based on some recomputation, the accounting, financial and tax parameters should be specified. Do you want 'net revenue' to be reduced by expenses that are unusually high and potentially unrelated to the generation of revenue?

Perhaps the seller might retain some percentage of the future sales price when and if the buyer resells the company within a specified period. Such a percentage does not need to be contingent on any action by the seller but merely reflects that the buyer and seller agreed on a price without appraisal, based on a 'drive-by' negotiation. If a third party buys in the near future, the price would be adjusted to reflect a true 'marketplace' value.

Joint Sale to Strategic Acquirer

A strategic acquirer is a mature business that already knows your business to a large extent. Exit planning should include identification of prospective acquirers. Professional contacts at trade conferences may help set the tone for a later solicitation of interest to buy. Public companies can use their shares as a deal currency, so they may have an edge over financial buyers in an auction process where the public company's stock has risen recently.

Types of Strategic Acquirers

Public Companies

Mature businesses want to buy smaller companies for various reasons: to capture a business opportunity where someone else took the risk of getting started. This might involve filling gaps in R&D, new product development, distribution networks (both online and physical), extension to a new line of business or new market territory. Every mature global enterprise has a 'business development' department responsible for identifying potential acquisition targets. From inception, every startup and family business should identify such enterprises as being in the orbit for possible exit sale. By identifying spheres of potential buyers, the founders can design their own companies for eventual integration.

Mature global companies face complex compliance requirements. Hence, when targeting a 'strategic' sale, the sellers should first ensure their company complies with all applicable laws and regulations. A compliance program will increase value, accelerate a sale, reduce risks of fines and penalties, help preserve brand value and shorten the time for due diligence and completion of sale.

There are several advantages to being acquired by a global company. For tax purposes, the sellers can choose between accepting, as consideration for their company's shares, securities of the acquirer (tax-free reorganizations) or receiving cash (taxable as capital gains). The public acquirer's shares are listed for public trading, so an all stock deal could generate cash by resale. As seller, you can hope to enjoy an increase in the value of the acquirer's shares, though care should be taken to avoid overconcentration in such shares that could expose the seller to serious portfolio risks upon a downturn. Finally, global companies are experienced in the acquisition process and post-merger integration and thus offer benefits of reliability for future employment depending on your goals and circumstances.

As a benefit to startups, global businesses are increasingly restructuring to reduce dependence on internal R&D departments and invite possible acquisitions of startups with disruptive business models, proven concepts and some value even without positive cash flow.

Global American Companies

American companies have an advantage as acquirers of technology-rich U.S. companies. Foreign acquirers must be vetted by the Committee on Foreign Investment in the United States ('CFIUS'). For tech startups, this means certain buyers should not be considered where CFIUS might conclude the sale would result in a transfer of sensitive technologies and national security concerns.

Foreign Buyer

A foreign buyer might offer a synergistic fit for your company. It could create synergies where the existing foreign organization can easily tack your operations on to its foreign operations in a consolidation roll-up. Your company could provide an American launchpad for the foreign business.

However, a foreign buyer presents challenges for legal compliance. If you have any sensitive U.S. technology or data, or if you want to conduct business as a supplier to the U.S. government, your stock purchase will be delayed by governmental reviews for national security and public policy.

Growth Companies

Growth companies offer an exit strategy for all stakeholders. A growth company in the same or adjacent service could create synergies from a merger, with higher revenues from the same customer base, extension of service offerings to new clienteles and both territorial and line-of-business extensions. A growth company could pursue strategies of strengthening its existing market position and developing (or acquiring) new services and products to support future growth. Such strategies imply a focus on growing existing services model, expanding geographically, developing new industry sectors, productizing market data assets, expanding managed services offerings and growing via acquisitions. Any synergies would need to be balanced against any challenges in transforming culture, processes and budget restructuring.

Foreign growth companies could be especially attractive for exit planning. In an optimal fit, a foreign company could bring technologies, management personnel, a new supply chain with new efficiencies for internal operations, a bevy of possible manufacturers with volume discount pricing, and foreign markets for the U.S. company

Peer-Level Competitors

You know your peers. You see them at trade fairs and conferences. Are they the right fit for a business exit? In contrast to growth companies, a 'peer-level' competitor may offer an exit solution with limited capacity to create new value. The peer competitor could thus solve a problem but offer lower value. A peer competitor might offer some employment to some divorcing owners but not to others.

Joint Sale to One or More Managers (Management Buyout, or 'MBO')

Sometimes, sale to a third party is not attractive or feasible. A third party might take too long to evaluate the operation and close the sale. Recapitalization is not feasible where the principal assets are not capable of being continued, such as for a professional services firms where disgruntled co-owners can easily jump ship to another firm. Where there are assets that are complex, or difficult to value, or difficult to realize the value in a sale to a third party, a buyout by management could resolve the exiting controlling shareholder's need to exit. The pricing for such a sale depends on many factors.

- *Leveraged MBO.* In a leveraged management buyout, the seller might seek a higher price and give 'seller financing' or allow the management to borrow (or the company to borrow, if it has borrowing capacity) to achieve the higher sales price. If the company borrows the funds, it can use the proceeds to pay the seller in various forms. The company could pay licensing royalties (assuming the seller has some valuable intellectual property). It might pay consulting fees (assuming the seller offers some consulting services). Or it might enter into purchase agreements (assuming the seller has other businesses that could benefit from post-sale commercial contracts). Maybe a lender might consider it wise to lend to a management buyout ('MBO'), since management will continue and thus secure the repayment through continuing operations using time-tested experience of this particular management team.

- *Controlling Shareholder's Buyout of Viable Assets before Restructuring Remaining Assets.* Sometimes a controlling shareholder might make an offer to buy viable assets as a ploy to reduce overall debt of the remaining assets. For example, in April 2018, Edward Lambert,

CEO of Sears Holding Corp., offered to buy the Kenmore brand for $400 million in cash, subject to obtaining equity financing, and likewise $80 million for Sears Home Services (home improvements). Such a buyout would have injected new cash for the core business while allowing the hived-off businesses to grow into new markets not limited by the troubled 'mother ship.'[118] Creditors objected to Lambert's pre-bankruptcy dealings, so the offer died.

From the Case Files

When a business is in irremediable chronic financial distress, a management buyout (MBO) might be the only possible buyer, assuming no insolvency. One of my clients was the U.S. operating subsidiary of a publicly traded Asian international technology services company. The parent company used the U.S. company to generate U.S. and international clients but, over time, the U.S. company could not generate sustainable U.S. clientele due to its dependency on the foreign parent for outsourced technologies. The U.S. CEO was a minority owner. The parties explored a scenario to transfer the U.S. company (and client contracts) to another foreign affiliate but decided ultimately to allow the U.S. manager's new company (co-owned by the CEO and three key employees) to acquire the assets, office leasehold and personnel for a nominal price. With the foreign company's consent, the CEO thus converted the foreign-controlled subsidiary to a U.S. startup with existing customers, cash flow and continued employment of workers who otherwise would have lost their jobs. There was no other potential buyer. (If there had been any other possible buyer, the exit might have taken advantage of a large accumulated net operating losses ('NOL') that are deductible against future revenues subject to limitations.[119])

---

[118] See Suzanne Kapner, 'Sears CEO Offers to Buy Kenmore,' Wall St. J., Aug. 15, 2018, p.B2, cols 4-7.
[119] Code § 170 (subject to Code §382's limitation if the company were purchased in the last 5 years).

Joint Sale to Financial Buyer

Sale to a financial buyer is unlike a sale to a strategic acquirer or incumbent management. The financial investor looks for companies that are undervalued and might cut costs, recapitalize, restructure, streamline and relaunch the business before reselling it. Unlike strategic acquirers, financial investors 'partner' with some or all of the selling owners for a long collaboration. Financial buyers often borrow from banks to finance the purchase, so the creditworthiness of your company becomes a factor. In turn, banks might issue collateralized loan obligations ('CLOs') to investors secured by a target company shares.

On an interim basis, the financial investor might bring in seasoned interim managers to restructure and repurpose the enterprise. If you want to continue in business after selling, you might seek such an interim manager role as advisor to a financial investor.

Private Equity Funds

Private equity ('PE') funds are financial investors with a business model to buy, grow and sell businesses. Under their agreements with institutional and other investors, PE fund managers charge investors annual management fees of one to two percent of fund assets plus a 'carry' of between twenty to thirty percent of a fund's profits on sale of a portfolio asset.[120]

As 'buyout firms,' PE funds create new value by developing or buying a platform company and extending its value by 'tack-on' acquisitions, extension of territory, new lines of business for the same customer base, cost reduction (automation, business process restructuring, reducing capital expenses, converting capital costs to marginal costs and shifting financial risks to suppliers).

To achieve such growth, PE funds assemble both professional managers to manage and integrate acquisition targets into a consolidated 'roll-up' enterprise. Middle-market PE firms drive transformation of individual companies into 'platform companies' that can extend the platform via 'tack-on' or 'bolt-on' acquisitions. Platform growth occurs from territorial expansion, finding new distribution channels and target customers for

---

[120] William Louch, *'Buyout Fund Raises Record Sum,'* Wall St. J. (Dec. 3, 2019, p.B9, cols. 1-5).

existing products or services, and using technologies for rapid scaling. Indeed, returns on investment in platform companies outperform standalone portfolio companies.

The roadmap for scalable growth depends on the readiness of the platform for bolt-on acquisitions. By adopting common tools and systems that can quickly integrate a series of new acquisitions, the platform company's managers can avoid distractions from its core business goals and operations and outsource some or all of the integration process. PE firms and their service providers can develop and adopt road maps for modeling and implementing post-merger integration ('PMI'). Using repeatable PMI tools and techniques, PE firms can deploy additional technical and administrative support on an ad-hoc basis in each bolt-on acquisition. A successful PMI can manage attrition, merge disparate corporate cultures and inspire all employees to achieve strategic goals and opportunities. Evaluating a financial investor's portfolio companies will provide insights into positioning your company for a sale. Unfortunately, financial investors like to maintain confidentiality of their 'secret sauce' and intentions, so investment bankers may need to be hired.

Family Offices

A family office is an entity, managed by investment professionals, that represents the investments of an ultra-high net worth individual or family. Often, a family office is established by a former business owner to diversify and manage the proceeds of sale of a business. Unlike PE firms, family offices tend to either be generalist investors (in market-liquid portfolios) or niche investors (in private portfolios). Their investment strategy generally does not include buying and rebuilding or restructuring businesses. Rather, they may be specialized lenders, providing bridge capital secured by adequate collateral. Or they may act as a private investment fund with only a few owners, seeking portfolio diversification to support lifestyles and favorite charities.

Distress Investors

Financial investors include those with an appetite for buying distressed companies. The companies might have suffered some setback that prevents them from pursuing reasonable opportunities. The question is how much distress has occurred. In each case, the value discount is significant and requires special effort to rebuild or liquidate. Distress investors generally like companies that have invested a lot of capital and created valuable assets (such as software or other intellectual property). Distress investors are problem solvers and fixers.

For the 'turnaround' or 'distress investor,' the hunt is for a fallen angel offered at a discounted value, for 'fix up' and resale in one to three or four years. Such investors may include ultra-high net worth individuals (who know a particular industry after having sold their own startups). For the 'vulture' investor, the company is beyond fixup. Its assets are worth more separately than as a going concern.

Leveraged Buyouts

In a leveraged buyout ('LBO'), the buyer uses the value of the target company as security to collateralize a loan for the purchase price. The lender may be a bank or other external financing source, or it could be the shareholders or affiliates of the buyer.

Leveraged buyouts pose legal risks for the company and the buyer. The leverage could be a voidable 'fraudulent transfer' under creditor protection laws. For example, a fraudulent transfer might arise where the buyer, not the target company, is receiving the loan, since the target is not receiving any substantially equivalent value for the lien on its assets. In another example, a fraudulent transfer might occur if the new securitization of the target's assets leaves it with no other unsecured assets.[121]

Where some 'new consideration' is given to the target company, it would be receiving fair value and thus not be reducing its assets in the transaction. 'New consideration' might include some right of subrogation by the purchaser to the lender's claims, guaranties by the buyer or its affiliates, or bringing new value to the target by offering business opportunities having new value (other than just bringing on new management), such as access to new markets, better financing teams or exclusive licenses from the buyer or affiliates.

---

[121] See Uniform Fraudulent Transfers Act, Section 1(2)(i).

To minimize the risk of avoidance by creditors, the purchaser must structure the transaction with due protection for creditors. Such protections invite alternative structures.

The purchaser might purchase the target company's assets, borrowing the purchase price by collateralizing such assets as security for repayment. The purchase price would need to be fair and adequate.

Or the purchaser could purchase the target company's shares and pledge the stock of the target's shares or other ownership interests.

Or, in a partial buyout, the 'lender' might buy a minority interest of the target and agreeing to resell it pursuant to approval or requirements of the real acquirer.[122] This structure imperils the selling owners, who might not collect if the leveraged company goes bankrupt.

Or the transaction could be structured so that one or more of the elements of a voidable fraudulent transfer do not exist. In one example, the target company was not 'insolvent' or rendered insolvent by the transaction because it had a positive net worth and could unquestionably pay its debts (including new debt) as they come due.

In short, LBOs need to be structured to avoid the risk of invalidation as a fraudulent transfer.

Which scenarios favor an LBO in a business exit? Generally, a lender will be happy to take collateral in long-lived assets, such as property, plant and equipment, or real estate, or potentially a famous brand. Lenders like stable businesses with reasonably predictable cash flow.

---

[122] See generally, Pease, '*Fraudulent Transfers under the Uniform Fraudulent Conveyance Act and the proposed Uniform Fraudulent Transactions Act*,' in Edward F. Greene and Walter G. McNeil, STRUCTURED RECEIVABLES FINANCING: MANAGING RISK MORE EFFICIENTLY IN SECURITY FORM, Law & Business Inc. (1985), p 45.

Post-Sale Relationships

Earn-out Variations

An 'earn-out' represents part of the purchase price that is collectible by a seller, usually from an escrow account, after the transfer of ownership. The delayed payment gives the buyer a tool to setoff newly discovered liabilities against the price and ensure the seller honors a non-competition covenant. Variables include:

- what services the seller will be required to perform after closing, as well as performance metrics for the seller and the company, and

- the accounting definitions used for computing the amount of the earn-out, and the potential abuses of accounting principles by either party leading to a post-closing dispute.

Relationships among Former Co-Owners

After a business exit, complete termination of any further business relationship between former co-owners might be desirable or even necessary. But relationships among former co-owners may continue, so long as they do not risk impairing the buyer's value.

Relationships after Sale to Strategic Acquirer

Employment Agreements. Some former owners will remain on Day One as employees to lead post-merger integration. The acquirer gets the benefits of continuity of operations. To avoid conflicts, the terms of employment should be fair to all, including former owners, and not merely a substitute for an earn-out or a special one-sided payment benefiting only one of the former owners.

Consulting Agreements. A post-divorce consulting agreement can help all parties and is very common. The enterprise benefits from the continuing availability of the departed co-founder's factual and historical knowledge, albeit with limited role for future strategic changes. The enterprise can tax-deduct consulting fees. The fees come from future cash flow (or future capital), thus deferring some expenses. The enterprise can offset any liabilities of the ex-owner against future payments, as a self-help tool to ensure the ex-owner does not breach any post-sale restrictive covenants.

The former co-owner benefits in many ways. Financially, the buyout price can be increased by relying on future revenue of the company to pay the 'true value' of the buyout. Fiscally, under the Tax Cuts and Jobs Act of 2017, the former co-owner can establish a pass-through operating company as the vehicle to deliver the consulting services. Such arrangements can reduce the federal income tax rate compared to a normal employee's remuneration to an unrelated employer. And the tax impact can be reduced by stretching the term of the consulting agreement to avoid income bunching that might bump the ex-owner into a higher tax bracket.

Commission Agreements. Most business exits do not include any incentive to the ex-owner to bring new business opportunities to the company. This represents a lost opportunity. The remaining owners usually justify their refusal to consider a commission sales agreement (or 'finder's fee' agreement) by denigrating the individual who left as untrustworthy or too much hassle. This attitude is surprising and short-sighted, since the same arguments in favor of a post-divorce consulting agreement can support a commission sales agreement. There may, nonetheless, be good reasons not to enter into this kind of arrangement, such as a continuing personal animosity from a sense of betrayal or a desire to avoid carve-outs that would confuse customers or reduce incentives to other sales agents or commissioned employees.

Tips for Joint Exit

Go shopping for investment bankers and prospective acquirers based on your industry, your strengths and known weaknesses. Look for a great fit. Pre-exit preparedness pursues prudent principles:

- potability (the ability of the acquirer to digest your company without adverse side effects);
- portability (the assets integrate and flow into the acquirer's platform);
- productivity (the ability of your assets to be productive in the new environment);
- process (for scalability);
- protection (for contingencies and risk management); and
- personality (to send the right message to customers).

Your Professional Advisors

In a joint exit by all, you pull out all the stops for preparation, due diligence, term sheet structuring, negotiation, documentation, closing and post-closing transition planning and escrow payments. Here, you will be calling on a team of investment banker (and/or business broker), attorneys in corporate, commercial, employment and intellectual property rights, accountants for audited financial statements and tax opinions, appraisers (for valuations long before the deal gets solidified) for personal wealth planning, insurance brokers and personal wealth planners. Remediation services to fix 'potholes' in your operations, assets or governance can be provided by knowledge managers, transition planners, forensic accountants and fraud examiners, and real estate brokers.

At closing, your prep for sale is normally confirmed by professional opinions of certain advisors. Lawyers may render opinions to the other party concerning capitalization, due authorization and legal compliance. Investment bankers support the business judgment of the board of directors in a 'fairness opinion' that, while not an appraisal, uses financial analysis of the fairness, from a financial standpoint, of the pricing. Customary for acquisitions of public companies, fairness opinions are also useful in acquisitions of private companies where some of the purchase price consists of the acquirer's shares and a minority owner might claim unfairness due to self-dealing or other conflict..

Your Self-Assessment

- Does the holder of a majority ownership want to sell? Under what conditions, anticipated timing and terms of sale?

- Have you begun preparations for a joint exit? What's missing in your mental checklist?

- What 'cleanup' operations have you identified? What is the plan for rectification?

- What 'pre-sale growth' strategies have you decided upon? What are the risks and rewards in the next 12–24 months? How much will be attributable to 'strategic accounting'? To new clients with long-term revenue potential?

- What synergies does your company offer to a potential buyer? How have you publicized your company's operating characteristics so that strategic buyers can find you (just like a 'keyword search'), without identifying or disclosing any trade secrets?

- Who are your potentially optimal buyers? What is each potential buyer's track record in M&A, post-merger integration, achievement of synergies, retention and future development of the personnel of acquired target companies?

- Have you optimized your 'pre-sale growth' strategy to your optimal target buyer?

- To 'ensure' your buyer achieves the desired synergies, who in your organization will provide ongoing management of such growth opportunities after your joint exit? Will such individuals transfer to the new owner without requiring a retention bonus or other golden handcuffs?

- What post-sale commitments do you and your co-owners wish to make?

12

Manifesto for Smarter Business Exits

Business exits impact so many stakeholders. Every stakeholder enjoys some legal or moral protections. But for business divorce to be intelligent, it must be cohesive, with generally applicable principles to minimize friction and delays and optimize value for all. For emotional, physical and economic health, improvements can come in thought leadership, corporate identity, corporate governance for contingency planning and risk avoidance or mitigation, training and checkups, divorce prevention, detection and response, communication, innovation, and stakeholder activism.

Create Shareholder Value by Design at the Start

Before Anything, Consider Eventual Business Exit

Before startup, think first. Evaluate the scenarios, risks, impact and possible risk mitigation tools relating to business exit. You will need multiple dimensions, including personal, family and legal perspectives. Identify your personal goals at the start, so you can identify how to pursue and achieve them.

Rather than focus on outcomes at the end, it's helpful to focus on 'what ifs' at the start, and to maintain constant attentiveness to evolving relations among co-owners and with critical customers and suppliers.

Design Your Business as an Investment to Protect

Your business may be the most valuable asset in your financial portfolio. Your wealth is not diversified and exposed to fluctuation in valuation due to economic factors. For your wealth planning, it is vital to plan for succession and/or exit, and to prevent or mitigate hostile exits by others.

Design Your Company as a Platform for Roll-Ups

For startups funded by VCs, your pathway may be simple: grow, scale and exit.

Maybe you could also design a company as a platform for roll-ups during this process. It might be even more rewarding for all.

Think bigger. You could combine an exit for some founders and a new global platform for others under a roll-up.

From the Case Files

We helped set up a self-rollup in several countries combined with an exit for some retiring founders and an entrance for a new global manager earning equity for services. It was an elegant succession plan with new talent, new growth opportunities, cost-efficient management structure and tax deferral except for some cashing out.

Through a process of tax-free reorganizations, we converted a group of three unrelated companies, in three countries, into subsidiaries of a new international holding company that became a platform for territorial extension into other foreign countries. For one of the operating companies, retiring founders sold their shares for cash and promissory notes, but retained some minority shares in the holding company for future appreciation. Each operating company has strong local management and business positioning in local markets but no international market openings. After the self-rollup, the global holding company then designated an experienced professional global business manager to integrate all operating companies as affiliates under a common information technology platform, common procurement and financial systems, centralized planning and global marketing, with volume discounts for volume purchases of products under a common brand. The holding company's board is composed of the active company founders worldwide. For good governance, they require a few supermajority voting rules as to change of control, sale of assets, M&A, corporate finance and other major events. They built a global platform, a limited exit plan and the possibility of a higher value and higher multiple of EBITDA for a future sale. Everyone wins.

Presto, you're a private equity company without having solicited capital from investors. You took operating companies and integrated them into a smartly run global company. Some founders cash out but retain a small stake in the new platform company.

Define Your Business Scope Narrowly for 'Best Tribal Fit'

By limiting the definition of the joint enterprise, you can retain autonomy to conduct unrelated business. The laws on corporate governance only apply to business opportunities reasonably within the board's power. In your business plan and shareholders' agreement, as founder you should limit the scope of the business to viable, yet narrowly defined, vision. If the financial, operational, management or technological parameters change, you can go back to your stakeholders and invite a 're-tribalization' exercise on how to respond to change. Conversely, if you are an investor, you should only agree to a narrow business scope if that's a viable business and you do not want your funds spent on 'unrelated' exploration.

Design for Global Dimensions

By designing your business for global impact, you and your business 'partners' will enjoy a global perspective on corporate opportunity, corporate governance and operational excellence. This will help avoid business divorce, but beware the risk of cultural divisions. A global presence could spark new opportunities for succession or exit.

Design Multi-Tiered Ownership

Typically, a closely held business consists of only one entity. By establishing a 'veil of tiers' at inception, you can help insulate your personal assets from creditors, facilitate mergers and acquisitions, permit new 'business partners' to share in ownership of different operating businesses, maintain control of all your business operations under one holding company and simplify estate and gift planning that includes a family trust. Your lawyer will explain.

Consider Alternative Business Models, such as Multi-Party Contractual Networks and Consortia

Before jumping into co-ownership, ask yourself whether the same goals could be accomplished by some form of contractual relationship with no equity or small contributions.

A multi-party contractual network might serve as a pre-agreed short-term 'test ride' for a more elaborate venture. The formal co-ownership might be agreed once the proof of concept (or other milestone) is achieved through joint R&D. Until then, the parties can agree to be mutually restricted from competing. This step-by-step basis is how some pharmaceutical companies agree to fund startups.

Alternatively, such a contractual network might be the chosen long-term business model. For example, where the value of a company depends on different inputs from people (or SMB's) with different skills, and the individuals (or SMB's) want to remain independent, they might form a consortium or trademark holding company to allow each to trade under a common brand and defined allocations for revenues. Multinational professional service firms adopt this model to limit vicarious liability and enable localized governance while formalizing inter-company payments.[123]

Define your Business Identity with an Exit in Mind

If you can, choose a corporate identity separate from anyone's family name. The separation up-front will avoid complexities later, on business divorce. The separation will prevent the founder from demanding compensation, disproportionate control, or special exit terms, all for the use of the name. And the goodwill of the business will not be slave to the personal reputation of any individual.

For startups, founders generally should choose an entity name capable of surviving a change of control in a joint exit to a strategic acquirer. For family businesses, adoption of a family business name just expands the risk that any family member might stupidly harm the family's brand by some personal misconduct.

For professional service companies, local licensing statutes may require a family name on the letterhead. In such cases, every business partner needs to know the personality faults, and the probability of personal or professional misconduct, of every individual whose name is on the door. And take care to ensure there is zero risk of reputational damage.

Can you afford to live with the reputational risk of the founder's family name?

To maximize value, founders should either give up any hope of perpetuating the family name in the business or manage the business under strict arm's length governance. This means adopting policies and practices for corporate leadership succession, with supervision and checks and balances.

---

[123] William B. Bierce, *Multiparty Contractual Networks: New Tool for Global Entrepreneurship and Supply Chains,* The International Business Lawyer (Int'l Bar Ass'n, Sept. 2019),

Build Your Agile Business

Develop Your Digital Business

Business exit intelligence requires an awareness of the benefits and risks of the current wave of 'digital transformation' of business operations. *'Digital transformation'* refers to the disruptions and redesign of 'smart' business operations to use computing and telecommunications for business process management. This includes the Internet, chat-bots, mobile applications, cloud computing and, in a second wave, Big Data, artificial intelligence, blockchain, agile and lean software development, DevOps, Internet of Things ('IoT'), virtual reality ('VR'), augmented reality ('AR') and robotic process automation ('RPA'). Digital transformation marries people managing technology for enterprise success, creating tensions for those who are neither curious nor willing to adapt.

Intelligent business survival and growth require adaptation and innovation, integrating internal core competitive strengths and external supply chain support. In a digital economy, businesses must either develop or integrate technologies, notably in both cloud computing services (e-commerce) and 'cognitive' services (such as business process reengineering guided by a team of subject matter experts, a/k/a 'artificial intelligence'). All this points toward more process automation and analytics to identify or predict potential problems and self-heal. As in business intelligence, the big data can be harnessed using dashboards which, in turn, are directed to particular roles of the employees who manage particular business functions. But even artificial intelligence needs to be guided by emotional intelligence, both for suitability and sustaining the robotic learning curve.

Develop Multiple Exit Scenarios

Likewise, intelligent exit strategies require innovation driven by emotional intelligence. Innovation in exit planning can be as simple as standardizing legal documentation for managing the high-risk, high probability scenarios and tacking on some novel customization. The up-front customization would add value on the back end by personalization, giving meaning, moral compass and hopefully a willingness to accommodate. If there is no innovation or accommodation, litigation and accompanying emotional, physical, financial and family distress will ensue.

Develop Project Management Tools for Resolving Unanswered Issues

You may use online project management tools for running a virtual business. If you do, identify in advance how you would like to use them for resolving issues and getting to closure.

Consider a Pivot to Add New Value

When circumstances change, you will need to act quickly. As your operations evolve, consider how your current shareholders or management provide value to the organization over the long term. If you need to pivot the organization, you may wish to invite some stakeholders to exit, with a fair valuation and fair payment terms for their voluntary exit.

Your business model should include some digital services, perhaps adding analytics that customers will pay for. Valuation can be higher for the same revenues, given higher multiples for digital revenues where you have annuity revenues, customer 'lock-in' loyalty and scalability. And keep innovating your core business models as you see disruptive competition. You would do this in any event, but you should keep focused on it because you will see a succession or exit soon enough.

Design a Robust Dispute Mechanism

Pre-Ownership: 'Test Ride' before Marching into Business

Whether you go into business with a friend, family member or new acquaintance, you should consider a 'test ride' in a project that resembles co-ownership but that does not constitute co-ownership. This could be a consultancy, advice or a project with a shared deliverable. Hold a post-mortem discussion to define and resolve relationship problems.

Co-Ownership: Creating an 'Undo' Button Early and Often

A little early planning for undoing the co-ownership relation can save a lot of lost value, unnecessary anxiety, family discord and stifled growth later. Every business that has more than one owner should include triggers and mechanisms for terminating every owner's co-ownership, even the majority owner's, depending on the 'unanticipated' scenario such as unequal contribution of services, dishonesty, honest disagreement, age, change in health or personal circumstances and insufficient operating capital.

Put Exit Strategies into All Your Agreements

Build your exit plan into every agreement, whether internal or external. Your shareholders' agreement and charter documents are the core for business exit. In addition, your employment agreements with owners should integrate employment terms (termination causes ('for cause' and 'for good reason')) with corporate ownership documents. Incentive compensation might best be handled as SARs or other general unsecured creditor's rights, rather than equity with possible claims for breach of fiduciary duty. Ideally, your supplier and customer agreements should not allow termination upon your company's change of control, since your value proposition could decline and wither.

Grow the Zone of Reasonableness (and Business Value) for All

Successful exits from a business require enough fairness to overcome a tendency for selfish outcomes. The best negotiations involve understanding the counterparty's position, gaining mutual trust, avoiding unnecessary confrontation, cultural and tribal respect, and expanding the zone of reasonableness. A healthy exit can thus come even from a stressed co-ownership.

Resolve Internal Conflicts

If you are having internal conflicts with other owners, you may wish to consider a joint exit (for an escape by all). Or, consider a buyout or sale. Try to avoid multiple simultaneous conflicts. You might resolve some conflicts and leave resolution for a scheduled further resolution by agreement. In any event, you need to maintain an organization that functions so that it can realize the maximum value. Be a peacemaker with a plan for change. Remember that internal conflicts can not only torpedo a joint exit, but can result in retaliation, litigation among owners and loss of future opportunities.

Get a Company 'Medical Checkup': Find and Plug Your Leaks

Prep for sale thus invites the exiting owners to review the entity's business health. You should identify and resolve persistent problems. Then you can align lines of business, to identify all factors that would create value in a sale, and even develop strategies for 'quick wins' in sales immediately after the change of ownership control. Do a 'SWOT' analysis of strengths, weaknesses, opportunities and threats. Identify opportunities that might be achieved under an acquirer's framework.

Look for anomalies with an expert. What you don't know can cost you a lot! To plug holes in compliance obligations and mitigate vulnerabilities, you should conduct a pre-sale internal investigation for legal and financial compliance. (Your lawyer or investment banker will have a checklist.) Then prioritize based on risk assessment and channel efforts at making your business clean, clear, compliant and cogent for your exit. This process will also assist you in valuing the risks that remain and disclosing what a buyer needs to know.

A 'checkup' can also identify risks that might kill an exit deal. For example, if you are considering sale to a large enterprise in a highly concentrated market, you should investigate the possible impact of anti-competition laws in any country. Generally, antitrust ('competition') laws seek to protect consumer choices by preventing excessive concentration in an industry (Sherman Act) and artificial constraints on competition (Clayton Act). Currently, prior governmental review is required for mergers involving assets or securities above a threshold.[124]

---

[124]   See, e.g., Hart-Scott-Rodino Antitrust Improvements Act, P.L. 94-435, 90 Stat. 1383 (1976). The current threshold is $90 million. The FTC adjusts the threshold annually.

Good Governance: Manage Operations for Smooth Post-Merger Integration

Governance, Compliance and Risk Management

Live by your GCR program, so you can choose when to sell and avoid 'catch up' and 'clean up' before going for a joint exit. Do your 'corporate housekeeping' so you can be ready for either blackmail threats or a sudden appealing exit opportunity.

Corporate governance consists of the policies, procedures, monitoring and supervision of the company's operations.

In closely held companies, corporate governance must be 'baked into' the ownership structure and operations, to allow for success and transition. The tools for formation and initial activation of a privately held enterprise should include an 'instruction manual' for replacing persons and personalities with roles, rights and responsibilities, with consequences for failure to continue playing the symphony in tune and tempo with the rest of the stakeholder orchestra. Thus, exits and new transitions must be a core goal of the new enterprise, even if the time horizon might be unusually long (not just five to seven years, but maybe twenty or thirty years).

Risk management sustains corporate resiliency. Vulnerabilities, like a blind spot in your field of vision, need identification, assessment and rectification. Without a clean house, other shareholders can assert irrational claims and extort their own one-sided happy exit.

Compliance with laws avoids costly and distracting legal disputes.

Ongoing Awareness: Training and Checkups in Business Continuity Management

Most businesses of training and coaching senior executives are driven by compliance mandates. For human resource management, everyone needs to be trained to avoid conduct (such as sexual harassment, hostile workplace, unlawful discrimination in hiring, promotion and discipline, and so on). Similarly, for business continuity management ('BCM'), CIOs and CFOs must anticipate and prepare for foreseeable disasters, such as loss of electricity, transpiration interruptions, illness of key personnel, supplier bankruptcy and Acts of God. In BCM and disaster recovery ('DR'), businesses need to develop and update such contingency plans.

For closely held business, there is usually no such compliance mandate to drive a BCM/DR plan. However, co-owners and other stakeholders can assist in BCM/DR planning. They can help design roles and responsibilities that obviate the entity's dependency on a single key leader. BCM/DR planning should start with the initial owners' agreement (founders' agreement, shareholders' agreement, LLC operating agreement) and be updated with every new capital contribution, new line of business and new strategic alliance.

Use Your Business Exit Intelligence

Divorce Prevention, Detection and Response

Prevention of a business divorce starts with the awareness of its roots, risks and impact. If all stakeholders have such awareness, they can act individually and as interest groups in a community to lobby the 'wrongdoers' for improved performance, greater commitment and accommodation to others to achieve a greater individual benefit from greater collective benefits. In addition to advocating for preventing a hostile business divorce, stakeholders can advocate for optimal rational solutions to redirect, restructure, recapitalize, revitalize, and realize the fruits of the individual and collective efforts. And when such advocacy fails, stakeholders can still pursue moral and personal suasion without immediately pulling the plug and litigating.

Once litigation starts, the paramount challenge is to achieve a mediated or negotiated resolution. If the stakeholders have diligently advocated against hostile business divorce, they will not be perceived as weak or capitulating merely by insisting on an 'intelligent business divorce.' Thus, by proposing creative resolutions, they can escape a disappointing legacy and relaunch.

Manage 'Key-Person' Risks

'Key person' risk occurs when one individual's involvement (or absence) disproportionately affects the enterprise's value. Companies dependent on one key person face the same fate as business operations run by a single hero. Even if they have repeatable, measurable and optimizable processes, they lack resiliency in case of personal disaster.

To deal with key-person risk, the other shareholders (and holders of options) should demand financial adjustments to equalize the disparity in control. The shareholder agreement might be adjusted to give the other shareholders a discount upon buy-in and a premium on sale of their equity. Such financial adjustments could offset the loss of rational control over the key person, the lack of a 'sunset' and transition, and the predictable difficulties and costs arising from sudden unavailability.

Second, board directors must acknowledge their personal risks of nonfeasance if they fail to govern. Being dependent on a single key person defeats the separation of board and officers, giving leverage to the key person even when they are not performing well.

Third, like fresh fruit or processed food, even the best performer must have an expiration date. Alternative succession plans can cover scenarios that might include a short-term crisis, an intermediate surprise and a definitive long-term plan.

Manage Intense Relationships with Stakeholders: Practicing Business Exit Intelligence

Practicing business exit intelligence can overcome the urge to litigate. How do you practice emotional intelligence at work? Given such analysis, what adjustments would improve your business exit or succession plan?

Digital technologies put co-owners and employees in constant contact for business purposes at any time of day or night, weekends and even holidays. With such intense and persistent contacts, we treat work more like marriage. We talk about work as our passion, purpose and fulfillment.

If you adopt 'tough love,' you might make a 'reasonable' demand based on the facts, but you use a confrontational approach. You hope the other owner (or stakeholder) will relent and acquiesce. Your harsh stance probably elicits shame and defensiveness, without resolution. Excessive aggressiveness might backfire.

You can get collaborative outcomes by practicing your emotional intelligence. Instead of demanding submission, ask questions, invite joint problem-solving and look together in the same direction. If you or your co-owner can't change, you might consider 'couples therapy for work relationships.'[125]

Beyond individual situations, you can set a framework for mutual practice of emotional intelligence. You and your co-owners and stakeholders could *set expectations for all relationships with your business*. It's just a matter of good governance, risk management and compliance for sustainable performance, with good policies, good people and good practices for a self-regulating business. Now you can sell and retire.

Keep Growing until the Exit

Some business exits are matches 'made in heaven.' When selling, consider how to increase value even beyond your valuation as of the date of sale. Take a broad global view, with a long-term perspective for ongoing growth after the change of control.

Be Nimble in Timing Your Exit or Succession

Do not miss your opportunity to design and implement your exit or succession plan. The opportunity exists throughout the business lifecycle. At startup, mutual goodwill and reciprocity will guide your business exit agreements. Upon accepting a new investor, you will have to negotiate new rules on governance and exits. If there is a shareholder dispute at any time, you might be foreclosed from effective personal wealth planning.

Don't be too early or late. A quick sale can be a disaster. Your acquirer (if you have one) will insist on risk allocations with escrows, earn-outs and perhaps consulting agreements. It may be too late to remediate any shortcomings. You will have missed your opportunities for tax planning, valuation with appropriate discounts, family wealth planning and succession.

---

[125] Nikki Waller, *'Couples Therapy for Work Relationships,'* Wall St. J. (Nov. 16-17, 2019), p. B1, cols.3-4, p. B4, cols 1-5.

Avoid Surprises for Your Acquirer

You cannot afford to surprise your acquirer, whether before, during or after the acquisition. You might get only one chance at the right deal. Identify your ideal acquirer and its key expectations so you can demonstrate a good fit from Day One. Before the deal, your business's value and marketability depends on its reliability. You cannot afford a sudden drop in revenues. Quality of earnings is the foundation for corporate valuation and finance. At closing, you cannot just offer to fix a 'material discrepancy' since it opens the risk of deal failure. After the deal, you cannot afford to lose any value from 'mistaken' misrepresentations. No surprises!

Design Your Best Joint Exit

Your best joint exit will probably take at least two years. You have time to prepare, but you should start now.

Communicate Succession Plans and Exit Plans with Stakeholders, and Listen

Communication about business succession planning can be an effective tool for retention of key stakeholders. Effective communications and listening depend on both timing and context.

For timing, transition planning should be a regular agenda item for all stakeholders to see, even if the planned transition is years in the future. Relevant communications should be considered for new hires of key employees, especially where one of the founders is over sixty or seventy, where one of the founders or owners is exiting (or has just exited), or where friction is public and inescapable. However, disclosures about the details, or the relevant 'corporate pre-nup' document, must be kept confidential under some form of confidentiality agreement.

For context, verbal and written communications like shareholder agreements are express and transparent. But what happens when one co-owner observes another co-owner acting in a potentially competitive, potentially unfair way, but the consequences will take time to evaluate? Where explicit communications are improbable or impossible, one should consider tacit communications in the form of some action that then might elicit an explicit dialogue. An 'action-based communication'[126] can pre-empt disputes by inviting cooperation and testing for acquiescence or minimal non-hostile responses.

Dress-up Your Company: Prep for Sale

You will need to present your company as credit-worthy and purchase-worthy. The creditworthiness will be needed if you do not have adequate cash to pay off a redemption price. (Maybe you forgot to get 'key person' life insurance.) The purchase-worthiness is to go all-out for optimal pricing, competition among bidders and terms of sale. Remember, your sale price should be a multiple of net cash flow (EBITDA), so every unit of cash earned generates a multiple in sale. Your pricing negotiations start with audited financial statements to justify your multiple.

Boost Gross Revenues: Growth Spurt

Accelerated revenue growth demonstrates customer satisfaction and scalable demand. Growth can come from increased sales or from acquiring a smaller company that provides synergies (assuming easy assimilation).

Reallocate Capital to Growth Segments

To the extent you have free cash, reinvest it in existing segments that generate the highest EBITDA multiples. (For new segments, you will need a separate risk-weighted ROI analysis).

File Patent Applications

Since patents give monopoly protections within limited scope, they are especially valuable to an acquirer that could use such patents for its existing operations added to yours. File patent applications but remain mindful of the countervailing need to protect trade secrets.

Supply Chain Management

Identify efficiencies and potential benefits from supply chain management when planning for a sale of the company.

---

[126] See generally, Thomas C. Schelling, *Strategy of Conflict* (1960).

Net Profits: Cost-Reduction Strategies

Paring costs is the first post-acquisition objective for a buyer. Sellers can increase their sale price by eliminating non-productive costs and helping the buyer more easily integrate the company into the buyer's organization. Well-advised sellers therefore apply lean management principles, concentrating on the core business and outsourcing the incidental, albeit essential, services.

Design for Transition, Post-Merger Integration and Delivering Performance Improvement

Think beyond the closing of sale ('Day One' for your acquirer). Your success at the bargaining table depends on the acquirer's comfort level that post-merger integration will proceed as smoothly as possible. If you identify how to cut the acquirer's costs and risks of a smooth integration, you can look like a better target with a better value. So be ready with a transition management plan for smooth transition and value preservation during post-merger integration.

For optimal negotiating leverage, the business owner should identify and quantify how the buyers analyze operations and potential synergies (both for revenue and expenses). To achieve the anticipated synergies, the seller can help fashion and facilitate the buyer's plans for post-merger integration ('PMI') and performance improvement. Some buyers even hire specialist advisors to design and manage such transition plans. Financial buyers may hire interim C-level managers to replace exiting senior executives. Such plans may include an 'integration management office,' synergy management, transitional services agreements, Day 1 Readiness operational plans and post-closing transitions. PMI requires 'blueprinting' and 'road-mapping' that identify, design and implement creative business and technology solutions for the buyer, especially for private equity buyers and their portfolio companies.

With such PMI and performance improvement in mind, a selling owner can anticipate PMI involving operational optimization, consolidation of back office services, integration of information technology and supply chains, customer and channel management. If you can show that your company will integrate extensively and easily, you negotiate a higher price, even though you might not control the company after Day 1 after the closing.

In short, whatever you did to 'prep for sale,' a selling owner can improve on the terms of sale by highlighting quality of operations. This means developing and managing your company's team for effective finance and accounting, effective organizational design of roles and responsibilities for all employees, optimization of pricing, margin and product mix, and knowledge management and transfer. Not surprisingly, such good 'prep' and negotiating focus represents involves the same good governance practices (suggested above) that undoubtedly made your company a desirable target in the first place!

Execute Your Best Joint Exit

Develop Your Digital Tools for a Transaction

Today, due diligence has become a digital art form. You upload your digital copies of your business documents and financial data into an online storage 'data room' that has a gatekeeper clocking who downloads what and when. You upload updates and remove outdated documents.

The sophisticated buyer may use e-discovery AI-assisted analytics to digitally read and analyze your documents for risk management (such as indemnification clauses and termination for change of control). So you should consider using similar tools, if the number or complexity of your documents is very high.

Know your Buyer: Selection Criteria for Your Optimal Acquirers

A company seeking to be acquired should define the qualities of prospective acquirers and thus the particular prospective bidders. Every acquisition is followed by transformation and integration of the target. In the transformation, the duplicative employees are terminated or redirected over time, while 'synergistic' employees are retained and integrated. In looking at prospective acquirers, the sellers should focus on the maturity of each potential acquirer's culture, processes and receptiveness for integration and employee retention, not just for acquisition and control.

In the sales process, the sellers thus should promote such optimization opportunities by selling not only to the CEO and CFO, but to the prospective acquirer's CHRO and chief marketing and sales officers.

In short, finding the right acquirer depends not just on pricing, but on alignment of corporate cultures, identification of go-to-market strategies and revenue growth in the first year after the change of control.

Select the Acquirer for Best Fit after Sale

Buyers in M&A deals often overlook the cultural elements of the target business. Founders seeking a joint exit can help obtain best value by understanding not only legal, financial and commercial integration, but also the likely psychological and behavioral responses of your employees to the acquirer's organization. Sellers should do their own assessment of 'good fit.'

For *a good fit on talent*, first, look at your employees' levels of anxiety about post-merger integration, loss of old identities, adaptability to a new organizational culture and new roles, perceived fairness to both surviving employees and displaced employees. Second, ask prospective buyers how they plan to integrate, with examples of successful integration and employee retention in the past.

For *governance*, take the lessons of 'best practices.' Find professional advisors to review your business and advise on decision-making. It does not matter how large your board is. It's the level of independent thinking, follow-up, accountability, transparency, risk management and resiliency that matter to the buyer for smooth post-merger integration.

For *the cleanest transaction*, be ready to deliver a clean suite of due diligence documentation. This will help the buyer to formulate core negotiating objectives at an early stage in the transaction and avoid the buyer's raising new issues in negotiations. Anticipate a request for a 'no-shop' exclusivity clause to prevent competitive bidding.

For *post-acquisition control*, be careful not to ask for substantial post-acquisition ownership. Your continuing ownership will interfere with the buyer's exercise of control and may be very expensive to the buyer if the minority must be bought out later.

For *the best fit*, look for an acquirer who will patiently take the time to get to know you and your business. Cultivate relationships with prospective acquirers long before you want to sell. Build personal relationships, even if you are not ready to sell. Listen to what they consider important.

Anticipate Your Buyer's Concerns and Tactics

In M&A, buyers fear making mistakes. This fear can lead to gamesmanship. You should expect your buyer to define a clean deal in the non-binding letter of intent and later identify the specks of dirt during due diligence, contract negotiations and pre-closing. Gamesmanship tactics may include anchoring a 'point' under a 'written rule' while ignoring the other party's concession for some implicit counterbalance. If your buyer has any justification to squeeze you into a better deal, you made a mistake. Having a good negotiating team can counterbalance the other's ploys.

Re-Trading the Price after Aggressive Due Diligence

Some private equity investors solve the puzzle of getting access to deals by overbidding a little and then seeking to cut the price based on 'discoveries' from due diligence investigation. Company founders should anticipate some haggling on price before the final agreement is signed, but investigation of the buyer's reputation might help avert shocking surprises. The impact of such shock is worst after the LOI is signed.

Breach of Representation and Warranty by Seller

After the closing, the buyer might 'discover' facts that constitute a breach of express warranty. The seller should define the maximum amount of post-closing price adjustments and other consequences of the breach of all covenants (an 'aggregate cap' on value at risk) and address other specific breaches with their own valuation caps. Conversely, sellers should expect unlimited liability for actions that could destroy overall value in the buyer's hands, such as fraud, breach of confidentiality as to trade secrets, and violations of law.

Setting an Earn-out without Management Control

If you agree to a low price with an earn-out, and the sellers have no way to govern or influence post-closing operations, you should negotiate the details on accounting. A buyer might be justified in charging your earn-out profits with some new cost that you had not anticipated. What you count you can keep.

Plan for a Possible Earn-out

Simple Earn-outs. An earn-out is a price adjustment contingent on some future revenue or cash flow of your company after you sell it. You hope to get a higher price by proving the company will generate future cash at a high level. You should analyze your revenue streams and decide whether you want to take such a gamble. Also, if you do agree to an earn-out, your contract should be written to clarify that the value involved is an additional consideration for the purchase price, and not just a consulting fee. And be careful to get the necessary management authority to implement the goals, or, the earn-out could vaporize.

Earn-outs with Long Tail Period and Deferred Transfer. In certain countries, the buyer funds the target company's operations while the seller remains in a managerial role to help grow the company.[127] In effect, the buyer and seller agree to a deferred transfer of title to the company's equity. For a period of months or years, the individual who owns control of the company (typically a founder) continues as company employee to manage the business. This manager must follow a business plan agreed between seller and buyer. But the buyer funds the company prior to transfer of equity ownership.

This long-term earn-out arrangement has many flaws.

- First, the business plan will usually need to adapt during the earn-out period, but the deal struck cannot be changed unilaterally. So the business plan becomes out of date and the company might fail to seize new opportunities or respond to market threats.

- Second, the buyer lacks the ability to exercise control over the seller and might not be able to terminate the employment agreement during the earn-out period. This sets up a dispute over whether a particular act by the seller was willful misconduct (and just cause for termination of employment) or merely a sloppy business judgment made in good faith.

- Third, the acquisition agreement might not have any meaningful metrics. This lack of definition prevents the buyer from imposing penalties for underachievement.

---

[127] In France, it's called *'location-gérance.'* It refers to 'rent to buy, with seller management and earn-out.'

- Fourth, until the completion of transfer, the assets are under the control of the seller, who may retain them if the buyer defaults on pre-transfer covenants, such as to fund operations, to support the seller as manager and to follow the business plan. In a power play over control, the seller wins and retains ownership of the company's assets and all intellectual property generated by the seller after the 'definitive' agreement is signed.

- Finally, in case of dispute the buyer's exit door is shut. The buyer cannot sell the company to a third party, since any third party would refuse to buy a hornet's nest tilted in favor of the seller. In short, a purchase deal that leaves the seller controlling operations leaves the buyer exposed to abuses, disputes, loss and lost opportunity.

Team up with Professional Advisors

In business divorce, succession, exit, divisive reorganization, recapitalization or restructuring, you may need various professional advisors at different stages. Most businesspeople lack skills, time or intestinal fortitude to be leading the process for an intelligent business divorce. Business exit advisors fill this gap. In buying or selling a business, professional advisors can guide you on valuation, manage the marketing of the business or conduct confidential research on potential targets or acquirers, negotiate, manage the sales process, structure the transactions for tax, value, HR, finance, legal and personal goals.

Be aware of the limitations of your professional advisors. To minimize blind spots, fill the gaps in perspectives by diversification of your team. Skilled practitioners typically focus on only one aspect of a single event, namely, the finalization and termination of the business or corporate relationship that involved joint efforts or joint venturing. Lawyers focus on rights and remedies, and maybe on narrow areas of the law like M&A, employment or litigation. Psychologists in a family divorce focus on the best interests of the children, but not (in business divorce) on the stakeholders.

Build your diversified professional advisory team for a smarter exit. Start with core advisors who know your business: your accountant, attorney, insurance broker and marketing consultant. As needed, complete your internal knowledge and institutionalize your organization with a forensic accountant, a knowledge management consultant. Keep your estate planners, wealth managers and personal advisors informed.

Start with a key personal advisor who is dedicated to you individually. This will avoid fights over conflicts of interest, breach of fiduciary duty. It will also protect the advisor's independence and the confidentiality of your communications. Look for a personal professional advisor with a broad and holistic overview of strategies, transactions and hurdles across the company's lifecycle.

Start Today

How can you avoid failure? Do something every day to get 'exit-ready.'

Good governance, succession planning and exit readiness are vital to your company's health, even if an exit is not imminent. By getting 'exit ready,' you can accelerate any exit process (thereby taking advantage of potentially favorable market conditions before they deteriorate). By conducting your own internal self-audits for due diligence, you manage business risks and compliance for remediation and loss prevention. You also train your employees that due diligence can happen at any time, and the corporate culture is based on governance, risk management and resiliency planning and compliance that will benefit all stakeholders.

Your readiness should cover regulatory compliance, privacy, cybersecurity and any other risk vector exposing you to potential liability), intellectual property, human resources liability (especially sexual harassment), contracts and business relationships with customers, suppliers, service providers and alliance partners, financial information and general operations and marketing.

Readiness for succession or exit also depends on your business's adaptation to changing business models. In turn, you must remain vigilant and act on your ability to identify and control risks and crises, pursue new opportunities and invent your company's future. This may involve re-investment in digital transformation or new lines of business that may require new capital investments, potentially with new investors. As you approach transformation, consider whether your business' timing, positioning and capital structure can withstand the change. If not, you should consider succession or a change of control.

So get ready now. Successful succession planning and exits can take longer than you think!

Your Life after Business Exit

What's next after your exit? How can you enjoy life now?

Consider your new community or 'tribe.' As business owner, you fulfilled core emotional needs to find purpose and meaning by adopting and contributing to a community. Analogous to making music together, people achieve meaning in living by starting with a 'design' (or plan) for what they want to accomplish. This enables them to tell others the 'story' (here, business plan) to build on that design and act as maestro to enlist others to create a 'symphony' of making music jointly (shared business governance). In turn, such collaboration leads to sharing feelings of 'empathy' that releases the spirit to 'play,' thereby giving meaning to both work and play.[128] You can build a new tribe that reflects your instinctive emotional attachments, common core beliefs and identity.[129] Your new community or tribe can help look forward and leave behind any residual distress.

Your Self-Assessment

- Looking at the various phases of the business exit lifecycle, where does your company fit now? What is the next phase, and when will it begin?

- Is your business ready for a sale or succession? What have you done to improve readiness? What is needed before you reach the next phase?

- What type of business would you be selling: talent, services or products? What is the best mix that will maximize shareholder value on change of control?

- Have you pulled all the levers for growth to maximize value? Have you positioned your business for best valuation? Have you optimized high-value assets such as a digital line of business?

---

[128] Thomas A. Pink, A WHOLE NEW MIND: WHY RIGHT-BRAINERS WILL RULE THE FUTURE (Riverhead Books 2006). See also Daniel J. Siegel and Tina Payne Bryson, THE WHOLE-BRAIN CHILD, (Bantam Books 2012).
[129] See generally, Daniel Shapiro, NEGOTIATING THE NON-NEGOTIABLE: HOW TO RESOLVE YOUR MOST EMOTIONALLY CHARGED CONFLICTS (Viking, an imprint of Penguin Random House LLC 2016).

- Is your business strategy adapted to the current and anticipated legal, regulatory, technological and competitive environments?

- Have you built a strong team that collaborates effectively? What vulnerabilities do you face as to key persons?

- Is this a good time to transfer your business to your family?

- Have you considered your obligations and risks after a transfer to your family or an acquirer?

- Do you have sufficient Business exit Intelligence™ to analyze your particular needs and identify and achieve your specific goals? If not, you might seek out a professional advisor.

- Who would be your best advisor for getting ready? It could be a current advisor, but you would want to make a special evaluation of the existing advisor's breadth and depth of knowledge as to strategies for successions and exits. Does your existing advisor have the capacity to brainstorm, listening, and propose creative and holistic solutions? Would you benefit from hiring a coach for succession and/or exit?

- Have your relations with your co-owners and stakeholders soured to the point of dispute? Could your business benefit from a coach to advise 'everybody,' serving informally as mediator among co-owners and other stakeholders with conflicting interests? In this case, you would hire a coach who has not been representing the company but who comes with a clean slate, an open mind, solid knowledge of corporate governance and enterprise competitiveness. Your instructions to the informal mediator would be to help all co-owners optimize value despite conflicting needs in a disputed or distressed exit scenario.

- How do you avoid embarrassment or public disclosure? How can you protect the confidentiality of your strategic planning (or dispute resolution method) for a succession and/or exit? What types of professional advisors have an ethical duty of confidentiality?

- Are your business records in good condition? Are you ready to assemble a digital data room for due diligence? If not, when do you plan to do so?

- When are you going to get started in updating your succession and/or exit plans?

Further Reading for Smarter Business Exits

Do you want additional articles or e-books that provide much more detail on the topics in this book? You can download them at the author's website www.biercekenerson.com/resources or contact us at wbierce@smarterbusinessexits.com.

International Businesses and/or International Ownership. You might own international business operations. You might have domestic and foreign owners. You might be considering a sale to an international business. These business configurations involve complex, difficult and uniquely sensitive challenges in exit planning.

Professional Service Firms and/or Consulting Firms. In today's service-based economy, professional service firms range from global firms to small, niche businesses. You might be a regulated professional, such as an accountant, architect, attorney, engineer, financial professional (such as broker-dealer, registered investment advisor or investment fund manager), medical doctor, psychologist or real estate broker. Or you might be in an unregulated consulting firm. Unregulated, your professional service firm might advise on digital media and marketing, digital transformation, management strategies (business processes, supply chains, value chains and/or other business strategies); branding and identity strategies (including environmental, sustainability and governance targets). Your professional service firm might provide outsourced services such as information technology, human resources administration, back-office accounting, family office administration, business knowledge management or interim executive services. In any form, professional service firms involve perhaps the most complex, difficult and uniquely sensitive exit issues for their owners.

Toolkits for Restructuring Ownership or Capital. Some liquidity strategies require restructuring before exit. For example, you could do a divisive reorganization to split up one enterprise into two or more separate businesses under a series of tax-free transactions. The chapter on restructuring in lieu of exit offers a variety of restructuring models for multi-step exit plans.

Additional Strategies for Smarter Business Exits™. Please check back from time to time for additional resources, strategies, checklists, webinars and other tool for smarter business exits. You might want to do this even before you start your next venture.

Conclusion

This book was written from an end-point perspective. But it offers the greatest value at inception, when you form and activate your new business. As business owner, board director and technology lawyer for founders, companies, investors and acquirers, I wrote it to help founders and investors understand the legal and operational frameworks for surviving, thriving and achieving liquidity in your closely held business.

As advisor, I also listen to other perspectives from different advisors. As owner and board member, it is your duty to do likewise. This explains why each chapter identifies other professionals for guidance, inspiration and legal protection at different phases in the business lifecycle.

I wish you the best of luck in your journey in business. While this book focuses on management succession planning and changes in ownership, the prize lies in building and solidifying your business from launch till exit. The change of control culminates one cycle and opens the door to your next venture, whether as owner or investor. If you have any questions, please feel free to e-mail me at wbierce@smarterbusinessexits.com.

About the Author

An award-winning international business and technology attorney, William B. Bierce assists companies, their owners, boards and investors throughout a company's business lifecycles. As business lawyer, he advises on organizational design, business formation, capital raising, equity compensation, governance, risk management, crisis resolution, resiliency planning, compliance, roll-ups, corporate sales and divestitures. As a technology lawyer, he assists domestic and foreign clients on digital transformation, e-commerce, privacy, cybersecurity and strategic transactions.

Bill has extensive experience in domestic and cross-border transactions for leading global companies in investments, banking and finance, consumer products, managed business services, manufacturing, transportation and digital media. He concentrates on mid-market niche companies, specialty manufacturing, services industries, family businesses, international businesses and tech companies.

In addition to legal services, Bill has also served as a business founder, corporate director, officer, litigation settlement negotiator, arbitrator, mediator, licensed insurance agent, graduate business professor of international business and tax law, mentor, executor, trustee, expert witness, investor, bar association committee chairman, public speaker, camp counselor and deckhand on a towboat pushing barges. Bill is U.S. delegate to the United Nations (ECOSOC) for a French-based non-governmental organization of experts, counselors and arbitrators. He has published over 80 articles on law and business in four languages.

Fluent in French, Bill has an undergraduate diploma from Yale and law degrees from New York University and the University of Grenoble, France.

www.ingramcontent.com/pod-product-compliance
Lightning Source LLC
Chambersburg PA
CBHW031920190326
41519CB00007B/362